Managing with a
Global Mindset

"Provides a truly global perspective from an acknowledged leader in the field of globalisation.

It contains many thought-provoking concepts and raises many fundamental questions about what it takes to develop a truly global mindset, and at the same time is practical."

P. J. Drechsler, Chairman & Chief Executive, Quest International and Executive Director, ICI plc

"Jean-Pierre has the enviable ability to reach out of any business and grasp the market needs and the key drivers.

There is only one Jeannet, if you cannot work with him first-hand, this book makes a great alternative, capturing the complexities of the global market with the clarity of the inspirational coach."

David Payne, Vice President, Huntsman Polyurethanes

"The global mindset is essential today. This book offers the first delineation of what this means, and it does so in a powerful, convincing manner, with plenty of examples and practical theories to build on. This book will be indispensable for executives and advanced students alike. Congratulations to Professor Jean-Pierre Jeannet for a pioneering job."

Dr. Peter Lorange, President, IMD

"*Managing with a Global Mindset* couldn't have found a more ideal author than Professor Jean-Pierre Jeannet. Thanks to his broad international exposure and long intercultural experience, he has realized that it is not sufficient to prepare your corporation for the global age by adjusting your organizational structure, your strategic skills and operational know-how, but that a change has to take place in the culture of your company, in the minds of your managers.

Whereas Professor Jeannet's recommended new forms of managerial and strategic thinking are open to every professional manager, the access to the softer aspects of the new mindset requires an international presidposition of the mind!"

Dr. Henri B. Meier, Member, Executive Committee, F. Hoffmann-La Roche Ltd

"An easy-to-follow road map for those seriously pursuing an edge in strategic global competitivenesss."

E. H. Schollmaier, Chairman, Alcon Laboratories, Inc.

"J.P. Jeannet has done it again! Developing a Global Mindset is both thought-provoking and pragmatic. The author clearly demonstrates why we turn to him both for intellectual stimulus and for practical advice."

Hein Schreuder, Corporate Vice-President Planning & Development, DSM N.V.

"In today's world, essentially every business competes for customers, resources, or both, in the global marketplace. J.P. Jeannet has the understanding, based on experience and research, to convert this hard-to-use generalization into a framework and logic to find a strategy relevant to a specific business."

John F. Magee, former Chairman, Arthur D. Little, Inc.

"A Global Mindset is a necessity in today's companies. It requires many changes in company processes, procedures and how people think and act. This book is a practical roadmap for all globalizing companies."

William F. Glavin, President, Emeritus Babson College and Former Vice Chairman Xerox Corporation

"This is not a flash-in-the-pan academic analysis, looking for the fast buck – this is history, reality, process, imagination and the future. I have worked with Jeannet, he's a class act, so is this book – this is the definitive article. This book is reality and the future – not just impactful for the first 50 pages like most "business books", but throughout. It's day-to-day usable."

Scott Davidson, Chief Executive Officer, ICI Acrylics

FINANCIAL TIMES
Prentice Hall

In an increasingly competitive world, it is quality
of thinking that gives an edge. An idea that opens new
doors, a technique that solves a problem, or an insight
that simply helps make sense of it all.

We work with leading authors in the fields of
management and finance to bring cutting-edge thinking
and best learning practice to a global market.

Under a range of leading imprints, including
Financial Times Prentice Hall, we create world-class
print publications and electronic products giving readers
knowledge and understanding which can then be
applied, whether studying or at work.

To find out more about our business and professional
products, you can visit us at *www.business-minds.com*

For other Pearson Education publications, visit
www.pearsoned-ema.com

Pearson
Education

Managing with a Global Mindset

Jean-Pierre Jeannet

F. W. Olin Distinguished Professor of Global Business
Director, William F. Glavin Center for Global Entrepreneurial Leadership
Babson College, Wellesley, Massachusetts

Professor of Strategy and Marketing
IMD Institute, Lausanne, Switzerland

FINANCIAL TIMES
Prentice Hall

London • New York • San Francisco • Toronto • Sydney • Tokyo
Singapore • Hong Kong • Cape Town • Madrid • Paris • Milan
Munich • Amsterdam

PEARSON EDUCATION LIMITED

Head Office
Edinburgh Gate
Harlow CM20 2JE
Tel: +44 (0)171 447 2000
Fax: +44 (0)171 240 5771

London Office:
128 Long Acre, London WC2E 9AN
Tel: +44 (0)171 447 2000
Fax: +44 (0)171 240 5771
Website:www.business-minds.com

First published in Great Britain in 2000

© Pearson Education Limited 2000

The right of Jean-Pierre Jeannet to be identified as Author
of this work has been asserted by him in accordance
with the Copyright, Designs and Patents Act 1988.

ISBN 0 273 63276 0

British Library Cataloguing in Publication Data
A CIP catalogue record for this book can be obtained from the British Library.

10 9 8 7 6 5 4 3 2

Typeset by Northern Phototypesetting Co Ltd, Bolton
Printed and bound in Great Britain by Biddles Ltd, Guildford & King's Lynn

The Publishers' policy is to use paper manufactured from sustainable forests.

Contents

Section 5 ● Implementing global mindsets

Foreword

My reasons for writing this book

The 1990s have been dominated by the rapid globalization of business. Global strategies have become issues of great concern to most international firms, and much has been written about the need to accomplish them. Despite the rapid globalization of many enterprises, the conceptual framework for strategy and management have not kept pace. Much of our current understanding of business strategy and management is, although well researched and articulated, relevant for single market companies only, regardless of their global spread. For that reason, I believe it is time for more contributions that focus on the global aspect of strategy and management, and complement the existing, more fundamental understanding of single-country business strategy, and is not intended to cover the fundamental concepts of strategy that apply to all business, independent of whether a company competes in a single market or globally.

When tackling issues of global strategy that go beyond our current understanding of single-country strategy, we have to realize that this is a new, emerging discipline. The prevailing views on elements such as business unit strategy, finance and marketing are quite mature, shared among many academics and practitioners, and already form a coherent body of knowledge. Globalization however, is a field where academics and practitioners alike have not yet formed a coherent, widely shared set of concepts that has found its way into business school teaching and business practice. Although globalization is frequently taught at business schools, academics tend to have more diverging views in this field than academics in other business areas. This is due to the still-emerging nature of concepts of globalization. My intention is to make a contribution to the global strategy area that may begin to converge existing views and help develop a more cohesive academic field.

Through my teaching and consulting work over the past years, I have been able to work directly with and observe at close range the struggle of many firms with the concept of globalization, its interpretation, implementation, and impact on the everyday operations of companies and the lives of their managers. The lessons learned and concepts derived from this close cooperation may benefit managers and the existing community of practising globalists. Most managers work in one industry, hone their skills to that industry, but have little time to look around for inspiration from others, or to rethink their own actions conceptually. It is the role of the business school professor to provide such cross-industry learning, and to challenge companies and managers to look beyond their own operations, so that they may improve their practice of global management beyond the experience provided by their own business.

It is my hope that this book can add clarity to many of the decisions companies and managers face, and thus contribute to the development of vibrant organizations able to contribute to the well-being of their own communities.

For whom is this book intended?

I wrote this book with several audiences in mind. First and foremost, this book was written for the practicing manager who needs to deal with the issues of globalization, from the manager with an extensive global background to the aspiring globalist tackling some of the concepts for the first time. The experienced globalists will, I trust be challenged beyond their existing experience. The less experienced will, I hope, find this book to be a useful guide through the issues to be resolved on the way to a sensible, competitive, global response. All those involved with issues of globalization will, I hope, find this book of interest.

This book is also written for companies. Some aspects are directed at firm strategy and firm behaviour, and are relevant for companies or groups of managers. I have not distinguished between large or small companies or whether they are experienced or new to globalization. In my view, the concepts explained are valid for any firm needing to develop a response to globalization, regardless of size, industry, national origin, or head-office location.

The third audience I had in mind were both students and faculty at major business schools addressing globalization, and global strategies as part of their coursework. Business school students are future globalists who need to develop a global mindset early in their careers. I hope that it may contribute to that important process. *Managing with a global mindset* was not developed as a testbook, but might serve as a supplement to existing courses and materials.

History of this book

Although most of the actual writing of this book was undertaken only over the last two years, the concept building and research that underpins it has been under way for many years. My academic career goes back to 1974 when I began teaching courses in International Marketing and International Business at Babson College. To those of us dealing with international business at that time,

Ted Levitt's writing published in 1983 served as the beginning for moving us into the global world.

Ever since, I have been able to develop individual concepts, or building blocks, not always connected, but all fitting under the umbrella of global strategies. My work on lead markets goes back to 1983. The concept of generic global strategies dates back to 1987. The first time I used the expression 'global mind' was in 1988. Our first text book using the title Global marketing appeared in 1992, followed in rapid succession by the new concepts on global mindsets and global logic in 1995. The vizualization of the global logic analysis in the form of the spiderweb began to appear in 1998, although I had been using it in several forms in the annual Orchestrating Winning Performance (OWP) conference.

What I want the reader to know is that this book is the result of a prolonged effort, spanning some 15 years, during which many of the concepts were created, usually as a response to some teaching, consulting or research assignment. Contrary to the background of many singe-issue books published today, this book was not based on a single research effort. Rather, it has come about from an extended research agenda.

The same can be said for the accompanying graphics. Although it may appear to the reader that these charts were created for this book, in fact most of the graphics were created, like the concepts, as part of my teaching of executives or business school students. The graphics preceded the text, and the text is in many ways the explanation of a series of graphs created when engaging both executive and student audiences.

My learning laboratories for this book

As mentioned earlier, this book was not created in a vacuum. Throughout the creation and learning process, I had the benefit of participating in important strategy discussion at global firms, and classroom discussion in unusual settings. Both acted in the form of essential laboratories where many of the book's concept were born.

The key sites that served as laboratories over many years were mostly European firms with extensive, global operations. Their challenges required new and different responses, and their executives needed to reach a level where they could deal with strategic global issues.

Listing these laboratories could only be an incomplete effort. However, there are some firms that stand out and that have become associated with the creation of specific concepts that are key building blocks for this book.

In the early phases, ABB and Electrolux were part of a multi-company research effort that led to the articulation of the difference between standardization and integration of global strategies. At Lego, I was able to first establish the concepts of global marketing. ICI was a company where, working with its many global businesses, I was given access to both case materials and executives that eventually led to the idea of global logics. At Nokia, I formed the idea of global focus that resulted in the concept of the 'horizontal tiger'. DSM challenged us to deal with the issue of global account management. My work with Sulzer brought about the realization of multiple 'industry codes' eventually leading to the ideal of multiple sets of global logic and their impact on company strategies. With the assistance of Ares Serono we developed the graphics on resource allocation across global opportunities in class. Finally, exposure to a number of executives from the Novartis OTC business led to the many 'Mondrian' type charts used to tease out differences and similarities across multiple geographies.

Other firms helped by inviting us to teach on their executive programs. This experience resulted in the essential validation of many ideas. Siemens of Germany for many years entrusted us with executives needing to deal with global strategies at their business levels. We gained enormously through executive education involving Deloitte Touche Tohmatsu, DSM, ICI, Zeneca, and Novartis. I am also grateful to speaking engagements that challenged me to articulate global strategic thinking at different moments in the development of this text, such as the assignments for Union Bank of Switzerland and Credit Agricole.

Further valuable experience was gained in a larger executive education conference environment. In particular, I would like to mention the experience teaching at IMD's annual program Orchestrating Winning Performance (OWP). Teaching several groups of executives in teams of 50, in multiple sessions each year, and developing new cutting edge materials for each of those sessions, provided an outstanding environment for innovation and conceptualization. Many of the graphs used in this book were initially created in this environment.

I am most grateful to all of these companies who have opened their doors to me over the years, and who have provided an engaging, searching, and challenging environment in which to go beyond the customary approaches to globalization.

Research methodology used for this book

Given the unusual history behind the creation of this book, it should not come as a surprise that its concepts are not the result of a singular, organized approach, such as a survey or other structured methodology. How then were the lessons and facts encountered in the many laboratory environments converted into a coded body of knowledge that bridges all the various companies and industries?

I would describe the principle research methodology as one of observation, generalization, validation, and conceptualization. Observations occur from the many contacts with firms dealing on a global basis. Every classroom contact, every lunch meeting, every formal research or case interview, is an opportunity to learn about something new, and an issue or challenge in need of a response. To go beyond mere factual observation, however, I have tried to generalize the issue isolated on the basis of the question 'If this were typical for many other firms, what would it mean?' Absorbing and resolving these issues then resulted in situational response, These responses were considered at the next event or contact with a firm. One is given a chance to ascertain whether the issue is relevant, important, and investigate how it can be dealt with. Since the initial generalization leads to a generalized response, trying this out on the next contact can generate new insights.

Finding that other firms or managers deal with the same issue is part of the process of validation. Taking it further and reporting on it again to a new, or larger managerial audience leads to a form of conceptualization that has a wider application. Managers confronted with new concepts do not, unlike academics, look for the proof in the concepts themselves. Instead, they tend to bounce the ideas off their own learning and experience base, thus giving an opportunity for rapid feedback on the nature of the ideas and concepts. At each step, the concepts get retested, refined and consolidated, until they become robust enough to be applied to different environments.

The process described has been the underlying research protocol for most of the concepts in this book. This means that the concepts described have been influenced by the nature of the learning, or laboratory experience. However, since they have been tested in sufficiently broad managerial settings with executives from all types of industries and countries, the concepts have proven themselves sufficiently general to be meaningful to a broad business audience.

➲ Acknowledgements

I would like to conclude this foreword with the recognition that this book would not have been published without the support of a number of institutions, colleagues, and individuals both part of and outside academic institutions.

First, let me extend my gratitude to my home institution, Babson College. For 25 years, my colleagues at Babson have supported my efforts to build global teaching material and have given me scope to design courses conducive to the development and teaching of concept in globalization. My assignments in teaching global marketing and global strategies at undergraduate, MBA, and executive levels have been crucial to honing the conceptual elements that are part of this book. Throughout this process, I have benefited form the support of several of Babson's Presidents, in particular Ralph Sorenson, Bill Dill, William Glavin, and Lee Higdon. Similarly, the support from the office of the academic vice president over the years has been crucial, and I wish to mention Walter Carpenter, Melvyn Copen, Gordon Prichett, and Allan Cohen for having tolerated an often difficult schedule on my part. Finally, I am grateful to Babson's major benefactors, namely to the F.W. Olin Foundation for having created the F.W. Olin Chair in Global Business, and to several Babson supporters for the creation of the W.F. Glavin Center for Global Entrepreneurial Management. Both the Olin Chair and the Glavin Center have been highly instrumental in making resources available without which this book would still be at the planning stage.

At IMD I have been able to benefit from access to many laboratories responsible for the creation of core concepts contained in this book. I am grateful to the support experienced from a number of present and past deans and presidents, in particular Derek Abell, and most recently, Peter Lorange. Their support, assignments to numerous executive programs, and interaction with faculty and executives on the Lake of Geneva have been part of my learning laboratory.

Both at Babson College and at IMD I have been supported by an excellent staff, ranging from administrative support, to program administration and case writing and research. The effort of our support staff has in no small measure, contributed to the completion of this project.

Finally, I would like to thank the many willing and unwilling members in my learning laboratories, namely students and executives, who in their open, spontaneous, but thoughtful interactions with issues of globalization have contributed to the sharpening, articulation, and generalization of the tools and concepts described in this book

Why this book is but work in progress

As this book goes to print and eventually reaches its readers, the work of conceptualizing global strategies continues. Every day, new learning opportunities appear. New companies will engage me and thus become learning laboratories. Different sets of students and executives alike will challenge our discussions, and conclusions. Clearly, the learning will continue and cannot be concluded with the publication of this book. By the time the reader will sit down and absorb some or all of it, new experiences will have resulted in either a sharpening of an explanation in the creation of additional concepts, or even in the elimination of some and their replacement with others. Such is the challenge of continued change, and the opportunities of continued learning. Keeping this in mind, I need to alert the reader to the fact that this book represents but work in progress. However, this does not require the readers to depend solely on this author for further elaboration or new ideas. Having engages in the concepts layed out in this book, it is my sincere hope and expectation that readers themselves, through a clearer and deeper understanding of 'things global' and absorption of a 'global mindset' will be able to do their own further development, updating of concepts, and creation of break-through ideas. All that is necessary is to engage in their own learning laboratories are open eyes, curiosity, and a willingness to conceptualize beyond daily business.

Providence, RI
October 1999

Preface

Background

The issue of globalization has been with business for some time. Much has been written about the companies, but far less about the managers who have to make global firms work. This book intends to close that gap. The concept of the global mindset has been the center of the author's writing for several years and has its origin in a need to describe the nature of a global perspective. The book takes a detailed look at the concept of the global mindset and contrasts it with other types of mindsets (domestic, international, multinational, regional). It makes an argument for managers to achieve a global mindset and for companies to create a sufficient cadre of such managers. It then goes about detailing the elements that might make up such a mindset: database, analytic skills, behavior, etc. In its orientation, this book is forward looking, describing future practice and future requirements, and yet is based upon examples of advanced practice firms.

The book also contains concepts, developed partly by the author as a result of his consulting practice, that are geared primarily to the global strategist and are different from concepts used for more typical country-by-country business practice. Frequent use of company illustrations is made.

This is a new topic and no major books are known to exist on this content. The closest books, in terms of content, are Ghoshal and Bartlett (*Managing Across Borders*) or Ohmae (*The Borderless World*, Collins, London, 1990).

Outline of the book

Section 1: Introducing the global mindset

Chapter 1 outlines the changes in the globalizing economic system which requires a change in the type of managerial mindset. Reference is made to previous types of mindsets and the need for a paradigm shift. Some winners and losers, big and small companies, will be analyzed.

Chapter 2 deals with the nature of the global mindset compared to other types of current managerial mindsets. In particular, the differences between domestic, international, multinational, regional, and global mindsets are emphasized. The issue of an appropriate pathway towards a global mindset is raised.

Chapter 3 presents five generic mindsets for consideration by the reader.

Section 2: The analytic skills of the global mindset

The emphasis in this section is on the analytical skills required to ferret out the extent of globalization that has taken place, or that will occur in a given industry. Global logic assessment is one of the core analytical elements presented in this book. The various chapters cover finding the sources of global logic within the customer base, finding global logic in industry and the competitive environment and assessing different patterns of global logic.

Section 3: Global market assessment

This section focuses on new types of market analysis needed for global analysis as opposed to single-country analysis. New tools proposed are the global chessboard, ripple effects, and lead markets.

Section 4: Global strategic skills

This section deals with the various types of generic global strategies managers need to understand. It takes the position that the world is much too complex to be categorized into "global" or "non-global," indicating that the relevant question becomes "Which global strategy do I adopt?". A multitude of different generic global strategies are described.

Section 5: Implementing global mindsets

Chapter 13 outlines the various types of new organizational forms companies will have to adopt in order to become successful with global strategies. Key new concepts are global mandates, the various types of permanent or semi-permanent global units formed today, and processes necessary to achieve global leverage.

In Chapter 14 we deal with the frequently asked question: "What does a global mindset have to know?". The difference between single-country knowledge and global knowledge in the realm of politics, economics, history, and culture are identified. Suggestions are included on how the individual manager can build a personal global "database."

The final chapter focuses on the actions companies can take to implement the ideas described in this book. It is intended to be a "call to action," or a "wake-up call" to managers anywhere, with any size of firm, and any industry.

Research and evidence base of material

The author has had some 20 years' experience in executive education, and spent much of the last ten years researching global marketing and global business strategies. Many of the concepts created and described come out of his teaching experience at Babson College in the USA, and at IMD Institute in Lausanne, Switzerland, as well as from teaching in many executive programs for international and global firms. The author has also had first-hand experience in guiding international firms in their strategy making and has had ample opportunities to test those concepts in real situations.

As part of the text, concepts are illustrated using leading firms. The author has had direct contact with many of these firms, either through management development teaching, research, case writing, or project consulting. Included in that list are US-based firms such as IBM, GE, Whirlpool, Citibank, Polaroid, Digital, State Street Bank, Johnson & Johnson, Exxon, AT&T, Nynex, and Hewlett-Packard. Among the European firms, the author's list of direct contacts includes Siemens, ICI, Zeneca, Nestlé, Nokia, ABB, Sulzer, DSM, Avebe, Ares-Serono, Neste, Tetra Laval, BAA, Union Bank of Switzerland, NatWest/Coutts, Telekurs, Deloitte Touche Tohmatsu International, Olivetti, St. Gobain, Ciba-Geigy, Philips, Logitech, Electrolux, Siemens-Nixdorf, Zurich Insurance, Swissair, SMH (Swatch/Omega), Curver-Rubbermaid, and Lego. The author has had intensive interaction with several of these companies, with regards to many of their business units. Furthermore, the author has access to a large inventory of examples from his secondary research. The author has also been Visiting Lecturer at Keio Graduate School of Business in Japan, and has worked with several Japanese companies, including Sony.

Previous publications of related concepts

The author has published several articles on globalization, and, most recently, added a chapter on this topic ("Developing a Global Mindset") in *Global Marketing Strategies: Text and Cases* (Houghton Mifflin, 3rd edn, 1995 (with Hennessey), a leading textbook on global and international marketing widely used in business schools, both in the USA and abroad.

Other relevant books recently published by the author include *Cases in International Marketing*, Prentice-Hall, 2nd edn, 1995 (with Gale, Kashani and Turpin), *Cases in Marketing Management*, Wiley, 1992 (with Dalrymple and Parsons), and *Competitive Marketing Strategies in a European Context*, Imede, 1987. A relevant recent article published by the author is "The age of the global mind", *Die Unternehmung*, Bern, Switzerland. The author has also written some 100 cases and notes distributed through the European Case Clearinghouse, Cranfield UK, and widely used in many business schools and management development programs. Many cases have been published in case books of other authors, and some have been translated into a variety of languages.

Section 1

Introducing the global mindset

1

Introduction: The global imperative

➡ To whom does globalization apply?

One of the questions most frequently posed by managers centers around the need to globalize companies. "Is this really for all, or only for some?", is the typical question. As a result of frequently having to analyze the necessity to pursue globalization, we have developed a series of diagnostics and responses. This book is aimed at managers, or companies, who have to deal with those questions. In general, we have found that the imperatives of globalization apply to most industries. Since those industries are made up of large firms, small firms, start-up ventures, and companies in different geographic regions, the global imperative has been found to apply to all. Regardless of the size of a company's operation, its location, or its role in the business system, the global imperative needs to be accommodated or the enterprise risks a decline in competitiveness.

The global imperative touches companies at all levels. It affects their strategy as well as the way they look at their global opportunities. It affects organizations at all levels, from the CEO vantage point to line managers, functional managers, and reaches into middle and lower levels of management. The concepts described in this volume are therefore relevant to a wide managerial audience, regardless of responsibility.

The global imperative touches companies at all levels.

As a result of the growing global imperative, we are describing a requirement for a totally new managerial mindset which we call the global mindset. This global mindset will need to be adopted both by companies and individual managers. It stands in sharp contrast to earlier managerial mindsets. In this first chapter, we intend to give an outline of that new managerial mindset driven by the global imperative and will introduce the major conceptual elements companies will need to master if they intend to accommodate the global imperative. As the book unfolds, each one of these concepts is described in greater detail in chapters 2 through 15.

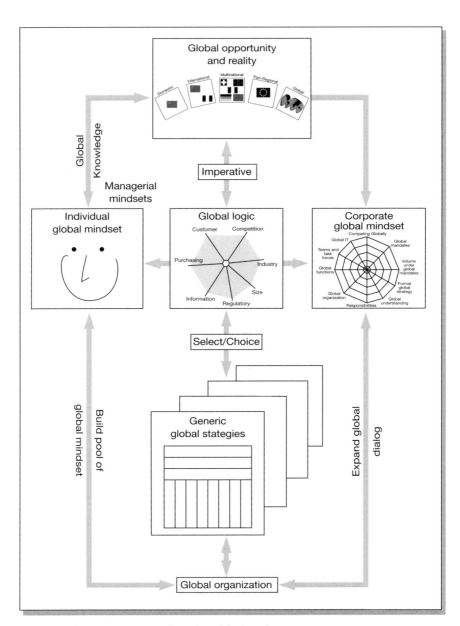

Fig 1.1   Conceptual outline for this book

¹ See Figure 6.4
² See Figure 15.1

Global logics: the key to understanding the global imperative

As the term imperative implies, we are faced with an era that subjects business to great, at times uncontrollable forces. The global imperative can be described as a absolute necessity that forces companies to embrace globalization or face extinction. Any company that faces a strong global imperative will have to pursue a path of globalization, although that particular path can vary under differing circumstances.

The global imperative, however, does not impact all companies in the same way. Following an anlysis of countless industries, a set of tools has emerged that allows us to categorize the particular global imperative and to use the patterns in shaping globalization strategies. Although some general global economic forces surround the entire world economy, we need to view the pressure to globalize on an industry-to-industry basis. The result is to classify the global imperative in terms of the particular global logic present in a given industry by understanding the various dimensions of the logic.

> The global imperative can be described as an absolute necessity that forces companies to embrace globalization or face extinction.

Global logic

Emerging as a central theme in this book is the notion that companies are under pressure to globalize. The presence of this pressure is described as global logic, causing companies to pursue global strategies of some form or risk a negative competitive impact. Some form of global logic is present in any company's industry and is germane for all firms that compete in that industry. It is therefore not company-specific. Global logic, when present, must be accommodated, thus becoming the compelling argument to move into the direction of globalization. It is central to understanding the extent of the global imperative.

When analyzing the global logic present in a company's industry, it is not sufficient to simply understand if the pressure is absent, present, or strong. We have identified several types of global logic, each one in need of deeper understanding. Identifying the specific source of dominating global logic pressure is necessary to guide the development of an appropriate global response. The sum total of all global logic forces make up the global imperative.

Customer-based global logic dimensions

The first group consists of global logics that center around a company's customer base. Fundamentally, we need to know to what extent the requirements, the purchasing practices, and the information acquisition patterns of a industry's customers translate into relevant global logic that could dictate the adaptation of a global strategy.

First, global customer pressure is an indicator of the similarity of customer demand. Customers might be similar across broad needs, leading to broad global product categories. Customers seeking similar benefits for products or services lead to global benefits. Finally, customers might demand similar product features which would lead firms to global products. Global customer pressure might exist at only one or two levels, and to a different extent.

Firms need to also understand the purchasing range of an industry. When customers, be they business-to-business or individual consumers, adhere to local buying, little global purchasing logic exists. When, however, companies begin to pool purchasing globally and even gravitate to global purchasing contracts, a strong global purchasing logic emerges. Managing with a global mindset demands that a distinction be made between the customers' requirements and the purchasing range as it will result in different types of global logic pressures.

Finally, the information acquisition range of an industry needs to be assessed. This requires an understanding of how customers in an industry go about the process of finding information, scan advertising, or obtain information of any kind that assists them in the purchasing decision. In industries where customers limit themselves to information available only locally, we can speak of very low global information logic. In industries where customers scan the globe, attend trade shows in foreign markets, and are keenly aware of developments no matter where they may occur, we can speak of substantial global logic pressure.

Industry-based global logic dimensions

Global pressure can also be found among the industry environment. In particular, we are differentiating among several types of generic global logics that measure the extent of pressure on all industry member firms with a different impact than those based upon customer understanding. Looking at industry, we find global logic pressure emanates from competitors, industry dynamics, critical mass, and the regulatory environment. Each of these forces creates its own specific global logic which must be understood by any firm wishing to compete in any industry.

When a company competes across the world and encounters consistently the same set of competitors, we have indications of a competitive logic. The competitive environment is further defined by the number of theaters a company encounters in an industry, ranging from many, basically locally defined with little global pressure versus a single global competitive theater signaling considerable global pressure.

Apart from the competitive dynamics, we need to recognize the require-ments of the industry. In particular, industries where the relevant key success factors are relatively similar across the world are characterized by a high degree of industry logic. For industries where critical mass, or minimal size, plays a role, we can speak of size logic. Finally, the regulatory environment may be dif-ferent by country, resulting in little regulatory logic or, where the regulations are relatively homogeneous, a strong regulatory logic may ensue.

Interpreting global logic patterns as spiderwebs

For a thorough understanding of the major source of global pressure, the vari-ous global logics dimensions need to be combined into an composite tapestry that helps in the identification of the dominant pressure. This we do this by assembling the analysis into a spiderweb-type chart that clarifies graphically the dominant source. Large "footprints" are typical of industries with extensive global logic. Each industry is likely to produce its own specific pattern, sug-gesting that this analysis needs be carried out on an industry basis. The global logic spiderweb will be employed as one of the core elements in developing global strategies.

Relevant for all

Since global logic is a concept that applies to all players in a given industry, it will have to be accommodated by all. This implies that it is not just for the large players in an industry, or those already recognized as international or multina-tional players. Global logic does not stop at size but engulfs even medium and small companies. Global logic pressure needs to be recognized by start-up ven-tures as much as by established firms. Global logic is also not restricted to any given geographic region of the world: it applies to all countries, large or small, developed or emerging. The only respite from global logic is granted to firms that happen to operate in an industry with small, or negligent global logic or imperative. The number of those industries, however, is becoming smaller. The reason for the dwindling number of "protected" industries lies in the nature of today's global economy.

⊛ The reality of the global economy

As the 20th century draws to a close, we are witnessing a historic sea change in the global economy and the global trading system. As individual country-based economic systems become submerged in the larger, more prevalent global econ-omy, this creates new imperatives for management. The type of managerial par-adigm that dominated in the 19th and 20th centuries is rapidly displaced with a completely new form of managerial and strategic thinking necessitated by the emerging global economy. With this book, we intend to challenge the international management community by confronting it with innovative managerial concepts researched, created, and invented for the single purpose of assuring the competitive survival of companies into the 21st century.

As the 20th century draws to a close, we are witnessing a historic sea change in the global economy and the global trading system.

When we speak of the merging global economy, our emphasis is primarily on the trading economy. We intend to view the world through the eyes of managers and companies who are considering if, or how, to compete globally through either products or services. We are delineating this difference for a purpose. Much has been made of the globalization of the world's financial markets, its capital and investments, and the freedom of capital to move from one country to another. Since mid-1997, substantial financial turbulence has been witnessed in those markets, commencing with developments in Thailand, Malaysia, Indonesia, and Korea, but encompassing also Japan, Russia, and Latin America. These changes might have a lasting effect on the capital markets of the major western nations. Along with this development, some voices are heard that call for a pull-back from free-wheeling global capital markets. The reader might wonder about the purpose of writing a book about global management at this juncture.

The world economy, measured by gross national product, has greatly benefitted from the growth of world capital markets and the liberalization of financial markets in key countries. This has brought capital, investments, and substantial economic growth into these countries. Although influencing the overall size of the global opportunity faced by firms marketing either products or services, we need to differentiate the need to accommodate global imperatives for firms from those of the capital markets. The issues raised in this book,

Globalization is not a fashion, or a temporary development. It is here to stay, and most companies or managers have yet to make their accommodation to it.

the concepts advanced to deal with them, and the necessity to transform companies to adapt a new managerial mindset are largely independent of the developments in the world's capital markets. Globalization, as advanced in this book, is understood as a response to fundamental forces, the global imperative, which are partially independent of the developments in the world's capital markets. It may appear that developments in Asia might depress the appetite around the world for investors, but the global imperative on companies is not necessarily mitigated by this development. Globalization is not a fashion, or a temporary development. It is here to stay, and most companies or managers have yet to make their accommodation to it.

New ways of assessing global market opportunities

The realities of the global imperative makes it necessary for firms to view their opportunity differently. Business opportunities are no longer to be viewed in local market terms, or on a country basis. Instead, managers and companies need to view the entire world as the economic opportunity. To this effect, we have introduced two principal concepts. First, there is a need to see the opportunity as part of a global chessboard where market size and value as part of an entire global strategy are more relevant than growth or investment climate as a determinant of where a company needs to go.

In a world dominated by the global imperative, a company needs to know which markets to enter, and to do so from a strategic necessity and not from an internal firm preference point of view. This is a world dominated by the nature of "must win" markets. The global chessboard consists of all markets that have been "joined" into the global economy, which means that there is reasonable freedom to move goods, services, funds, profits, people, and capital. Countries that maintain closed economies and therefore are not part of the global chessboard have little or no strategic value when it comes to responding to the global imperative. Over the past 20 years, we have seen a tremendous expansion of the global chessboard, as a successive number of countries previously separate have joined in. This includes China, through trade liberalization and market opening processes, India, by allowing international firms more open access to its markets, Latin America, through dismantling barriers to trade, and the series of countries that used to operate under state-trading systems such as the countries of the former Soviet Union and Comecon agreement.

In a world driven by the global imperative as indicated by the global logics, a company needs to be clear on the strategic importance of each country, or territory. With more than 200 different territories in the world today, a global strategy needs to be focused on the core markets. Depicting the world opportunity as a global chessboard drives home the point of size, and challenges companies to define the relevant metric that determines market size by industry. Each industry thus faces its own global chessboard, in line with the earlier observation that each industry develops its own global logic.

As the world remains a highly dynamic place, companies will be challenged to configure their chessboard not only in today's terms, but to do so in terms of future metrics, future size and future importance. The basis for understanding how an industry's future chessboard might be configured is a sense of the trends in the industry and how developments ripple through the chessboard – with the aid of the concept of the lead market. Lead markets are markets, usually countries, where developments occur first and eventually reverberate through all other markets. Managing lead markets is important under the global imperative as it gives any company an indication of how the global chessboard might evolve, thus helping in placing crucial bets in the form of investments, product launches, market selection, etc.

The need for a new managerial mindset

Today's globalizing economy rose out of the previous international trading system. As the world economy developed, it moved through different phases, progressing from a trading economy based upon exporting in the 19th century towards a economy that made it easy for companies to set up operations in many countries. At each turn of the economic development, the type of companies that dominated the scene changed. Earlier, it was the international trading firms that dominated. Then we saw the rise of the exporters, eventually giving way to the multinational firms of the 1960s and 1970s which dotted the world map with plants. With the emerging global imperative fueled by the liberalization of the world economy in the 1980s, the dominating organizational paradigm changed from the multinational firm to the global firm.

The globalizing economy has had a tremendous influence on firms, forcing them to adapt to new realities. Expanded competition meant that firms would be able to enter many markets, and local or domestic firms were increasingly faced with competitors from far away. A relentless pursuit of efficiency, partially driven by new realities among investors and capital markets, forced companies to adopt new ways of management. Management in firms faced with global competition cannot expect to cope using the managerial philosophy from the past.

The global mindset as a new managerial paradigm

Managers can be categorized into different type of mandates, ranging from domestic to international, regional, and multi-domestic. Each of these mindsets represents a particular point of view and is the result of different type of experiences. For the new merging competition in the globalizing economy, the old mindsets will not suffice and a global mind will become necessary. The capabilities of this new type of mindset are the main concerns for this book. But first, let us look at how managerial mindsets progressed over time.

The domestic mindset is characterized by a reliance on one market as the key reference and is the mindset most managers are born with. Domestic mindsets rely on a single reference point, their domestic markets, for judgments. For successful managers, who need to act in a globalizing economy, working with a domestic mindset tends to limit the point of view.

Representing the next level up is the international mindset characterized by one or few experiences in another country. The international mindset might come with different levels of international experience, ranging from casual international exposure through travel all the way to extensive foreign stay resulting in a capacity to integrate in a foreign country or environment. The international mindset, with a limited, but in-depth exposure, is, however, not identical to the more extensive global mindset.

A manager with extensive regional experience, such as throughout Latin America, or across Europe, may possess a regional mindset. The regional mindset is of interest because it includes experiences across a score of countries. Still further up the scale is the multinational mindset typical of executives who have been on successive international assignments in different countries. Although representing the backbone of the executive pool of many of our largest multinational firms today, executives with multinational mindsets are still not necessarily possessing true global mindsets.

For the purpose of this book, the global mindset is defined as a state of mind able to understand a business, an industry sector, or a particular market on a global basis. The executive with a global mindset has the ability to see across multiple territories and focuses on commonalities across many markets rather than emphasizing the differences among countries. Companies which find themselves engulfed by extensive global pressures will need to acquire a large pool of executives who possess a global mindset and who are able to view business opportunities from a global perspective. Part of this global mindset is an entire set of new and different analytical tools that would not be needed by the previous domestic or multinational mindset. New strategies, resulting from responding to new market opportunities, are another part of this toolkit.

This global perspective differs substantially from the more traditional single-country, or domestic, and multinational perspective so much more typical today. Much of this book is devoted to explaining the abilities of the global mindset, both in terms of conceptual or analytical skills, as well as in terms of knowledge and organizational abilities.

Accommodating the global imperative

When referring to the global imperative, we have made several references to the need to accommodate such forces. The meaning of accommodation is important as it connotes a sense that different types of accommodation are possible. We have made it clear that the global imperative, as characterized by the global logic, impacts on firms large and small, domestic and international, start-up and established, and unrelated to geographic location. However, accommodation may differ by firm. We will make the point in the context of this book that there can be different ways of accommodation, and that the major challenge of a company lies in finding the appropriate form. The question is now shifting from whether or not a global accommodation is necessary to one of searching for the best accommodation. We have long left the age of questioning if a company needs to adopt a global strategy to the era where we must decide which of many potential generic global strategies to pursue.

The pathway to globalization had traditionally been viewed as a last step in the internationalization process of a firm. Typically, it was assumed that a firm would first conquer its domestic market, then try its hand at exporting, establish an international posture, and eventually move towards the state of multinational strategy. Globalization was viewed as the last step in this pathway. We are arguing that "global" is the latest of a series of managerial paradigms. The fact that it had not been adopted by most firms was primarily related to the fact that it was an unknown approach.

The global imperative will not stop at the doorstep of multinational firms.

Once the global imperative has been established, companies will have to move towards globalization regardless of where they happen to be in the development process. The global imperative will not stop at the doorstep of multinational firms. It affects all companies, domestic firms, exporters, and firms from little to extensive international coverage.

One of the important discoveries of our research was the realization that companies had actually a choice among a full range of different types of global strategies. No longer were firms restricted to the "global or not global" syndrome where global meant "doing everything everywhere in the same way". Generic global business strategies are prototype or archetypal strategies, ranging from shallow levels of globalization all the way to full integration. Fully integrated global strategies encompass globalization of the key strategic elements, as well as the major functions. A company would pursue the global opportunity with one single integrated strategy rather than pursuing individual country opportunities with separately created strategies.

Other types of generic global strategies introduced in this volume are global category strategies which allow firms to globalize more broadly across a given product category while keeping many decisions, such as product, segments, or branding, for local management. A company might find it attractive to integrate further and drive a global segment strategy, keeping the customer segments constant and coordinating and leverage across global segments. In some cases, firms have adopted a global customer strategy focusing all products or service offerings on a given customer globally and integrating all activities around the world on a single account. All of these generic global strategies reflect different levels of integration and more or less control at the central or local levels.

Observing many internationally active firms, we have also uncovered a series of global functional strategies. These functional strategies challenge the firms to determine the appropriate level of global integration across a business function. Firms must assess whether they need to adopt global manufacturing strategies, selecting from a number of different types of integration levels. Research and development (R&D) is another function that has challenged companies in terms of finding the appropriate global integration level. Finance and control offer a multitude of globalization decisions, forcing companies to come to terms with issues in control, treasury function, accounting, and information technology.

Finance and control offer a multitude of globalization decisions, forcing companies to come to terms with issues in control, treasury function, accounting and information technology.

More than any other function, marketing has received attention in the globalization debate. Companies have to select from a series of different generic global marketing strategies, each with different levels of integration. Although a company may adopt a completely integrated global marketing strategy, many companies will find it more suitable to adopt partially global strategies. Global product strategies emphasize the similarity of the physical product, or service, and similarity in functionality or features. Global communications strategies cover a range of options, such as global advertising, global branding, or global audience strategies.

Adopting generic global business strategies

The major new development is the shift in debate from the completely global versus completely local strategy to a more sophisticated understanding of the notion of partially global strategies. With the understanding that for most companies the effective choice will be somewhere in the middle ground, the selection of the most suitable partially global strategy becomes central. To approach this selection process, we fall back on the concept of the global logic, introduced earlier, as the linchpin in these discussions. Depending on the strongest global logic source, the partially global strategy will have to be suitable to accommodate the latter's imperative.

Accommodating strong global customer logic will make companies adopt global segment, global product, and global benefit strategies. By the same token, strong global purchasing logic will demand global customer strategies, global account strategies, and global branding, as well as a globalization of the pricing strategy. When the global information logic is paramount, global communications strategies, such as global branding, global themes, global positioning, or global symbols will become required.

The implication of strong industry-based logics is different. Where a strong global industry logic persists, global category or global assets strategies are called for, as are some of the global functional strategies to allow for leverage. Accommodating critical mass logic will drive companies towards global reach strategies or global niche and focus strategies. Companies facing strong global competitive logic will need to fall back on global category, global segment, and integrated global strategies.

Setting global strategic priorities

The fact that a myriad partially global strategies exist places a premium on understanding the matching process against the global logic pattern of a given industry. With each industry showing its own global logic pattern, and thus presenting a different form of global imperative for accommodation, multi-business unit firms should be prepared to tolerate a number of different generic global strategies. This has been, and continues to be, a source of difficulty as many companies are still in the mode of equating globalization with one single strategy. When faced with multiple global logic spiderwebs, the tendency is to mandate the form for the largest business to all, thus constraining growth for the other businesses.

When comparing firms' present global posture in terms of meeting the imperative based on the global logic faced, any existing gap becomes apparent. Firms whose own posture is not yet as developed as global logic demands would be suffering from a reduction in competitiveness, essentially leaving money on the table. Firms who over-globalize incur the opposite risk, strangling their operations with procedures and strategies beyond their competitive need.

Getting it right is no easy task. The essential dilemma in pursuing globalization for any company is the tremendous demand on resources for the global build-up. Firms, even some of the largest, are unlikely to be able to live up to the demands for globalization of all of their businesses. Choices will have to be made. Presently, many corporations still have a strategic posture that results in a number of businesses with partial globalization, or many businesses resting on regional positions. In this fight for resources, the firm with superior focus is likely to come out on top. Caught between the need to feed globalization on one hand and to maintain advances in technology, innovation, and managerial practice on the other, companies will have to understand where to "go long," and where to "go short." Inevitably, resources have to redirected towards building strong global positions across all relevant key markets. Only focus will help companies achieve that.

Focus in the context of global resource allocation means that the advantage has shifted to companies who are able to field a multi-regional or multi-country business, thus geographically broadly based, but limiting their business to a single, or selected set of segments, sectors, or categories. We have called them the "horizontal tigers," and call the descending companies the "vertical dragons." The future is with the horizontal tigers, and companies will have to carefully pick the businesses they desire to globalize while finding ways to reduce their exposure to others by divesting or floating them off. As we observe the changes among large, traditional corporations through reorganization, we are witnessing a wholesale shift from the broad-based, unfocused business to the focused niche company with their superior promise to accommodate the global imperative.

Implementing global mindsets

Strategy direction, even when couched in terms of a compelling argument, cannot be implemented in a vacuum. If companies want to deliver on the global imperative, they will need to make major changes in their organizations. The managerial talent pool will have to be brought up to the demands of globalization, and the companies themselves as organizations will be in need of adopting a global mindset.

> **Strategy direction, even when couched in terms of a compelling argument, cannot be implemented in a vacuum. If companies want to deliver on the global imperative, they will need to make major changes in their organizations.**

Building global organizations

To adapt the organizations in line with the demands of pursing the global logic in their industries, companies will increasingly create deliberate opportunities for global responsibilities. These positions, which we call global mandates, can be found at any level in an organization. Managers occupying such global mandates will be asked to execute their responsibility on a global scale, rather than regionally or domestically. In addition, business units also will be asked to pursue global mandates. Corporations will move towards issuing global strategic mandates to strategic business units (SBUs) and measure progress accordingly.

As business units receive their global mandates, companies will be asked to change the responsibilities between central head office and business units. Increasingly, the newly freed SBUs will be disentangled from the corporate webs and allowed to make their own arrangements in their key markets, freeing them from corporate international divisions. Regional managerial responsibility, as is already the trend, will be relegated to lower levels and many more business will receive unencumbered global mandates. Regional and country-level operations will have to learn how to implement the global strategy locally, or contribute to its success more specifically. This will lead to a wholesale change in the organizational charter of businesses, where many managerial parameters controlled locally up to now will be coordinated from a center, or at least in a coherent integrated manner. This major change in how international firms operate is already underway in many companies. The process is not yet complete, however.

Creating global mindsets

Hand in hand with the organizational redesign of the future global firm is the change in the dominating managerial mindset. We have already made it clear that this new type of competition will require the adoption of a global mindset, both on the part of individual managers, and by entire firms. Both types of global mindsets are relevant to the successful implementation of globalization.

First, let us turn to individual managers. Moving them from a domestic, international, or multi-domestic mindset requires the understanding of new global strategies and a clear sense of the forces behind the global imperative. That is largely a cerebral process and can be understood analytically. The new global mindset requires managers to master knowledge not only of key markets, ranging from the background of a country to its current economic situation, but also an understanding and appreciation of the overarching global structure, be it in history, economics, politics, or a related field. Global knowledge is more than the summation of knowledge of the world's top markets.

Adding this new type of knowledge to the individual manager is part of the process of globalization, but global mandates on their own will fail unless they are supported by an organization that, judging from its behavior, *breathes* global thinking. This has prompted us to pay attention to the global mindset of individual firms, as opposed to individual managers. Calling this the corporate global mindset, it has become clear from working with and observing many of those firms that corporate global thinking is often several steps behind requirements as signaled by the global imperative. If the corporate global mindset cannot expand, opportunities will be missed because the organization will inevitably fail to respond fully to the demands of the global imperative.

If the corporate global mindset cannot expand, opportunities will be missed because the organization will inevitably fail to respond fully to the demands of the global imperative.

We have proposed both a full diagnostic, which companies or managers might want to apply, and a set of moves firms can undertake to expand their own global mindsets. A principal assumption underlying our suggestions is the realization that managers will find it difficult to learn to think in global terms if their present positions, and future ones, do not actually require that. In other words, too many of today's existing firms select for major executive appointments managers who may have had successive single-country assignments, but who did not have practice thinking across multiple markets. We maintain that a major step into the direction of rectifying this, and making companies think and behave more globally, is to create a series of managerial positions for temporary assignments or permanent assignments, which allow firms to move its managerial talent through those positions equipped with global mandates, thus forcing young managers to think globally. Placing managers in a situation where they have to think or act globally remains one of the strongest remedies to balance the need for more globally thinking talent with the reality of managers typically raised in single-country stovepipes. Achieving this balance will be a core element in achieving competitiveness in the global business world of the 21st century.

The organization of this book follows closely the argument advanced in this introductory chapter:

- In Chapters 2 and 3 we begin the exploration of the new world economic system and the need for a new managerial mindset. In particular, we make the point on the differences between existing mindsets and the future, global mindset.

- Section 2 is focused entirely on the global logic. We take the readers through a detailed description of both the customer-based (Chapter 4) and industry-based global logic dimensions (Chapter 5). Combining this analysis, Chapter 6 demonstrates how global logic patterns can be analyzed for an interpretation of the global imperative.

- Section 3 is devoted to the assessment of global market opportunities. In Chapter 7, we review the concept of the global chessboard and its use as a strategic tool. The dynamic market interpretations and trend analysis using lead markets is the core of Chapter 8.

- Section 4 deals with the required global strategic skills. We first review the various pathways to globalization in Chapter 9. Chapter 10 is devoted to the various generic global business strategies. In Chapter 11 the generic global marketing strategies are reviewed and the relationship between global logic and selection of generic global strategies is demonstrated. The section ends with Chapter 12 dealing with prioritization and focusing resources against a whole set of demands.

- Section 5 addresses implementation issues for global strategies, and how companies and individuals can adopt more of a global mindset. The new forms of organizations and the ideas of shaping global mandates is the core of Chapter 13. Chapter 14 deals with individual requirements and steps individual managers can take to move towards the adoption of a global mindset. Chapter 15 concentrates on how companies as such can adopt global mindsets and the actions they need to undertake to foster an environment that is conducive to global thinking. Chapter 16 provides a conceptual summary and outlines a step-by-step approach on how to perform a global analysis on a business.

The need for global minds

During the past decade significant changes have affected the world economy forcing both business and government institutions to adapt to a new world, the world of the global economy. This new economic order with its new imperatives requires substantial changes in the practice of management. Adapting to these changes is no longer a matter of learning new tools. Instead, we need an entirely new managerial outlook. When companies change, their managers must change. This new mindset, the global mindset, is a requirement for companies competing in the new global economic order.[1] Availability of a sufficiently large cadre of global minds will become as much a key success factor (KSF) for future success as technology, market power, or other more traditional business expertise.

Development from Trading to Globalized Economy

Before exploring the global mindset, we first examine the forces reshaping our economies, producing competitive upheaval all over the world.

The international trading economy

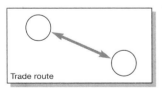

Trade route

The global economy differs radically from the previous international economy which developed for centuries in the era of trade. Passing through several phases from trade in agricultural products to trade in manufactured goods, managers bridged business practice across two countries.[2] The trader needed to understand foreign trade practices, specifically market access, transactions, and payment. Profit was derived largely from efficient management. The trader's key was identifying where demand for goods existed, and where to find supply to meet this demand. Business was conducted through "correspondents" or agencies with knowledge of foreign languages. Communication was hazardous, and travel was difficult and time-consuming. In the Middle Ages, prominent firms such as the Medici[3] and the Fugger[4] developed. Later came the age of the Yankee Clipper, of international trading houses such as East Hanseatic of Denmark, Volkart of Switzerland and the Hudson Bay Company of the UK. Much later, Japanese trading firms such as Mitsubishi, Mitsui, Sumitomo, and Marubeni became major forces in international business-building up large networks of subsidiaries spanning the globe.

Although there is no agreement as to when this trading era actually ended, it was probably some time in the first half of the 20th century, possibly with the advent of World War I. Today even the largest Japanese firms no longer dominate exports of manufactured products and instead play a role importing raw materials and metals. With operations all around the world covering activities such as finance, distribution, mining, and oil and gas exploration, the large trading companies act as intermediaries for as much as two-thirds of Japanese imports. However, many exporting firms, such as Honda, Sony, and Toyota, have preferred to run their own sales networks. The Japanese trading companies are increasingly engaged in non-merchandise trading activities as a result.[5]

In some commodity sectors, such as grain or wheat, western trading companies such as Bunge, André, Cargill, and Continental dominate the grain trading sector.[6] Once the dominant force in international business, the share of these companies has declined and other types of international firms have assumed a more dominant role.

The era of the international exporting and importing economy

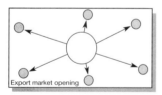

Export market opening

With the advance of the manufacturing economy, a new form of enterprise emerged, manufacturers exporting products into many different markets. The classical export company developed a new product for its domestic market, improved it, and began to export as demand grew. International expansion occurred as an afterthought rather than as intentional strategy. Market success depended on technological or innovative product quality and on demand in other parts of the world for a domestic product.

Although many firms continue export operations today, few companies may be classified as pure exporters with production marketed internationally from a single production point.

Although many firms continue export operations today, few companies may be classified as pure exporters with production marketed internationally from a single production point. Boeing of the USA assembles jet planes in Seattle but sources components worldwide. Boeing consistently remains the largest US exporter with $11.844 billion worth in 1996, accounting for slightly more than half of total business. For the commercial jet segment, the export share was considerably higher still.[7] Among European firms, Volvo[8] of Sweden sells some 87 percent of passenger car volume outside its home market, Daimler-Benz mar-kets a large percentage of its volume outside Germany, having only recently begun production abroad with the opening of its new assembly plant in the southern USA.[9] Among Japanese firms, Toyota Motor company sold 2.343 million vehicles abroad. Of those, 1.379 mil-lion were manufactured in the local markets, and almost 1 million exported from Japan. This represented about 22 percent of Japanese production. In total, international sales accounted for almost one-third of total output.[10]

> **Once a dominant form of international business, exporting declined when companies realized that for reasons of efficiency, market entry, or service, plants were needed in or near the markets served.**

Managerial skills of the exporting company, particularly those relating to international business, consisted largely of market opening, market explo-ration, and market building. Executives traveled to foreign markets and identi-fied distributors or sales companies. Once a dominant form of international business, exporting declined when companies realized that for reasons of effi-ciency, market entry, or service, plants were needed in or near the markets served.

The era of the multinational enterprise

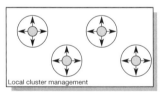
Local cluster management

The period following World War II saw rapid expan-sion, with US firms initially and later European and Japanese firms leaving exporting to build factories and operations in foreign markets. Although export-ing to some small markets continued, dedicated man-ufacturing operations began to serve the larger markets. Firms with manufacturing enterprises all over the world, now called multinational companies (MNCs),[11] began to dominate the international econ-omy. Companies built local plants to protect their market interests and tailored strategy to the local situation by developing multi-local strategies.

Nestlé, the Swiss-based international food company, is a leading example of the MNC. Active outside Switzerland, its home country base, since 1868, Nestlé transacts only 2 percent of sales in Switzerland.[12] Of nearly 500 factories oper-ating around the world, only 12 are located in Switzerland, indicating that most of Nestlé's international business is produced locally and that exporting plays a minor role. Nestlé consists of a large number of operating companies, each controlling its own local strategy. At Nestlé, input from the head office is mini-mized, controlling the local effort rather than directing it.

MNCs had a keen interest in forming managers able to run their numerous local operations with knowledge of national operating conditions. Managers

were often sent overseas for long periods, some with successive assignments of 3 to 5 years, usually moving within a given region of the world. Eventually local managers were hired, and the need to move expatriates diminished. Today, fewer and fewer managers at MNCs are expatriates.

Since the MNC gave operating freedom to local managers, many firms experienced duplication of effort. The MNC adapted to local requirements to the point where diseconomies occurred. As a result, companies described as MNCs changed operations to become "global" in approach, for example ICI of the UK, Philips of the Netherlands, Siemens of Germany, and ABB of Sweden/Switzerland.

The era of the global economy

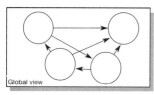

Global view

Few people would disagree that we are living in the era of a global economy.[13] But it is important to understand that the global economy is not simply an extrapolation of a "more international" or a "more multinational" economy.

The global economy operates on fundamentally different principles and therefore has different requirements. First, in the global economy, participation in the economic space is open to all, and some of the barriers still present in the multinational economy are rapidly disappearing. Sanctuaries such as protected markets were the hallmarks of the multinational economy previously described. Second, markets are characterized by growing homogeneity of customers, which should not be confused with similarity or standardization.[14]

Few people would disagree that we are living in the era of a global economy. But it is important to understand that the global economy is not simply an extrapolation of a "more international" or a "more multinational" economy.

Many local economies have opened their borders to liberalized trade, enlarging the potential scope of a firm's international activities to a point where true global market coverage can be achieved.

The merger of Swedish-based Asea with Swiss-based Brown Boveri in 1988 resulted in the creation of a truly global firm with a organization adapted to the new competitive environment, Asea Brown Boveri (ABB).[15] Made up of many small units, there are clear global leaders defined by industry, sector, or segments, who have to cooperate with regional or local managers in a complex matrix structure. The company has extended global goals to its more than 50 key operating units, spread around the globe. Electrolux, another Sweden-based firm leading in the home appliances industry, was also an early leader in the 1980s, acquiring operations across Europe (Zanussi of Italy) and the USA (White Westinghouse) to form a global business with centrally coordinated strategies in various sectors, application areas, and different price levels.[16]

Whirlpool, the US competitor of Electrolux, was actually inspired by the same model and created its own global operation, breaking out from what was previously a largely national, or US-based, business. With the purchase of Philips (of the Netherlands) home appliance business in the early 1990s, Whirlpool also adopted a global strategy for its business and extended it to Asia and Latin America.[17]

Drivers of the global economy

The drive to a completely global economy comes from several important factors. These drivers, present to a varying degree in different parts of the world, push the world economy into a global and integrated system, reducing that part of economic activity which can be described as domestic, local, or regional.

Liberalization of trade

A significant phase of international trade liberalization is currently in progress. Over the past 50 years the international community has reduced trade barriers in the form of customs or duties to an almost inconsequential level. The GATT negotiations serve as an example. Non-tariff trade barriers have also been reduced, although they are still significant in some pockets of the world. The new World Trade Organization (WTO, successor organization to GATT) in Geneva deals with non-tariff barrier issues.[18]

Liberalization has occurred between countries, across regions, and among trading blocks. European Union (EU, formerly EC or EEC) efforts culminating in barrier-free trade among member nations have profoundly affected businesses located in the EU. The intent was to reduce barriers and create an even level of regulation in order to open markets further, especially impacting insurance, banking, and airlines. More limited to trade but important nonetheless was the formation of NAFTA in North America, LAFTA in Latin America, and ASEAN in Asia.

With communist economic systems being swept away throughout much of the world, economies have liberalized and opened to foreign business. Political changes have contributed to the fact that today's trading range for international business is far greater than it has ever been in the past, almost eliminating from business discussion the term "closed economy". These political changes have allowed firms to penetrate foreign markets, thus closing former "sanctuaries" where companies enjoyed monopoly positions behind government protected trade barriers and regulations.

> Political changes have contributed to the fact that today's trading range for international business is far greater than it has ever been in the past, almost eliminating from business discussion the term "closed economy."

The push for deregulation

While liberalization of trade has made the import and export game more practicable, the recent impetus in many countries to deregulate entire industry sectors has further opened access for international players. As a result, many firms have discovered international opportunities in places where once they barely dared go.

Deregulation has taken three major directions. First, sectors previously reserved for state-controlled enterprises, such as telecommunications, postal services, energy, transportation, and utilities, have become privatized. Privatization began with the Thatcher government in the UK during the early 1980s and spread to emerging economies of Latin America and Asia. Newly privatized firms moved from a government-dominated style to a management style resembling that of an international company dominating the private sector.

Many of these companies, such as the former Bell System telecommunications in the USA, have become global players in their own right. BAA, a UK-based firm that owns and operates major international airports such as Heathrow outside London, became very profitable and developed a specific expertise. Following initial success in operating in the UK, BAA began to expand its operations internationally with an initial assignment in the USA. There, the company assumed responsibility for retail operations in the Indianapolis and Pittsburgh airports.[19] Bell Atlantic, one of the regional telephone companies formed as a result of a merger with Nynex in 1997, has a separate operating firm for mobile or wireless service, the Bell Atlantic Global Wireless Group. This unit maintains operating interests in more than 20 countries or about half of its subscriber base. Operations range from countries such as Mexico, to Italy and Indonesia.

The second form of deregulation is reduction of industry-specific regulation where the general economy has been open. Examples are banking and insurance where private ownership in most countries was subject to stringent regulations. Regulators have loosened their grip, leaving banks in the Netherlands, for example, almost without regulation. Less regulation promotes international expansion and globalization of the economy.

The Dutch ING banking group exemplifies the new type of financial institution created by these forces. Itself a combination of a Dutch insurance company and a Dutch retail bank, ING integrated these two financial services in one company, not running merely a holding firm with two separate organizations. ING aggressively pursued markets outside the Netherlands, such as emerging financial markets in Asia and Eastern Europe. Finally, upon acquisition of Barings, a UK-based investment company in difficulty after catastrophic losses from unauthorized speculations, ING expanded its service lines into investment banking. None of these expansions would have been possible without extensive deregulation in the domestic market, and in many international markets as well.

Finally, governments, particularly members of the EU, have sought a level playing field by standardizing existing regulations. As with many directives the EU adopted under its Europe 1992 drive, the goal has been to harmonize existing regulations, often combined with a push to liberalize by harmonizing minimally. This was a specific goal in pharmaceuticals and insurance. The EU adopted a single filing policy in pharmaceuticals whereby one common application could be filed for the entire EU, thus permitting simultaneous launch of a new drug product in different countries. Previously firms had been required to obtain regulatory approval country by country, adding cost and time to the process. Harmonization facilitates entry into multiple markets, thus driving a globalized economy. One of the first firms on record to take advantage of this new type of regional filing was Ares-Serono, a Geneva-based biotechnology firm that filed its Serostim AIDS-wasting drug with the European Medicines Evaluation Agency (EMEA) in 1997.[20]

> **Harmonization facilitates entry into multiple markets, thus driving a globalized economy.**

Expanded worldwide communication capabilities

While liberalization and deregulation expanded the reach of business around the world, the communications revolution made it possible to follow up on these opportunities with both physical travel and rapid communication. Expansion of world travel via air has contributed tremendously to the ability to move quickly from one part of the world to another, thus extending management and control capabilities to far corners of the world. No longer are transatlantic or transpacific trips planned well in advance, nor do they take weeks. Managers can now travel abroad frequently, staying for ever shorter periods. Using supersonic Concorde service across the North Atlantic makes it possible to cross the Atlantic, have a meeting, and return home on the same day.

Shortening the time for covering large distances allows management to project ideas to other parts of the world without a permanent presence, or even a physical presence, as formerly required. It expands the action radius of management and diminishes the need for local presence, or decision making.

The telecommunications revolution has impacted the conduct of international business. In previous stages of economic development, mail and telegrams dominated international communication. Interactivity, or immediate response, was almost impossible. The telex changed much, creating dependable communications at a time when the

> **The telecommunications revolution has impacted the conduct of international business.**

telephone service on an international scale was lacking. The real break-through came with simultaneous direct-dial capability of most phone systems, combined with low cost fax technology. Both developments allowed business quick access to persons or institutions worldwide and reduced response time.

Today, our ability to communicate is further enhanced by mobile phones and the Internet. Mobile communication has now reached most parts of the world, making access to any person almost instantaneous. As more businesses use the Internet, local communication tools such as electronic mail can extend to most parts of the world.

A key point to understand is how these technologies change the job of management. Just as more effective air travel has expanded the geographic reach, or radius of action, of managers, so has the telecommunication revolution expanded management ability to control details at great distance. Technology has nearly eliminated space barriers to management and business, facilitating rapid follow-up on the potential created by trade liberalization and deregulation. While trade liberalization has given business a reason to act on the global economy, communication changes have given business the means to do so. Some of the more recent breakthroughs in the common use of electronic mail, the accessibility of the Internet, and the spread of video conferencing are just some examples of this trend. In the software industry, development for a company in the USA or Europe might take place in India with frequent satellite transmissions, thus creating new operating forms and separating units in ways previously unknown.

> While trade liberalization has given businesses a reason to act on the global economy, communicatioin changes have given business the means to do so.

In some more tangible ways, a similar revolution has taken place in the logistics area. Physical shipments of products are now much more efficient with the ready availability of air freight, container ships, and express delivery services such as Federal Express or UPS. The common trade of completely assembled cars or trucks would be unthinkable without the existence of the modern Ro-Ro carrier, where some 3000 to 5000 cars can be efficiently transported across oceans and loaded and unloaded in a matter of hours. The physical shipment revolution has also extended the reach of firms, making it easier to access far-away markets from concentrated production points.

Customer homogeneity

Few arguments in business today are as heated as those about similarity or difference in market requirements and customers. Ignited by writings from the early 1980s, early debate focussed on customer similarity in countries or regions.[21] More important is whether differences where they still exist are

diminishing. Clearly, customers are becoming more similar in taste and requirements, although they have not yet reached complete similarity. Differences are
narrowing in established product categories (personal
ones such as food) and are almost absent for new,   **The trend continues toward**
highly technological products such as semiconductor   **homogeneity, creating a**
manufacturing lines for personal computers. Aided by   **greater payoff for global**
                                                         opportunists and
rapid information transfer around the globe, customers   **cementing bonds between**
worldwide demand products and services that are far   **local economies.**
more similar today than they were just a decade ago.
The trend continues toward homogeneity, creating a greater payoff for global
opportunists and cementing bonds between local economies.

Extending technological applications worldwide

In high technology applications, whether industrial production equipment or
recently developed products, the technology used around the world has
become more similar. Products are based on new, often identical technological
solutions, narrowing the difference between products offered. As a technological solution discovered in one part of the world becomes applicable elsewhere,
economic links are forged. These links help form the globalized economy where
similar technical solutions, or technologies, can be marketed everywhere.
When markets are less segmented or less categorized by different technological
approaches, incentives for extending global reach are created and become a
powerful driver toward the global economy.

Impact of the global economy on business and managerial practice

The major drivers toward the globalized economy have already been described.
These drivers create forces that bring economic activity into the globalized, as
compared to local or regionalized, economy. The globalized economy, with
requirements different from the previous models of international, multinational, or trading economies, creates new business realities which must be recognized by business and management. In particular, this has led to expanded
and intensified competition for most companies, a relentless push for ever
greater efficiency, leading eventually to a new management paradigm.

Expanded competition

Two prominent characteristics develop in a globalized economy. The first is a
constant sense of intensifying competition. This competitive intensity experienced by companies today springs from the sudden appearance of new players

whose range has expanded into new markets, rather than from efforts of traditional competitors. This heightened level of competition results from increased business range fostered by liberalization and new communication technologies as described earlier.

The "club" of competitors expands daily. While major competition used to include members of the so-called "Triad" (USA, western Europe, and Japan),[22] new entrants have since joined the field. Traditional players from the core Triad areas now face companies from Korea, India, Mexico, China, Thailand, the Philippines, Taiwan, and Indonesia, not only when they enter those markets, but also as rivals in their home markets. Companies based in emerging economies have reached into the developed markets of North America and western Europe, aided by liberalized trade practices. This creates the sense that a company might compete in any place with any firm from a number of countries. Distance, the traditional barrier, has been wiped out. Examples abound. Even in a high technology application, such as fine chemicals used for building blocks in pharmaceuticals, emerging players in India and China compete effectively worldwide with traditional American and European suppliers.

Distance, the traditional barrier, has been wiped out.

While this competition is export based, information technology-based competition takes a different route. India, known as the source of many excellent software engineers, has become a major software development center. One European firm operating a software group in India transfers information regularly via satellite phone lines to its European centers where the work is integrated. In this case, competition has expanded to include any specialist with the capability to achieve a presence in the global arena.

One European firm operating a software group in India transfers information regularly via satellite phone lines to its European centers where the work is integrated.

This intensified yet more international competition raises the stakes in many industries. As more competitors enter, the outcome hinges on the competitiveness of the players and on the cost efficiency base of their operations. This leads directly to the second prominent characteristic of a globalized economy.

The continued push for efficiency

In traditional competition, competitors evolved from similarly developed areas or countries and often had a similar cost base. With expanded globalized competition, new entrants may have different cost bases and thus gain competitive advantage over established players. It is precisely this pressure that inspires efforts to improve efficiency and profitability within firms that already appear profitable. In the globalized economy, it is the efficiency of the most competitive that sets the benchmark for "world-class efficiency" and pressures firms else-where, even if they appear profitable (see Fig 2.1).

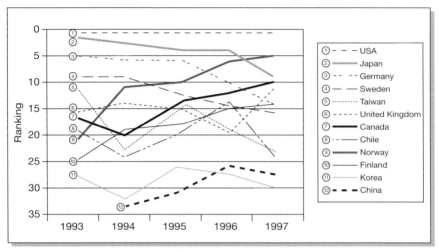

Source: The World Competitive Yearbook (1997), IMD, Lausanne, Switzerland

Fig 2.1   Competitive ranking of selective national economies, 1993–1997

World-class standard in key markets is required, and firms that do not achieve this standard often find themselves destined to disappear. In the past, trade barriers or regulation buffered such circumstances. World class was defined as best practice in a certain area, function, process, or sector. Because emerging economies particularly in Asia continuously generate new players who advance the comparative efficiency benchmark, all other players are forced to assume a constant adaptation mode. Few firms can avoid this com-petitive imperative.[23]

In a recent study carried out in Europe and sponsored by IBM, IMD reported on manufacturing in Switzerland and compared it to manufacturing in the rest of Europe.[24] The report clearly demonstrated that less than 3 percent of investigated plants in Europe performed at world standard. The survey cov-ered European plants that in earlier times had probably done far better. In recent years a rapid shift in standards had occurred with "best of class" no longer defined by country or region, but worldwide. Rival newcomers in other countries, Asian firms in particular, had surpassed European plants in effi-ciency, standards, and performance.

The power of the managerial philosophy

Parallel to development in the business community, transformation has also occurred in government and quasi-government institutions. Increasingly, government services are accountable for efficiency, and public administration is expected to perform at competitive levels. This drive toward efficiency is fueled by tight government finances worldwide. As a result, global best practice in business has its counterpart in the public sector, now spurred to higher levels of performance. The managerial mindset has developed in public service.[25] In sectors such as health, pension funds, and transportation, business or managerial frameworks have been introduced. The push to managerial philosophy, coupled with the drive to globalization, may force dislocations when foreign or global standards of efficiency are suddenly imposed on organizations that view themselves as performing at domestic or single-country standards. For example, France experienced public sector strikes at the end of 1995. Promotion of monetary union throughout the EU will further aggravate this issue.

> **Increasingly, government services are accountable for efficiency, and public administration is expected to perform at competitive levels.**

The emergence of a new managerial paradigm

The twin forces of intensified competition and the enormous push toward world-class efficiency will dominate the globalized economy. These forces are recent and demand a new managerial paradigm. The traditional approach of viewing data, trends, or developments on a country-by-country basis will no longer suffice. Instead, managers who aspire to lead firms into the 21st century must develop a different, more global mindset. For this reason, I have created the term "global mindset," and it is the purpose of this book to define and elaborate the contours of the Global Mindset.

> **The twin forces of intensified competition and the enormous push toward world-class efficiency will dominate the globalized economy.**

The need for the global mindset does not come only from the urgency to absorb new information or more data. Rather, the complexity of impending competitive forces requires managers to absorb experience and knowledge within different frameworks, beyond existing frameworks for management, many of which were initially conceived for single-country environments.

Then why not write a book exclusively on strategies for firms in the global economy? While this is an important issue as well, I feel that the impetus for change must come from managers who design those strategies. With the world changing around us, these managers would have to think, analyze, and conceptualize their experience differently, so that new strategies for their firms can emerge. Needless to say this book contains much that deals with global strategy, as the global mindset must encompass strategy formulation and global strategic thinking. However, strategy alone is not the issue, but rather the new mindset providing global strategies with a chance to succeed.

Notes

1. Jean-Pierre Jeannet "The age of the global mind", *Die Unternehmung*, 45 (2), pp. 132–142

2. Fernand Braudel, *The Wheels of Commerce*, University of California Press, Berkeley, 1992.

3. Christopher Hibbert, *The House of Medici: Its Rise and Fall,* William Morrow & Co., New York, 1975.

4. Eugen Ortner, *Glück und Macht*, Ehrenwirth, Munich, 3rd. edn, 1977.

5. "The Japanese trading companies: the giants that refused to die", The *Economist*, 1 June, 1991, p. 72 –3.

6. John Freivalds, *Grain Trade: The Key to World Power and Human Survival*, Stein & Day, 1976, New York.

7. Boeing, Annual Report, 1996.

8. "Alliances fuel Volvo's drive to survive", *Automotive News*, Vol. 71, 17 March, 1997, p. 20G.

9. "Companies and Finance: The Americas: Daimler Benz may increase US output," *Financial Times*, 23 May, 1997, p. 28.

10. Toyota, Annual Report, 1997.

11. Aharoni, Yair, "On the definition of a MNC", Quarterly Review of Economics and Business, Vol. II, 1971.

12. Ray A. Goldberg and Elizabeth Ashcroft, "Nestlé in the twenty-first century", Case Study, Harvard Business School N9–596–074, 1996.

13. Kenichi Ohmae, *The Borderless World*, Collins, London, 1990.

14. Theodore Levitt, "The globalization of markets", *Harvard Business Review,* May–June 983, pp. 92–102.

15. William Taylor, "The logic of global business: an interview with Percy Barnevik", *Harvard Business Review*, March–April 1991, pp. 91–105.

16. Stephen Allen, Electrolux Case Study, Babson College/ECCH.

17. Stephen Allen, Whirlpool Case Study, by Babson College/ECCH.

18 "Antagonists Que For WTO Judgement", *Financial Times*, 8 August, 1996, p. 6.

19. "Ready to Export", *Air Transport*, 1997, p. 77.

20. Ares-Serono, Company Press Release, Geneva, Switzerland, 17 March 17, 1997.

21. Levitt, op. cit.

22. Kenichi Ohmae, *Triad Power: The Coming Shape of Global Competition*, Free Press, New York, 1995.

23. *The World Competitiveness Yearbook (1997)*, IMD, Lausanne, June 1997.

24. Robert S. Collins, *Made in Switzerland: A Benchmarking Study of Manufacturing Practice and Performance in Swiss Industry*, IMD, Lausanne, 1996.

25. William F. Enteman, Managerialism: The Emergence of a New Ideology, University of Wisconsin Press, 1993.

From domestic to global thinking: five generic mindsets

The purpose of this chapter is to confront the reader with the notion that a global mindset is not only something new, but that it is different from the traditional international or multinational mindset. The categorization into 5 distinct generic models is my own and the key to keep in mind is that the last stage, global, is viewed as a new and different category, independent from the other intermediate stages.   ·

The domestic mindset

Most executives are born with a domestic mindset. Some observers might call it a single-country mindset. For the executive with a domestic mindset, all reference points, or experiences, come from one single culture or business environment. The person born in Japan goes to school in that country, is raised with Japanese as a language, and attends university in Japan, so most reference points are from Japanese society. The same is true for a German born and raised in Germany, an American born and raised in the USA, or a Brazilian in Brazil. The reference points are shaped by the social environment in which a person is raised, the school system, and the professional or work experience.

For the executive with a domestic mindset, all reference points or experiences come from one single culture or business environment.

What are the problems with the domestic mindset? For one, executives with single-environment reference points usually have more difficulty absorbing developments and ideas from other parts of the world. The tendency to fall back on one's own experience is referred to as the self-reference criterion.[1] This automatic reflex causes managers to refer unconsciously to their own culture, or experience base, and rely on basic facts or truth that they never had to challenge because in their own country there was no need to. Whenever managers face an unknown situation, or need to make a decision they have not faced before, they tend to fall back on their own experience, i.e. domestic or home base, to fill in the blanks for their underlying assumptions.

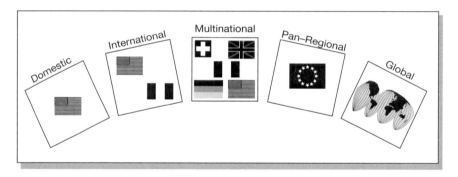

Fig 3.1   Generic mindsets

Although management journals are full of stories where managers or their companies made poor decisions or behaved inappropriately, we often fail to understand how automatically, and without much thought, we, too are filling in the blanks based upon our domestic experience.

A colleague experienced in management development related his experience with a well-known management development situation, the desert survival situation, where groups of managers are asked to make decisions on how to proceed if they were stranded, following an airplane accident, in the middle of the desert. My colleague explained that for the use of this material with participants from developing countries he always needs to note where reliance on government help is not assumed, and therefore their options chosen tend to be the same, making the simulation of less value. In his experience, these participants always try to resolve the situation on their own since it is not in their experience to rely on government agencies for help. In comparison, executives from developed countries, such as the USA, with extensive rescue capability available from government agencies, propose different strategies.

Another example was passed to me by a manager from a European multinational chemical company with a sizable animal health business. This European manager, who had recently been asked to take over a US subsidiary, was relied upon by the entire business to obtain US Federal Food and Drug Administration (FDA) approval of new drug products, as US approval meant approval in many other countries, particularly where substantial meat exports to the USA were the norm (Argentina, New Zealand, Australia, Canada, etc.). When the newly appointed US general manager approached his first new product introduction, it got turned down by the FDA due to laboratory methodology. In his words (simplified): "They used 20 rats for the test in the European country where the company had its R&D base, and Washington required 24 rats!" To overcome the situation, new tests were performed in the USA, promptly resulting in approval. As his colleagues in other countries began to reap the benefits of the new approval by obtaining sales for themselves, this manager thought he should avoid dual testing which ended up on his own profit and loss account. A trip to Europe revealed that the laboratory testing procedures were performed with 20 rats "because our government only requires 20 rats!". According to this manager, it took considerable effort and time to convince the research staff to change the procedures. Clearly, what we have at work here is the domestic mindset, frustrating the performance of the international company.

Limitations of the domestic mindset

Many experienced international executives would be able to recall their own favorite stories. However, what is important here is to appreciate the danger of having companies populated by "domestic minds" at a time when our economy is globalizing. The first impact is the constant danger of using the self-reference criterion to fill in the blanks with invalid data, or to approach a business situation on the basis of domestic experience. This is particularly true where complete lack of knowledge, or international naiveté is at work.

A second, and often cited side effect of domestic minds is the preponderance of the not-invented-here (NIH) syndrome. Again, it should be expected that the experienced international executive among the readers would immediately be able to recall instances when this attitude frustrated good intentions. Usually described as the rejection of a new idea on the basis that it was not invented here, it used to be attached primarily to engineering or technical concepts. However, the NIH syndrome applies just as much to business practices in areas of production, finance, marketing, information systems, or human resources. The domestic mindset, with its inability to check the validity of new ideas from other countries or regions, and its reliance on domestic or home country facts only, has a high tendency to fall prey to this well-known state. In a world where interconnected economies lead to new managerial requirements, companies, or even societies, with a high degree of NIH syndrome are clearly at risk.

> In a world where interconnected economies lead to new managerial requirements, companies, or even societies, with a high degree of NIH syndrome are clearly at risk.

However, there is one additional aspect that needs to be considered when discussing the domestic mind. The element often missed is international curiosity. By that we mean the innate willingness of a person to learn more about other parts of the world, by demonstrating or engaging in activities that expose the domestic mind to other types of thinking. Contrast international curiosity with international disinterest, indifference about what happens elsewhere, and outright apathy. A domestic mind infected with international curiosity will move to a different level. The domestic mind with a complete international disinterest will most likely remain subject to a high degree of self-reference criterion combined with an unhealthy dose of the NIH syndrome.

Businesses that have become part of the globalized economy cannot possibly be led successfully by managers who are subject to a domestic mindset. These companies need access to a sufficient cadre of lower level executives who also must step out of the domestic mindset. Companies expecting their fortunes to remain secure in the hands of a few highly enlightened and globally experienced managers, while the rest of their business is led by managers with domestic minds will experience sooner or later the type of situations we have examined so far. In countless examples retold to the author, managers have complained about the lack of international understanding among their lower echelons which caused mistakes, bad decisions, or even worse, lack of progress on important projects. As our companies become streamlined into small decision-making units with responsibility increasingly placed at lower levels, a large number of domestic minds can frustrate a firm's progress into the globalizing economy.

For successful business leaders, it will become an imperative to move out of their domestic mindsets into a more internationalized, or even globalized type of thinking which we will explain in more detail in the rest of the chapter. But it is the overall level of domestic versus non-domestic thinking present in a company that is decisive, and not only the dominant mindset of a few senior managers.

The international mindset

The international mindset is formed by an individual having had at least one major experience in a second country. The effect of this experience promotes additional reference points for the manager, reducing reliance on the home country experience. As part of the expanded experience in one or possibly several other countries, the international mind may acquire foreign language or cross-cultural skills in a second country or region.

Although people might become internationalized as a result of casual travel, we are talking about a capability to conduct business in another culture. This experience may have come at different stages in a manager's life. For some, it comes rather early when they move with their parents between two different country assignments. Others might study at a university outside their own home culture. Some might be exposed to foreign business environments as a result of travel on behalf of their firms. Most typical is to be assigned by one's own firm to work abroad for an extended period of time by assuming the role of an expatriate manager.

The international mind is much less likely than the domestic mind to supplant "blank facts" with home country facts, as this manager knows circumstances are not always the same. At the extreme, international minds with experience in one country as a result of a lengthy stay can become so much in tune that they become part of the new culture. This is often the case for managers who are very much enamored by their new experience. Over time, they may stay, becoming part of the group of permanent expatriates who do not even return home upon retirement, assuming the role of "deep moles."

The importance of international minds lies in their ability to serve as a bridge between home country (i.e. head office country) and host country environment, playing the role of cultural interpreters on both sides. They can deal with the home office in the language of the home office and as they pass on the realities of their host country. They become the "guides in the fog" and trusted advisors because of their interpretations of the host country scene. Conversely, these same managers are able to interpret for host country locals, or intercede with head office on their behalf, and can provide interpretations of head office intent. International managers frequently have limited territorial responsibility, often limited to the country or region for which they have experience and knowledge.

Needless to say, there are different levels of international mindsets, some with only scant international experience, and others with great depth. These earlier comments pertain to those with significant international experience in another country, which is understood to have come as a result of stays lasting several years. The effectiveness of such an experience is not only determined by time, but when in a career the international experience took place. Senior executives whose careers evolve in a single economy and, before assuming higher responsibility, who suddenly take an international position, often do not benefit as much because it came relatively late in the game.

But is such knowledge equal to a global mindset? It appears that in-depth understanding of another country, or region is not to be equated with a global perspective, or having a global mindset, as we are calling it for the purpose of this book. The international mind has a radius of activity that is limited, and is best applied to a narrow geographic area. A Japanese manager who has worked for an international firm as an expatriate in Italy for a long period of time would probably not become equally effective when moved to Germany. However, it would be expected that such a manager would be more effective in Germany than someone else coming directly from Japan without any international experience.

The major challenge for the international mindset is to keep up with the complex demands of the

> **Managers with an international mindset, particularly those with a deep understanding of a local culture or business environment, will remain important for firms with operations spread across the globe.**

global business environment, placing a premium on viewing issues across a series of countries, rather than between only two countries. Managers with an international mindset, particularly those with a deep understanding of a local culture or business environment, will remain important for firms with operations spread across the globe. But such knowledge alone will not suffice if a company needs to compete on a global scale in the rapidly globalizing economy.

The multinational mindset

While the post-World War II environment gave birth to long international assignments, some for life, thus creating international minds, the rapid expansion of the multinational corporation (MNC) beginning in the 1960s led to the rise of the multinational mindset. "Multinational" refers to managers who have had a series of international assignments, frequently within the same general region.

The following case offers an example of multinational formation. Our first example came to business school in the USA from Europe where he had already worked in two different language regions. After business school, he joined a US multinational firm in the consumer goods area and was given his first management responsibility in his country of origin. After several promotions in the area of marketing, he was assigned to France for a period of two years before being given the next higher job in his home country. A second international assignment in Belgium followed, succeeded by a promotion into a higher position in Switzerland. Joining another company as country manager of a small country, he was promoted into a large market, again with country responsibility. Eventually, this manager found his way into a MNC, leading a division with worldwide responsibility.

Our second example followed a different path. Although starting out in Europe and coming to the USA for business school followed by entry level management assignments in his home country for international firms, he then joined a second firm and moved to Asia where he had country responsibility in both Japan and Taiwan. Next, he moved back to Europe where he took over responsibility for a large European market for the same firm.

Many companies have created a whole cadre of such managers. Nestlé, the Swiss-based MNC serves as a typical example. Its top management consists of managers who typically have held a succession of international assignments, sometimes covering more than one region. Nestle's new CEO, Peter Brabeck-Letmathe, had been promoted across several different geographic areas prior to assuming his new position in 1997.[2] As part of his career, Brabeck spent seventeen years in various management positions in Latin America, starting with marketing director in Chile, then managing director of Ecuador, before eventually assuming the same position for Venezuela. At that point, he was transferred to the head office in Switzerland to assume leadership of one of the product divisions, then of global marketing for the entire company.

Similar experiences are the case for other members of Nestlé top management. At the local level, the company employs a large cadre of managers with deep sensitivity to the local environment. These managers are sometimes rotated for international experience, either to the company's international head office in Vevey, Switzerland, or to another local company.

Managers with a multinational mindset are often characterized as more internationally experienced than those with an international mindset. They have spent a considerable amount of time outside their home country or home culture. However, their assignments are usually on a country-by-country basis with strategy responsibility for a given territory. Their experience is multi-domestic, which means that they have experienced the workings of several markets, largely on a market-by-market basis.[3]

The great strength of the manager with a multinational mindset is the ability to move into a new country on the strength of having managed such a challenge on several previous occasions. They may not be experts at first, but they are very fast learners and tend to end up on their feet. As the "workhorses" of many MNCs, these managers have been crucial to the rapid deployment of MNCs in many countries and in building up a local infrastructure where a firm might not yet have its own operation. Over time, they were supplanted by locally hired managers.

How is a multinational mindset different from a global mindset? The difference stems primarily from the fact that the multinational mindset operates on a multi-domestic basis, having one country or market in sight at a time and not geared to worldwide responsibility where different rules apply. Managers with multinational mindsets are experienced internationally, but often they are very keen on displaying their superb knowledge of all the differences among countries they know. Their discussions are frequently centered around one market at a time, and they are less skilled, or focused, in discussing regional, or even global business issues in their firms.

> Managers with multinational mindsets are experienced internationally, but often they are very keen on displaying their superb knowledge of all the differences among countries they know.

The regional mindset

The executive with a regional mindset is characterized by a deep understanding of a region comprising a number of individual, but similar, markets or countries. This understanding can be gained from first-hand experience in such a region through a series of assignments, or alternatively through management responsibility for a regional operation, and in the latter having developed a deepened understanding. Regional responsibility typically includes supervising a number of local country organizations for either a large region, such as Europe or Asia–Pacific, or for a sub-region, such as the Nordic area in Europe (Scandinavia and Finland) or South East Asia in the Asia–Pacific region.

Regional managers are the first group to develop a business across several countries, as this is the nature of their assignments. In Europe, where the region includes some 20 plus markets, characterized by a high level of economic integration, regional managers have been at the forefront of building pan-European business strategies. Their experience makes them skilled at integrating business across several countries and at thinking about business strategy as it applies to a number of countries. This is a substantial difference from the single-country manager with the responsibility for one country only.

At many large international firms, regional executives are among its most experienced operating managers. In Europe, these executives have sometimes been referred to as Euro-managers, although that term is also used to describe any manager whose responsibility for a part of a business spans Europe.[4]

> **At many large international firms, regional executives are among its most experienced operating managers.**

The regional mindset is still different from the global mindset. The difference stems from the nature of the assignment. A manager responsible for Europe only, and who has never held management responsibility in the USA or Asia, has had little opportunity to develop a global mindset. The regional mindset, however, has one important element in common that we did not encounter in the previous international or multinational mindsets: a need to think simultaneously across several countries. Conceptually, the task of a regional manager is more closely related to the task of a global manager than it is to the other mindsets.

> **Conceptually, the task of a regional manager is more closely related to the task of a global manager than it is to the other mindsets.**

⮞ The global mindset

Now that we have moved from domestic to international, to multinational, and to regional mindsets, what then are the unique and defining characteristics of the global mindset? The global mindset is not simply a linear extension of the multinational mindset. Instead (and this is the main purpose of this book) we intend to demonstrate that the global mindset has unique dimensions and perspectives not present in the others.

The global mindset is able to understand a business, an industry sector, a particular market segment, or a business function on a global basis. This ability is different from comprehending those tasks within limited, specified territorial borders. In other words, the manager exhibiting a global mindset can discuss the business in global terms rather than simply one country at a time. That manager displays a global attitude, sometimes also called global view, which is a vantage point different from managers with the other mindsets described earlier.

> **The global mindset is able to understand a business, an industry sector, a particular market segment, or a business function on a global basis.**

Since it is the purpose of this book to provide insights into the workings of the global mindset, we do not intend to give a complete definition and explanation of it at this time. Rather, an outline of some of the following chapters is offered that will take core elements of the global mindset and illuminate them in greater detail.

A glimpse into the global mindset

If the global mind is different from others, then this mindset must be able to deal with different problems. In Chapter 3 we look in detail at the analytic skills required of the global mindset, beyond those skills needed for a domestic or international mind. In particular, we will describe the ability to think and understand in terms of global logic, resulting in an ability to appreciate the global forces on a given business.

The market assessment skills of the global mind are also different from those of other mindsets. Market-by-market assessment is the hallmark of other mindsets, but the global mindset must be more at home with multi-market analysis and the corresponding new type of assessment. Chapter 4 will highlight innovative concepts such as lead markets and the global chessboard.

The global mindset must be comfortable with the various types of global strategies pursued by business today. In particular, because global mindsets are a pre-condition for successful dealing with worldwide responsibility, the global mindset must be able to select for a given business the appropriate generic global strategy. Those strategies are detailed in Chapter 5.

> **The global mindset must be comfortable with the various types of global strategies pursued by business today.**

As firms develop new types of organizations when adapting to the rapidly globalizing economy, the global mindset must be able to keep up with new organizational designs. Issues of global mandates are central, and the relationships among organizational units spread over the globe needs to be appreciated. We have therefore designated Chapter 6 to the particular organizational skills of the global mindset.

The manager with a global mindset might also be required to have unique and different behavioral skills. These skills are primarily important for managers about to assume global responsibility for some part of their business. Chapter 7 will focus on the new type of teams the global mindset will have to able to deal with, as well as with more operational issues of travel and time zone management. It is here where we will also discuss the hotly debated issue of foreign language.

No mind can operate without its specific database. In Chapter 8 we attempt to describe the database, or knowledge base, the global mindset needs to cope with the unique new assignments created by the modern global company. This covers both market knowledge, and also general knowledge about history, geopolitics and culture, as well as how to acquire and update it. In Chapters 9 and 10 we deal with the implications of the global mindset for public policy, companies, and individuals. In these chapters, we will cover how one can achieve a global mindset, and which development path from one generic mindset to another might be most appropriate.

It would be presumptuous on our part to suggest that these are the only dimensions, or features, of the global mindset. The reader must take into consideration that we are embarking on an exploratory voyage into an emerging global business system just now beginning to take shape. The concepts, skills, and capabilities raised in the succeeding chapters are but a glimpse into the future. They are based on close observation of practicing managers, emerging global companies, and their needs. For some readers they might at times appear speculative or even futuristic. It is therefore hoped that one of the principal effects of reading the next chapters would be for readers to be challenged to reflect on their own experience.

> **... we are embarking on an exploratory voyage into an emerging global system just now beginning to take shape.**

Notes

1. James E. Lee, "Cultural analysis in overseas operations", *Harvard Business Review*, March–April 1966, pp. 106–114.

2. Peter Brabeck, "Un Président élevé au lait maison", *Les Echos*, 6 June, 1997.

3. For a definition of multi-domestic strategy, see Jean-Pierre Jeannet and David H. Hennessey, *Global Marketing Strategies*, Houghton Mifflin, Boston, 4th edn, 1998, p. 286–288.

4. Roger Darby, "Developing the Euro-manager", *European Business Review*, Vol. 95, No. 1, 1995, p. 13–15; Gillian Ursell, "Euro-manager or splendid isolation? International management: an Anglo-German comparison", *Organization Studies*, Vol. 16, No. 3, 1995, pp. 538–541; "The elusive Euro-manager", The *Economist*, 7 November, 1992, p. 83.

Global analytical skills: analyzing and understanding global logics

If we claim that the global mindset is significantly different from the international, and certainly from the domestic mindset, we need to be able to describe some of the features that are different. One of the critical elements of the global mindset is the ability to appreciate the degree of globalization that exists in a given industry, or sector, and to provide the required strategic response. We call this understanding the global logic in a business or industry.

Globalization, as many companies have found over the years, is a concept too often simplified, and applied without sufficient understanding and caution. Global logic can be described as a methodology to measure globalization with successive measurements, each taken separately, and interpreted for telling patterns. The presence of a global logic in a business or industry indicates that management recognize the need to find a suitable response to issues regarding globalization. The absence of sufficient global logic would indicate that globalization is not being properly addressed.

The understanding of the concept of global logic has proven helpful in appreciating the need to globalize a company or business. To globalize a firm adds complexity to a business, and often incurs costs as well. Furthermore, for managers, working in a global firm is often more demanding and tends to stretch their resources. To play globally can be fun, but has its risks as well. No firm should play globally simply because it is the current fashion. It must be ascertained to what extent a globalization path is required. Managers must always be on the lookout for the need to globalize. Where global logic is present, the argument for globalization can be assessed and justified.

Over time, we have found it useful to look for global logic in a number of areas. Global logic might be present among customers, competitors, or among the regulatory forces of an industry. As global logic is analyzed in the different elements of a business, managers often find that the extent of globalization is quite different. The following section deals primarily with the various different types of global logic and with the relevant questions that need to be asked.

Finding the sources of global logic within the customer base

Ever since Levitt's thought-provoking article on the "globalization of markets," companies have been struggling with the question: "Do we have global customers?".[1] The early response was an attempt to categorize customers either as global or non-global, with the assumption that global customers wanted standardized products and the others wanted products that were tailor-made to country-specific requirements. This simplified version of globalization among customers soon provided some well-known difficulties leading to extensive criticism of both the concept of globalization and of Levitt, author of the leading article.[2]

Exposure to the challenges of various firms soon indicated that the simple question "Do we have global customers?" was not refined enough to obtain differentiated answers. A far more subtle view was gained from the realization that a better question was "To what extent, and in what areas, are my customers global?". Once the question was asked differently, the response changed and the implications for management also varied by the type of response.

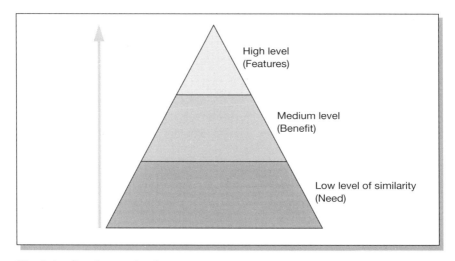

Fig 4.1 Customer logic

⟳ Global customer logic

Among customers, globalization can occur at three different levels: customer need, customer benefit, and product features. Each of these levels might return a different answer, and the manager with the global mindset needs to interpret the pattern of responses into a differentiated globalization strategy.

First, let's look at customer needs. On a generic level, we can investigate customers in different countries in a given category to understand if their underlying needs are similar or different.[3] For example, the need for protection of wooden surfaces is probably global. Equally, the need for children to play is present everywhere. These simple examples indicate that paint (wood surface protection) or toys (child's play) on a need level face global customers (needs). In our view, it would be appropriate to describe products facing worldwide needs as globalized on a need level. For that matter, many products face that test, and the vast majority of companies face global need customers. It is not a very deep form of globalization and still leaves room for a considerable amount of differences on other levels.

> **Among customers, globalization can occur at three different levels: customer need, customer benefit, and product features.**

Companies that face customers exhibiting global needs have a chance to capitalize on this but their strategies will have to recognize this rather shallow level of globalization. It is typically the most common form and would not allow a firm to run a very integrated global strategy. Products that are aimed at customers with global needs can be called global product categories, as they are present, or needed, in most parts of the world. That they would differ extensively based on local factors is to be expected, unless globalization goes beyond global needs.

The next layer of globalization might occur around the concept of customer benefits. Here we need to ask the question: "Are customer buying our products for the same reasons, or with the same benefits in mind?". Even if we find ourselves in a global category, there is still ample room for the customer to purchase our products, or services, with different goals in mind and for different purposes. Take a simple product such as bicycles. Purchased by customers around the globe, and thus a global product category, they are a transportation vehicle in a country such as China and are purchased for the purpose of physical fitness in a country such as the USA. Similar differences can be found with motorcycles, which are outselling cars in countries such as India and are used as the primary transportation means for someone who cannot afford an automobile. In general, fewer differences in benefits exist in industrial products; and the more we deal with high technology products, the more likely that the reason for the purchase and the use intent are similar around the globe.

For a product to be classified as "global benefit," the marketing task on a global scale is different compared to classification only in the global product category. Customers exhibiting global benefit behavior require therefore a different strategy than those who are simply part of a global category but purchase for different reasons.

Finally, there is a third element of interest to potential global firms. The question turns from use and rationale for buying to focus on the particular features needed. For products where the features are largely identical across the world, such as for 35mm film, the physical product standardization has a chance to succeed. We can start to speak of global products where the features of the product are essentially the same around the world.

> For a product to be classified as "global benefit," the marketing task on a global scale is different compared to classification only in the global product category.

It is not difficult to find examples where the use conditions are such that differences in the environment dictate different product features. In fact, it is not common to find standardized products in the consumer goods industry, whereas for technical products used under specific manufacturing conditions, the similarity tends to be much greater.

As we review our global customer logic, it is important to avoid the trap of asking the question "Are you facing a global customer" on a simplified basis and to distinguish between the various levels on which globalization might occur. We may face customers who consistently display the same general need (global category), but purchase the product or service for different reasons. Or we may have customers who want the same physical products (global product) but purchase it for different reasons in different countries. Several combinations exist. What is important is to differentiate the question and begin asking it in a different form: "To what level is your customer global?" is often a more appropriate question than to force it into the binary global/non-global category.

The presence of significant global customer logic, particularly when benefits, or features, are very similar, dictates action on the part of the company. Ignoring strong global customer logic risks losing business. Similarly, companies need to understand that if they market products as if there were a strong customer logic, but in reality it is weak or not present, the risk becomes over-globalization and loss of attractiveness due to over-standardization. Finding the proper balance is the challenge for companies with global ambitions.

When the global debate first began, partially fueled by Levitt's article of 1983, the common assumption was that companies would globalize because customers became more similar. Over time, it became clear that global customer logic may be one reason for globalization, but others may be even more important.

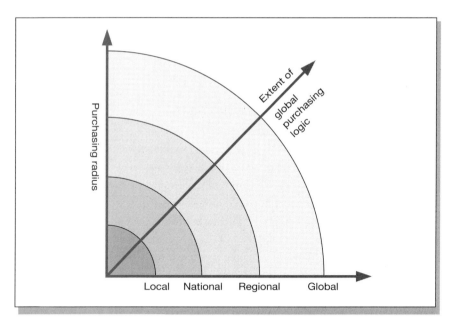

Fig 4.2   Global purchasing logic

⇢ Understanding global purchasing logic

When looking at customers, not only what they want to buy but how they buy it is of importance. Here we are really asking the question: "How do your customers buy your products?". We need to know if there is any global logic streaming from the purchase behavior.

The analysis of global purchasing logic has its roots in the purchase range, or the distance customers are likely to "travel" to search for the best buy. Here we need to understand the purchasing behavior of the customers. Several factors may be used as indicators for the presence of global market logic: distance or range of buying patterns, distribution or delivery arrangements, and the phenomenon of gray markets. Each of these is now described in detail.

> Several factors may be used as indicators for the presence of global market logic: distance or range of buying patterns, distribution or delivery arrangements, and the phenomenon of gray markets.

Global purchasing logic is present when customers search in a wider radius for their products or services. When such logic is completely absent, customers would only contract locally or nationally for purchases. In many industries today, corporate purchasing is still restricted to national markets. At times, local legislation fosters such practices. The local buyer does not chase around the world for best bargains, and is not likely to be influenced by competing offers in other countries. By the same token, we can speak of the presence of strong global market logic where customers scour the world for best bargains and are not reluctant to cover large distances to obtain the best deal for their firms.

Developments in the automotive industry offer an excellent example of this changing practice.[4] Car assemblers purchase about half of their cost base from outside component suppliers, some captive and others independent.[5] For decades, the purchasing pattern was to source such components from nearby suppliers, usually located in the same country or region. US companies tended to buy from US component suppliers, whereas European and Japanese firms formed their own. This created a myriad smaller component firms with relatively small volumes. Once car assemblers became aware of the opportunity to save on costs through better purchasing, components were increasingly purchased by the most cost-effective firm, even if that firm was located on another continent. This trend toward global sourcing, which extends the supply chain for the purchasing company beyond its country or region, has become a major factor in affecting global purchase logic in the automotive industry. Other industries, such as the electronic component industry, have shown similar patterns. Automotive component suppliers thus faced increased global purchase logic as a result of this development.[6]

The need to supply worldwide, with consistency but in separate locations, is another trend that is indicative of global purchasing logic. In many industries, companies want their operations spread over the world supplied by a consistent supplier that can cover all plant locations. The purchasing strategy of these customers is for global purchasing contracts almost eliminating competitors who cannot be present in all locations.

In a recent example, Groupe Schneider, a French-based firm with a major interest in the electrical power distribution business, acquired manufacturing operations in Europe and the USA (Square D). Rather than operating the various businesses on an independent basis, Schneider realized that major production efficiencies might be effected if the production and sourcing strategies of the company were integrated worldwide. As a result, Schneider approached several of its materials suppliers with a request to offer a package of products across all of its worldwide operations. Preferred suppliers were to be selected on the basis of long-term commitment to Schneider and global coverage. This request caught some suppliers by surprise as they discovered that they did not have complete coverage of all the regions in which Schneider operated.[7]

Professional service businesses offer good examples of the effect of global purchasing logic. Multinational firms, when selecting their statutory auditors, exhibit strong preferences for auditing firms that can deliver an integrated audit simultaneously at its various locations around the world. This requires the audit firm to have its own delivery system around the world. Audit firms without such an international network are forced to join with other firms or be left out. This notion of a strong purchasing logic in their industry was one of the drivers for the rash of global mergers announced in the fall of 1997.

Within a few weeks, Price Waterhouse had announced a merger with Coopers & Lybrand, and KPMG announced its intentions to merge with Ernst & Young, forming the world's biggest and second biggest firms. Eventually, regulatory hurdles caused the KPMG/E&Y merger to be called off.[8] There were voices, of course, even among customers, that the mergers were going too far and that other drivers existed than those exerted by customers. Similar trends can be seen in advertising, where contracts increasingly go to advertising agencies that can provide global coverage, thus creating a powerful Global Logic that forces agencies to adapt by building large, international networks with a capacity to serve clients on a worldwide basis.

The impact of these mergers is very powerful for all industry participants. Even small, single-country accounting firms are affected by this. Recent information indicates that "Big Six" firms accounted for a significant percentage of statutory auditing in most European countries, typically above 50 percent. Small firms, not affiliated with any international networks, would find it close to impossible to become auditors of internationally active firms.[9]

In all of these cases, clients, through their purchasing polices, exhibited strong global customer purchasing logic requiring suppliers to adapt their strategies or ignore them at their own peril.

Some sectors view customers largely on a business-to-business basis. However, many firms market through intermediaries, such as independent distributors, wholesalers, or retailers. The purchasing characteristics of these intermediate channel members thus partially determine the extent of a global purchasing logic. In the past, most of these intermediate channel members viewed their markets as local or regional. Typically, companies appointed country-specific distributors with exclusive territories. Wholesalers, to the extent that they played a role, were country specific. And most of all, retailers, in their own operations, rarely spread across several countries. As a result, traditionally, very low global retail or wholesale purchasing logic was exerted from this direction.

> Some retailers, especially category killers such as Toys-Я-Us, Wal-Mart, and Carrefour are coordinating their purchasing policies on an international scale, forcing suppliers to adopt new strategies. This trend creates new global pressure from a direction where traditionally very little has been noticed.

In recent years, we have seen the emergence of internationally active retailers, wholesalers, and distributors. Coca-Cola has adopted a strategy of purposely favoring bottlers with a regional focus, such as Europe, Asia, or Latin America. These bottlers in turn create a global purchasing logic, as their scope of business is very wide.[10] In areas such as drug wholesaling in Europe, we have seen the emergence of regional distributors who take the responsibility for a product across several countries. Some retailers, especially category killers such as Toys-Я-Us, Wal-Mart, and Carrefour are coordinating their purchasing policies on an international scale, forcing suppliers to adopt new strategies. This trend creates new global pressure from a direction where traditionally very little has been noticed.

In many consumer markets, strong global consumer purchasing logic emanates from the "traveling consumer." With international travel continuing to experience substantial growth rates, the world is developing a group of roving consumers who require their preferred services wherever they travel. Products that have had to respond to this emerging trend are telephone services. With more people on the move, telephone operators not only offer mobile phones, but also new technology such as the Global System for Mobile Communications (GSM)-type digital phones which allow consumers to acquire a phone in one country and move with it across Europe and Asia. Hotels, and even banking, as demonstrated by Citibank's global consumer services, are other examples of the traveling consumer looking for products and services everywhere.[11]

> With international travel continuing to experience substantial growth rates, the world is developing a group of roving consumers who require their preferred services wherever they travel.

The emergence of gray markets, sometimes referred to as parallel imports, is a third indicator of global market logic. As most international firms have experienced, gray markets develop when price differentials between two countries become large enough that some other company or agent can engage in arbitrage and profit from the difference. Gray market behavior has existed in the air ticket market where consumers and executives alike have learned that the booking location determines prices, and thus from where to book for the best deals. The gray market phenomenon exists for both consumer and industrial products and emerges particularly when two currencies move apart and prices begin to vary. What is important is the signaling effect of the emergence of gray markets. They are indicative that customers buy not only locally but also react to offers from different parts of the world. Gray markets signal that global market logic, although dormant prior to the event, may actually be present.

> As most international firms have experienced, gray markets develop when price differentials between two countries become large enough that some other company or agent can engage in arbitrage and profit from the difference.

We currently live in a world where the purchasing range of companies and consumers alike is extended due to better and more rapid spread of information. As a result, many companies experience increasing global market logic, and this phenomenon has even appeared in industry sectors previously known for strictly local buying. Some of these changes are also driven by legislation,

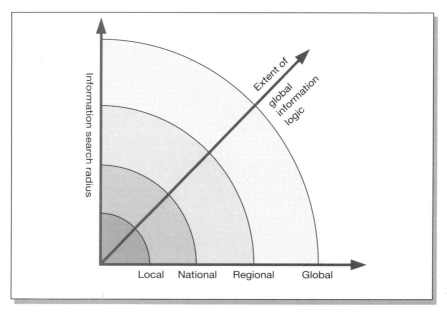

Fig 4.3   Global information logic

and the well-known efforts of the European Union as part of its Europe 1992 integrated market initiative have contributed to push many sectors to a more regional and even global market logic.

➔ Global information logic[12]

In the previous sections we have concentrated on how customers purchase (global purchasing logic) or what they actually desire (global customer logic). Recently, we have come across another type of logic that is different from the first two but yet relates to the customer base, namely the information acquisition strategy of a company's customers. By information acquisition we mean the way customers scan the environment, the type of media they read or are exposed to, and to what extent they go to obtain information about products and services a long distance from home.

Traditional coverage of information acquisition is well documented in standard marketing textbooks.[13] Typically, consumers or business customers would scan the local media before making a particular purchasing decision. There was very little global information logic in the customer base that influenced international firms.

More recent developments, however, have made such influences more pervasive and thus affect the presence of a global information logic. Many business-to-business customers in technology-driven sectors tended to read specific magazines or publications mainly from the USA, thus making that information available to buyers in other countries. A Japanese buyer, reviewing a US-based industry publication, thus acts to acquire information on a global scale, not merely locally. This is particularly true for such sectors as information technology, communications, computers, and medical instruments where the US market is viewed as the lead market and developments in the USA are quickly spotted elsewhere.

As a next step, buyers might go to specific trade shows with a global following. Such shows exist in both the USA and Europe, and for some industries they are most important events. Telecom is a major show taking place every fours years in Geneva, Switzerland. Visitors come from all over the world, thus creating a global information acquisition opportunity. Other important trade shows can be identified for many specific industries.

The ever more frequent travel by business executives exposes many buyers to information outside their home country. To the extent they follow up and actively pursue such information, a global information logic exists.

In consumer industries, this development has been even more pronounced. Information sources have geographically spread through cable TV channels and satellite TV, making it possible for consumers to sit in their living room in Germany and watch a program transmitted from the UK. To reach such consumers, companies in Germany may have to advertise via a foreign channel, although the customer is in many ways viewed as a domestic customer. Sports events, such as the Olympics or World Championships, create other strong global information logics. The commitment of advertisers to the Olympics in Nagano, Japan, was not driven primarily by the potential exposure to event visitors, or even the Japanese market. Instead, these companies were pursuing customers looking in via television from many countries. The actual event site is immaterial. The companies are primarily interested in the audience generated by the event.

> Consumers anywhere can log onto the WWW and locate product information in a different country, thus creating strong global information logic.

Maybe the most important change in our information acquisition is the development of the Internet and the World Wide Web (WWW). This electronic tool, which is taking the world by storm, is rapidly becoming a new mode for looking for product or service information. Consumers anywhere can log onto the WWW and locate product information in a different country, thus creating strong global information logic. Furthermore, it is even influencing the global purchasing logic to the extent that actual product purchases are becoming more common.

Any company seeking to thoroughly understand the forces that shape the global marketplace must recognize the changing way by which customers acquire information. Neglecting global information logic in a business would put the company's entire communications strategy at risk, and any global strategy designed will need to be based upon a thorough understanding of this logic.

When the debate on the merits of globalization began in the early 1980s, the predominant assumption among proponents of globalization was the belief that consumers or customers were becoming more similar, thus driving the trend toward globalization. This chapter was largely devoted to these trends and explained in detail sources of the various pressures that might compel firms to adopt some form of global strategy. That said, there are still many firms where pressure from the customer base itself is not sufficiently strong to warrant all-out global strategies. However, as our experience with countless firms has shown, other forces, often related to an industry's competitive behavior, or inherent economics, may outshine customer-based forces as a source for globalization. These industry-based global logics will be the focus for the next chapter.

Notes

1. Theodore Levitt, "The globalization of markets", *Harvard Business Review*, May–June 1983, pp. 92–102.

2. Ibid.

3. Notice that the term "similar" is preferred over "identical" or "the same". Similarity in the context of global customer analysis is more meaningful, and identical often connotes the term of an absolute.

4. "The World Automotive Suppliers", *Financial Times*, 28 June 28 1993, Survey, sec. IV.

5. Jean-Pierre Jeannet, "Siemens AT: Brazil Strategy", Case Study, IMD Institute, Lausanne, 1993.

6. "Consolidation in auto-parts industry globally has shifted into high gear", *Wall Street Journal*, 20 February, 1998, p. B98.

7. Groupe Schneider, Case Study, proprietary (Babson College).

8. "Accountancy merger called off", *Financial Times*, 14/15 February, 1998, p. 1.

9. "Virtual firm stays in realm of the unreal", *Financial Times*, 14/15 February, 1998, p. 23.

10. "Internationalizing the Cola Wars (A): The Battle for China and Asian Markets", Harvard Case Study, 9–795–186, Richard Seet and David Yoffie, Boston, 1995.

11. "Capturing the global consumer", *Fortune*, 13 December, 1993, p. 166.

12. This might also be called the global media logic.

13. Philip Kotler, *Marketing Management: Analysis, Planning, Implementation, and Control*, Prentice Hall, Englewood Cliffs, NJ, 9th ed., 1997.

5

Finding global logic in industry and in the competitive environment

Global customer logic, global purchasing logic, and global information logic all focus on customers, either what they want, how they purchase, or how they search for information. The next generic global logics focus on the industry, either on competition, industry structure, key success factors (KSFs), critical mass, or regulations. Clearly, these forces on companies to globalize are different from customer-derived pressures.

Global competitive logic

Competition is a potent force requiring globalization. When competition generates a compelling argument to pursue globalization, we speak of a global competitive logic. The principal question to ask in assessing competitive logic is: "Are we meeting the same competitors around the world?" In some industries, a company might be present in many markets but always finds a different set of competitors, indicating low global competitive logic. In other industries, and this is increasingly the case, companies run into the same competitors wherever they go. In many industries, particularly where industrial products are concerned, only a handful of firms compete everywhere, and global players always encounter the same firms. When a company faces the same players worldwide, a good argument for global competitive logic can be made.

Over time, we have also learned that presence of competitors alone is not the only indicator to watch. Even more telling is whether the company encounters the same strategy. This would signal a more coordinated competition and would enhance the need to respond. In some sectors, global competitive logic is so strong that it may overtake other global logic dimensions and become an end in itself. Several examples exist where global competition is reduced to two major players, staking out territory in chess-like fashion. The experiences in soft drinks (Coca-Cola versus Pepsi Cola), photographic film (Kodak versus Fuji), or construction machinery (Caterpillar versus Komatsu) are typical examples of such global competitive constellations.[1]

Global competitive logic develops along a vector ranging from a strictly national competitive pattern, where firms compete nationally, and different sets of firms compete in different countries, all the way to the pure global competitive form where very few compete everywhere. It is therefore helpful to regard competition in the form of different theaters. Country-specific theaters imply that the competitive situation of a firm is determined country by country, and that a competitive situation in one country is independent of that in another country. In this case, each market requires a new and different game with a separate starting gate. This type of locale for local competition is still prevalent (but not exclusively) in service industries, in retailing, contracting, and small artisan shops. Here, little can be leveraged from one market to another, and the competitive strength of a firm is not enhanced by positions built elsewhere. Competitive strength can be measured solely in terms of local market share.

In some industries, the relevant competitive theater may be regional, with different players in Europe, North America, and Asia–Pacific. Regional competitive theaters are characterized by a lack of competitive synergy across regions, i.e. global, as competitive positions cannot be leveraged into other regions. Competitiveness could be measured in regional market share, whereby local shares would be less important than the regional share. Conversely, the global competitive theater is characterized by the capability of all competitors to reach into one another's home territory, thus eliminating carefully coveted "sanctuaries" or protected markets. When a global competitive theater situation applies, competitive position is not simply the addition of various local strengths. We can now think in terms of global market share to measure competitiveness, and local or even regional share as less indicative of competitive strength.

The difference between national, regional, and global competitive theaters can be illustrated using examples from the world of sports. Most readers can be assumed to be familiar with bicycle road racing. Some races, such as the *Classiques* raced in early spring in Belgium (Liége–Bastogne–Liége, Tour of Flanders, etc.) are one-day or single-stage events. Here, only the placing on that day counts. The rider winning in one race carries over no advantage to the next race. Quite different in the multi-stage races such as the Giro d'Italia or the Tour de France. The eventual winner is the racer with the lowest elapsed time over all 20 or more stages, and the daily placings are largely irrelevant for the overall winner. The global competitive theater encountered in a situation with strong global competitive logic can thus be compared with the Tour de France, whereas the national or local competitive logic is more comparable to the single-stage races.

The global competitive theater encountered in a situation with strong global competitive logic can thus be compared with the Tour de France, whereas the national or local competitive logic is more comparable to the single-stage races.

In today's rapidly changing environment, industries can quickly migrate from one type of theater to another. The white goods industry serves as an excellent example.[2] In the early 1980s, the white goods industry structure in Europe was characterized by 70 or more players, most of them locked into small country-specific markets. In the USA, there were a few large players (GE, Whirlpool, Maytag, White-Westinghouse), and a similar structure existed in Japan. Clearly, the relevant theater was regional, but in Europe country-specific theaters could be said to exist. When Electrolux concluded that for cost reasons, the company needed to break out of what was largely a regional market in Nordic Europe, major acquisitions were made in Europe (Zanussi) and in the USA (White-Westinghouse).[3] Thus moving towards a view of a global theater, this prompted major moves on the part of many key players. GE, up to that time the largest company, quickly became affiliated with other European firms. Whirlpool acquired the Philips business in Europe and became itself the largest player, moving Electrolux to second place and GE to third. Within a short period of time, the dynamics of the market had changed from that of a national to regional, and then to a global theater.[4]

Companies need to keep in mind the dangers of ignoring significant global competitive logic. When such logic exists, companies are well advised to keep competitive viewpoints in mind when embarking on the decision whether to adopt a global strategy, or which global strategy to adopt. Obtaining a clear

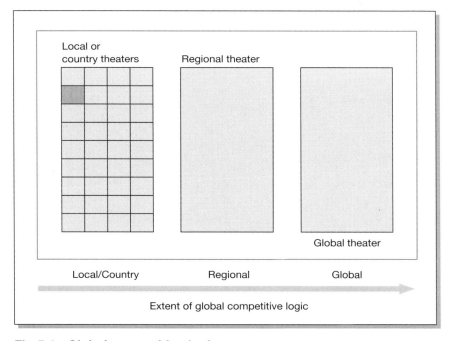

Fig 5.1   Global competitive logic

view on the type of competitive logic involved is thus a prerequisite for forming an appropriate strategy.

➔ Global industry logic

While the presence or absence of global competitive pressure is relatively easy to spot, global industry logic is one of those forces not easily visible, indeed it can be labeled "non-visible" globalization. The question we need to answer is: "Are we competing in a global industry?" Remember, we already deal with competition separately, so the unit of analysis is the nature of the value chain and the overall structure of the industry and the relevant KSFs.[5]

Conceptually, every industry requires some basic dos and don'ts of its participants. A company violating these competitive rules would invariably suffer competitive disadvantages and, in the long run, go out of business. These basic rules of competition, required for any player that wants to be a member of this industry, have traditionally been called key success factors (KSFs). Most competitive firms deliver on these KSFs in their home markets. However, when a company faces a situation where its industry KSFs apply to many markets, or even globally, we can say that there exists a global logic to apply those skills across the world. Transferring such performance from one country to another would create leverage on skills already learned, and thus add to the competitiveness of the company.

It may be easier to think of the set of KSFs required in an industry as an industry "code."[6] Most companies crack this code for their home markets. Firms expend great effort to crack the relevant industry code, measured in terms of expertise, time, skills, and investments. Once the code of an industry is cracked and the road to success lies open, companies have to ask whether the same code applies to another country, region, or even the world. An industry with a global code is characterized by a similar set of KSFs governing success in that industry. Understanding that, a company can leverage this into other areas, thus obtaining more "bang for the buck." Industries where the same set of KSFs applies worldwide are thus said to experience a greater amount of global industry logic. Conversely, industries where the KSFs differ substantially from country to country can be said to experience very little global industry logic. The implications of global industry logic are important for the development of global strategies. Having successfully navigated the code for an industry with worldwide application, a company has an incentive to take that experience elsewhere and obtain additional return on a lesson already learned. This reduces the cost of the original lesson, or "code cracking" experience.

The implications of global industry logic are important for the development of global strategies.

Having understood the basic concept of industry codes, KSFs, and the need to ask the question: "Does this code apply to one country alone, or are the codes essentially the same around the world?" managers will find that few industries exist where this can be answered in absolute terms. Global industry logic does come in intervals, and not only in "yes" or "no" terms.

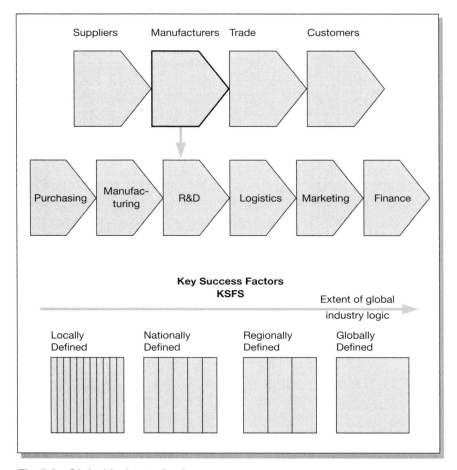

Fig 5.2 Global industry logic

Let us use the paint industry as an example.[7] In paints, there are a number of dimensions along which the industry can be segmented: geographically, by application industry (automotive, marine, decorative), and by technology (water borne, solvent based, powder). For a company such as ICI Paints, which runs paint operations around the world, would the KSFs encountered by each regional or country organization be similar?[8] Although there is a need to adjust paint to the local operating environment (climate, substrata), running paint operations *per se* might be considered largely similar. Significant differences may, however, exist in the various application segments. The automotive industry, with its particular needs and its globalizing customer base, experiences a high degree of uniformity, suggesting that automotive Original Equipment Manufacturer (OEM) paint operations can be run with a high degree of similarity, and the relevant code to crack that segment is likely to be very similar across the globe. In decorative paint, however, an industry that still differs substantially from country to country and in which a substantial amount of paint moves through the retail sector, the relevant segment code might be more different.

The paint industry example illustrates the need to look not only at the industry, but also at the relevant sub-segments, and to ask questions regarding similarity of codes on several levels. In most instances, as companies go through such an exercise, they will find that the important judgment to be made is an assessment of how different or similar the industry is. Once similarities have been identified, however shallow, the next step requires the company to take advantage of these similarities in codes through leverage. Since global leverage is one of those terms frequently used but often applied in a cavalier fashion, it is important to look at leverage in more specific terms to see how this might apply in the context of global industry logic.

Leverage means that we get additional effectiveness from doing it a second time, or we might be able to do it better by spreading it over more business volume. The first type of leverage comes from applying lessons from one part of the world to another. I am reminded of the similarity with tuition, the educational fees to be paid for attending university in the USA. If a company wants to obtain such leverage through its global network of companies, the firm must provide for a process by which the lessons, and the related cost for learning them, get paid only once and others learn from them. This is much easier said than done as we have seen earlier with the not-invented-here (NIH) syndrome, requiring managers who can evaluate lessons for their applicability regardless of their home base or experience base. Many opportunities to gain leverage under global industry logic are thus under-utilized, and many global firms remind us of classrooms where many students attend, all paying high tuition, but it is not clear whether anyone is learning the lessons taught.

> **Leverage means that we get additional effectiveness from doing it a second time, or we might be able to do it better by spreading it over more business volume.**

The second form of leverage, namely the sharing of resources so that you can do something better, is also a difficult task to achieve. If all local units of a worldwide operating firm were left to their own devices, there would be a substantial duplication of resources. A firm applying this strategy well would gain additional competitiveness.

One of the most telling examples of this type of leverage is Electrolux, the Sweden-based white goods manufacturer which transformed industry competition through its assessment of KSFs. Electrolux concluded that, while customer requirements differ from country to country, each of its appliances had nevertheless a substantial amount of components "under the hood" that were identical. Leverage thus came from building volume in "same components," or sharing them across a diverse line of products, thus gaining efficiency.[9]

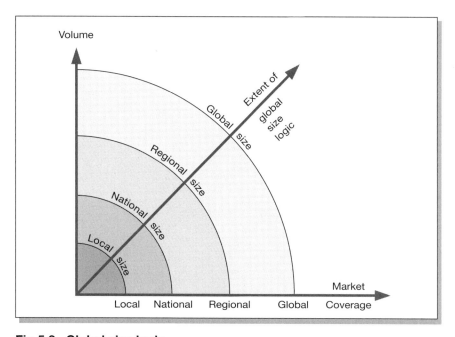

Fig 5.3   Global size logic

Global size logic

Related to global industry logic is global size logic. Often referred to as the need to build critical mass, global size logic is an important driver in the global strategies pursued by many firms. In many industries, a minimal size of a key activity is needed to compete effectively. In some ways, it is part of a KSF or "industry code." The presence of any form of critical mass clearly relates to globalization, because strong global size logic typically forces companies to adjust by spreading market coverage to gain the required minimum size. In many industries, the presence of size logic even means that no single market can pay off the fixed investments needed to enter.

Companies need to search for global size logic by finding out if anywhere in their business some steps, departments, or functions exist that would be inefficient below such a critical mass. Some of the easiest examples to understand stem from the pharmaceutical industry. For pharma companies, the typical investment required to bring a new drug from molecule development to market introduction is about $250 million.[10] Given that a pharmaceutical company cannot spend an unlimited amount on research, this minimum fixed investment needs to be amortized within the research budget (15 to 20 percent of sales). In addition, patent filing early in the molecule development stage, and long lead times for market introduction, mean that effective time in the market is cut to about ten years. If the drug is to earn sufficient profits, the pharmaceutical company needs to obtain sales of about $1.2 to $1.5 billion over the product lifetime, or $120 to $150 million per year. To obtain such volumes, pharmaceutical companies need to have distribution in many markets to generate the required minimum amount.

> **The presence of any form of critical mass clearly relates to globalization, because strong global size logic typically forces companies to adjust by spreading market coverage to gain the required minimum size.**

Recent merger activity in the pharmaceutical industry has clearly been driven by a global size logic strongly perceived by many of these players. In the early phase of consolidation, the mergers were between a large acquirer and smaller firms who had become marginalized by the strong global size logic. The acquisition of Wellcome[11] by Glaxo, or Syntex and Boehringer-Mannheim by Roche[12] fit these categories. Other mergers took place between mid-size firms in an effort to leapfrog into the Big League. Pharmacia/Upjohn would be part of this trend.[13] Finally, the latest trend has been the mega-merger between members already part of the Big League: Ciba-Geigy merging with Sandoz to form Novartis, thus coming close to global leadership in pharmaceuticals and creating the world biggest life sciences company, is the most outstanding of these examples. Later attempted mergers between SKB and American Home,[14] then SKB and Glaxo, all fell apart not for their absence of global size logic but for their inability to overcome internal hurdles to capitalize on the opportunity.[15]

> **Later attempted mergers ... fell apart not for their absence of global size logic but for their inability to overcome internal hurdles to capitalize on the opportunity.**

In the financial sector, we have witnessed major mergers between large companies. Among financial institutions in Europe, 1998 saw the merger between Union Bank of Switzerland and Swiss Bank Corporation to form United Bank of Switzerland (UBS), becoming the largest European bank and one of the largest in the world.[16] This merger was caused by the perceived need to gain more critical mass in the investment banking area which requires a considerable amount of capital. The two banks were already among the leaders in private banking, commercial banking, and domestic retail banking. The combination of Zurich Insurance of Switzerland with the BAT financial services arm of BAT of the UK is a second major merger in the insurance sector. This combination creates a more global coverage in insurance and fund management, where both firms strive to achieve sufficient size to compete globally.[17]

> **As more and more firms face an increasing amount of fixed expenditures, particularly in the R&D area, many firms find themselves pushed into a new game through increasing global size logic.**

Minimum size pointing to the presence of global size logic may exist in different parts of a firm's business. For an airline, it may be in the reservation system applied worldwide. For other companies, this critical mass may be dictated by high fixed costs in a logistic system, a required sales presence, or other elements. What is needed is to understand the business system and the industry of a company well enough to ferret them out, identify them, and be clear of the strength of the size logic. As more and more firms face an increasing amount of fixed expenditures, particularly in the R&D area, many firms find themselves pushed into a new game through increasing global size logic.

The need to achieve critical mass on a global scale has created a substantial

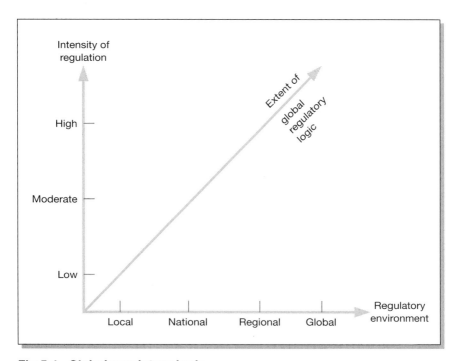

Fig 5.4 Global regulatory logic

momentum toward mergers that improve both the global ranking of a firm and the global size of a business. We can expect many more of these mergers in the near future.

Global regulatory logic

For some industries, the regulatory environment is one of the most important elements. This is true for many of the healthcare industries, but also for industries such as banking, insurance, airlines, telecommunications, and much of the new media. Global regulatory logic exists when a company faces a need to extend itself globally due to different regulatory forces, or would face competitive disadvantage for not doing so.

Looking at the healthcare industry helps illustrate the concept. Regulatory affairs, such as for pharmaceuticals or medical implants, are still dominated by country-specific regulatory bodies. For the USA this is the Federal Food and Drug Administration (FDA). Some of the regulations, or permissions granted to market a drug in the USA, at times differ from those in other countries. In general, regulatory practice in the USA has been accused of being slower than in Europe. Because the time period between patent granting and market entry is important in determining the economic success of a new product, companies planning to operate in the USA alone would be limited to exploiting new products, compared to others able to launch earlier in Europe or elsewhere.

The presence of global regulatory logic would therefore require the company to have a launching pad in more than one area of the world, but in particular in those countries where approval might be gained first. Ares-Serono, a Swiss-based biotechnology firm with a global leadership position in fertility drugs, was the first company to seize upon the opportunity to apply for approval under the new European regulatory arrangement. The new body, the European Medicines Evaluation Agency (EMEA) approved Serostim, an Ares-Serono growth hormone to fight AIDS wasting.

In the production of many drugs, the US-based FDA has become the de facto standard for manufacturing processes. The FDA goods manufacturing process (GMP) approval is necessary for any plant shipping drug products into the USA. Since it is increasingly impossible to dedicate factories to individual markets, the globally or regionally focused factory must be able to master GMP to ship to the USA. A manufacturing base for a firm in Europe exporting to the US market thus becomes subject to the FDA GMP approval. When building a plant, or designing a new manufacturing process, GMP has to be factored in from the outset. This tends to level the playing field for more firms, albeit at a higher level, thus increasing the global regulatory logic. Once the most difficult regulatory hurdle is overcome (USA), a company might as well ship worldwide because it has cleared the hurdles for many other countries as well.

In the telecommunications industry, traditional standards for telephone signaling, equipment, and network systems were nationally configured. This was also true for cellular networks. As a result, a cellular customer in Finland, for example, could not use the phone when traveling to France or to the USA. The move to newer standards, and in particular the Global System for Mobile communicationi (GSM) standard pioneered by European telephone carriers, meant that customers could begin to use their phones wherever they traveled. Rather than finding regional, or local standards, the world is rapidly moving to the adoption of one standard. This creates a strong global regulatory logic and makes it possible for equipment manufacturers to market their equipment across multiple markets. The rapid growth of Ericsson and Nokia in mobile telecommunications networks in the USA is a result of these changes.

> The move to newer standards, and in particular the GSM standard pioneered by European telephone carriers, meant that customers could begin to use their phones wherever they traveled.

The financial services sector is another area where standards or regulations were typically national. Both through the WTO and the integration movement in the European Union, regulatory affairs have become more closely coordinated. As local barriers disappear or are reduced, global regulatory logic makes it possible for players to cross borders. This is one reason we are witnessing cross-border mergers in insurance (Allianz, Axa, Zurich Insurance), banking (ING and Barings),[18] and the many acquisitions of financial institutions on a global scale.

> Low regulatory global logic exists, therefore, where significant differences in regulatory behavior exist, and is high where the approval or regulatory practices are similar.

Low regulatory global logic exists, therefore, where significant differences in regulatory behavior exist, and is high where the approval or regulatory practices are similar. The past decade has seen enormous shifts in how national or local governments regulate industries. The result has been an overall reduction of regulatory barriers, and a general increase in the global regulatory logic, which impacts on the competitive behavior of firms active in previously highly regulated sectors.

Notes

1. See case series by Stephen Allen, "Note on the Construction Machinery Industry", (ECCH No. 393–068–5), "Caterpillar and Komatsu in 1988" (ECCH No. 393–069–1), "Caterpillar and Komatsu in 1992", (ECCH No. 393–070–1).

2. See case series developed by Stephen Allen, "Note on the European Major Home

Appliance Industry – 1990" (ECCH No. 393–091–5), Whirlpool Corporation (ECCH No. 393–095–1), "Electrolux" (ECCH No. 393–094–1), "General Electric: Major Appliances" (ECCH No. 393–093–1).

3. Christopher Lorenz, "The birth of a transitional", *McKinsey Quarterly*, Autumn 1989, p. 72.

4. "On the verge of a world war in white goods", *Business Week*, 2 November, 1987, p. 41.

5. Kenichi Ohmae, *The Mind of the Strategist*, McGraw-Hill, New York, 1992 [1982], Chapter 3.

6. Jean-Pierre Jeannet, *Understanding Your Industry*, Note/Working Paper, 1996.

7. Jean-Pierre Jeannet, *The World Paint Industry (1992)*, Industry Note, IMD, 1993.

8. Jean-Pierre Jeannet, *ICI Paints (A) and (B)*, Case Studies, IMD, 1990 and 1993.

9. "White goods empire: 400 villages crown Electrolux market king", *Business International*, 11 August, 1986, p. 250.

10. "Research moves to sharper focus", *Financial Times*, 23 March, 1994, p.5, Survey, Pharmaceuticals: Research and Development.

11. "Cost savings expected from creation of world's largest drugs group. Glaxo in £9.4 bn Wellcome bid," *Financial Times*, 24 January, 1995, p.1 and 6.

12. "Roche in $5.3 bn agreed bid for Syntex," *Financial Times*, 3 May, 1994, p. 1. and "Companies and Markets: Roche confounds the analysts: Acquisition will make Swiss group joint leader in world diagnostics," The *Financial Times*, 27 May, 1997, p. 23.

13. "Pharmacia and Upjohn form $13 bn drugs group: Swedish/US merged company to have London headquarters," *Financial Times*, 21 August, 1995, p. 1.

14. "Shares in sector boosted: SmithKline and AHP in $125 bn drug merger talks," *Financial Times*, 21 January, 1998, p. 1.

15. "Glaxo Wellcome and Smith shares fall sharply: Dispute over power ended merger plan," *Financial Times*, 25 February, 1998, p. 1.

16. "SBC comes out on top as UBS boosts shares: Deal will cost 13,000 jobs," *Financial Times*, 9 December, 1997, p. 1.

17. "Zurich sets out terms of £23 bn deal with BAT: Financial Services tie-up expected to take a year to get regulatory go-ahead," *Financial Times*, 17 October, 1998, p. 21.

18. "A Premium on Size." *Financial Times*, 15 August, 1996.

6

Assessing patterns of global logic

The previous chapters have concentrated on providing companies with an approach for probing the intensity of global logic in different parts of their business. Following that analysis, a company would have an appropriate reading of each of the chosen global logic dimensions. This chapter is devoted to the conversion of these separate global logic readings on each dimension into a meaningful pattern for guiding global strategy. To accomplish this, the use of the "spiderweb" is suggested. We also discuss approaches to assure that the global logic analysis is performed in a sufficiently forward-looking manner so that future trends can be incorporated.

Selection of generic global logic dimensions

The previous two chapters gave the reader a chance to review several global logic dimensions. However, we have to note that these were generic dimensions, or global logics, that occurred in most industries we have reviewed. Whenever we do this, we tend to make these generic global logic dimensions seem the only ones possible. This is far from actuality. While typically present in most industries, we suggest that each industry be separately analyzed and that there may well be other dimensions more relevant for further analysis. Some creativity is thus required, and business teams facing a thorough analysis of the relevant global logic present in their industry are well advised to use a measure of judgment in terms of applying generic dimensions in a "cookie cutter"-style approach.

> ... business teams facing a thorough analysis of the relevant global logic present in their industry are well advised to use a measure of judgment in terms of applying generic dimensions in a "cookie cutter"-style approach.

Our experience with the creation of the global logic concept is of value to aspiring globalists elsewhere. Originally, we recognized only four generic global logic dimensions. As our analytic experience grew, additional dimensions emerged. It is to be expected that over time, additional generic global logics dimensions will be uncovered.

Apart from the specific generic global logic dimension, experience also shows that some generic global logics are in reality a composite of several related logics, forming broader rays, or vectors. As we have seen, the global purchasing logic can be measured at the business-to-business level, the individual consumer level, the retail level, or the wholesale and distribution level, thus combining into a vector with several dimensions. The global purchasing logic may not be of equal intensity in all of these dimensions. Consequently, any analyst must take care to understand the depth and breadth of these vectors before committing to a detailed analysis.

Measuring global logic intensity

Rather than reducing global intensity to a single denominator, or measurement, we suggest an approach that might accept different measurements along different global logics dimensions. To realize this, we will have to reduce the various global logic dimensions to some comparable measurement.

From the diligent performance of global logic analysis, a company would be facing a considerable amount of data, or experience, that on its own is not yet comparable across the various different dimensions. Some care must now be taken to convert the analysis into more standardized measures. The rationale for using measurements stems from the experience that the forces for globalization as captured through global logics are not equally spread throughout the business environment of a firm. To isolate the sources of strongest global logic, the analyst has the choice of two principle types of measurements: either measure in absolute terms or in ordinal/rank order ratings.

Working with absolute measurements, we would have to convert each of the identified global logic dimensions into a measurements, such as a rating along an index of 1 through 10 or 1 through 100. This would be a judgment based upon global management experience by a company, business team, or an experienced executive.

> **Although managers are quite used to making judgments about environmental conditions, experience has shown that on many scales managers have difficulty separating global intensity across the various global logic dimensions.**

Although convenient and easily implemented, the use of absolute ratings, such as scales from 0 to 100, is to be discouraged for two reasons. First, it gives a semblance of precision that is simply not present in the real world where the situation is much more complex. Although managers are quite used to making judgments about environmental conditions, experience has shown that on many scales managers have difficulty separating global intensity across the various global logic dimensions. As we will see later, it does not serve a useful purpose if the dimensions are all rated "highly global," or all are a "10" out of 10. Under those circumstances, ties can develop and prioritization is made difficult.

Global logic dimensions	Ratings									
	1	2	3	4	5	6	7	8	9	10
Customer logic										
	1	2	3	4	5	6	7	8	9	10
Purchasing logic										
	1	2	3	4	5	6	7	8	9	10
Information logic										
	1	2	3	4	5	6	7	8	9	10
Competitive logic										
	1	2	3	4	5	6	7	8	9	10
Industry logic										
	1	2	3	4	5	6	7	8	9	10
Size logic										
	1	2	3	4	5	6	7	8	9	10
Regulatory logic										

Fig 6.1   Global logic ratings

Measuring global logics using rank order

Since it will be of great importance to a company to understand the relative pressures emanating from the various global logics, we are much better served if we look for relevant, or comparative rankings. Such comparative rankings allow us to rank order the global logic intensity of each of the selected global logic dimensions. Ranking would require a business team to agree which one of the dimensions experiences the highest global logic pressure, which one the second, and so on.

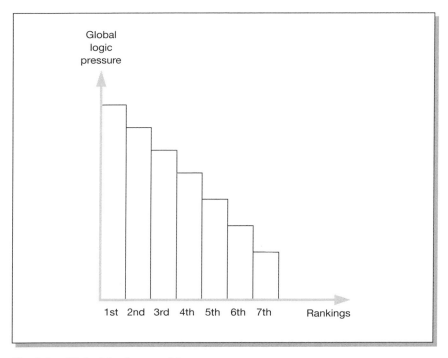

Fig 6.2   Global logics rankings

Assembling global logics into meaningful patterns

How then are we to conceptualize the various global logic measurements into a coherent pattern that will help companies appreciate the global pressures in their industries? When searching for appropriate ways to depict the complexity of global logics in different industries, we discarded traditional histograms, bar charts, and other composite measures. Instead, we adopted the "spider-web" chart so often used in business and economics journals.[1]

Depicting the generic global logics dimensions starting in the center of the chart, we can indicate extensive global pressure by the relative distance from the center. A company facing an industry with little, or even zero global pressure, would show a small footprint. A company exposed to extensive global pressure would show a large, extensive footprint.

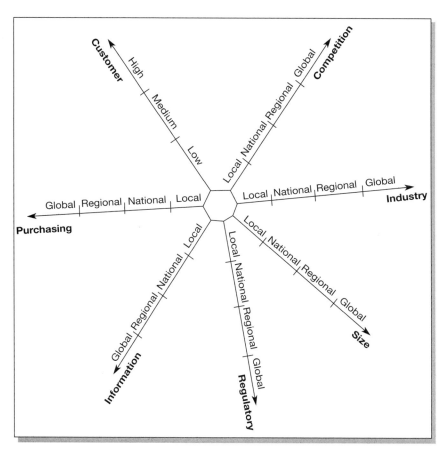

Fig 6.3   Generic global logics spiderweb chart

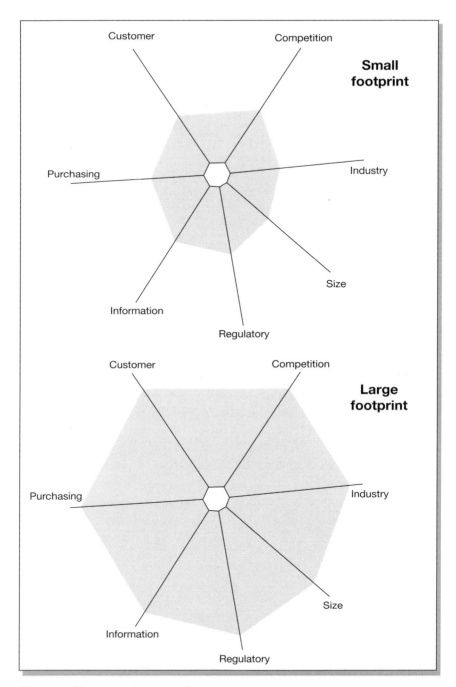

Fig 6.4   Global logic footprints

Categorizing generic global spiderwebs

For a complete and meaningful analysis, it is not sufficient to denote the size of the footprint alone. It makes a real difference to know the actual source of the dominating global pressure, thus forcing companies to identify the extreme ends of their spiderwebs.

As we pointed out in Chapter 4, the initial debate surrounding globalization centered around markets and customers showing increasingly converging patterns of consumption. This "Levitt"[2] argument, if translated into our conceptualization, would indicate that global pressures would primarily emanate from the consumer side, or global customer, purchase, or information logic. With a view that globalization was primarily driven by customers, the typical spiderweb chart would be heavily weighted in favor of customer-sensitive dimensions.

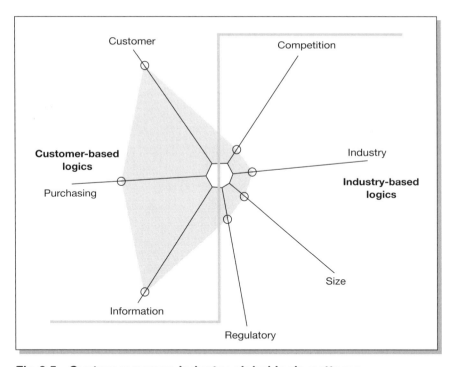

Fig 6.5   Customer versus industry global logic patterns

Experience indicates, however, that the measurements for global logic differ by industry. We found customer-based global logics were not always the strongest. In many sectors, industry-based global logics (industry, competitive, size, regulatory) are relatively more pronounced and often outrank customer-based global logics. Industry-based logics are strong in those industries where significant differences exist among the global customer base but where the realities of competition and industry economics dictates a non-domestic approach. Typical examples of such industries would be cement, forestry, basic chemicals, and other basic industries.

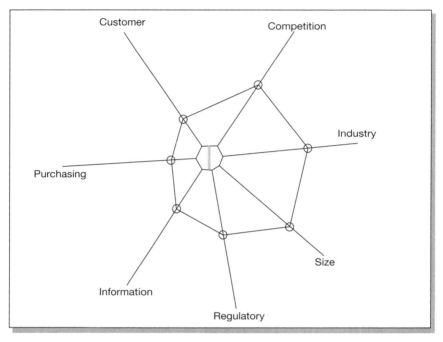

Fig 6.6   Global logic patterns: industrial versus customer logics

Visible versus invisible globalization

Different patterns exist, and we can point out but some of the generic patterns. In fact, the dimensions, though sometimes correlated, can describe different orthogonal patterns that often act independently of each other.

From the experience of working with different firms operating in many different industry environments, we have observed that the ratings for the chosen generic global logics are usually different. The chances of running a business where all elements show the exact same global intensity are small. Rather, the intensity differs by global logic, and the patterns exhibited by most firms will differ by the industry they are facing. However, given the fact that we are measuring the global intensity of an industry, not a company, firms operating in the same competitive industry environment are expected to face an identical pattern of global logics.

Treating the various global logics as partly independent, or orthogonal, is based on the observations that companies face radically different globalization patterns in different industries. In some industries, the external factors, such as global customer logic or global purchasing logic may be experiencing greater pressure to globalize in a business. In other situations, companies face largely hidden, or industry-based global logic factors which leads to globalization in spite of differentiation forces among the customer base. For many industries, global logic stemming from industry factors is more important and relevant than that from customers or markets. This is particularly the case for some of the more technologically oriented industries, and for many business-to-business situations.

> **For many industries, global logic stemming from industry factors is more important and relevant than that from customers or markets.**

Having a clear idea of the relevant "spiderweb" is a precondition to engage in an articulate and informed globalization debate in any business or company. Managers should be aware that the spiderweb is highly industry specific, and in some instances even segment specific. How the spiderweb analysis output may be used to chart an actual globalization strategy will be the main point in the following chapter.

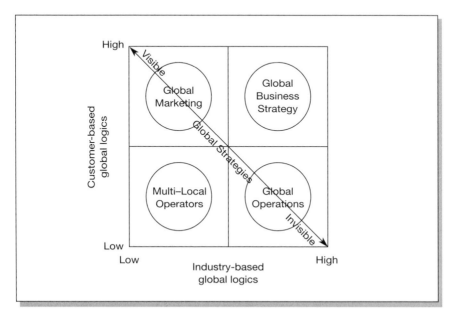

Fig 6.7   Visible versus invisible global logic patterns

➲ Global logic trends over time

Careful analysis of the relevant dimensions of globalization, or its logics, should also lead to an understanding of the present and future state of an industry. We might be able to paint an accurate picture through an in-depth spiderweb analysis for a company for this moment in time, but there are forces at work that cause patterns to change. Typically, the forces at work in our rapidly globalizing economy tend to enhance the global logic working on firms. In some instances, the changes can come about rather quickly, as we have seen in the case of global competitive logic where a move by one player can make all others change strategy.

> Typically, the forces at work in our rapidly globalizing economy tend to enhance the global logic working on firms. In some instances, the changes can come about rather quickly, as we have seen in the case of global competitive logic where a move by one player can make all others change strategy.

In the major home appliance, or white goods industry, the impetus given by Electrolux led to similar global strategies by Whirlpool, Maytag, and GE. In the end, when the original industry vision of Electrolux became reality, it was difficult to tell if this was as a result of a solid strategy or simply because all players followed suit and thus made the vision a reality.

Outward moves on our spiderweb chart have been most prevalent in the areas of purchasing logic and competitive logic. For both dimensions, we have witnessed considerable changes in business practices which have had more effect on the global logic than in other areas. Customers have changed, and will continue to change their requirements. However, movements along the customer logic are taking more time, moving more deliberately, and changes are often only noticeable over a longer period of time. In the areas of purchasing and competition, a single move by an important customer, or the acquisition strategy of a major competitor, can throw an entire industry into a globalization turmoil, effectively changing the overall global logic in a short period of time.

> In areas of purchasing and competition, a single move by an important customer, or the acquisition strategy of a major competitor, can throw an entire industry into a globalization turmoil, effectively changing the overall global logic in a short period of time.

Equally, we should consider it possible for global logic forces to diminish along a given dimension. Although all of our examples have pointed to the direction of outward, or increasing global pressure, we should not eliminate out of hand the possibility that global logic pressure might diminish across a given dimension as a result of different industry environments.

Anticipating global logic changes

Having made the comment that companies needed to understand the future global spiderweb as a basis for their forward strategies, we need to understand how such forward predictions can be made with some sense of authority. For that purpose, we suggest that the particular relationship of the various global logic dimensions can be such a bellwether, indicating imminent changes.

A first indicator can be a relatively high degree of global industry logic combined with low competitive logic. This would signal that, while substantial opportunities for global logic exist, the industry *per se* has not yet stepped up and is not conducting itself as globally as required by the industry. In such situations, it would take only one major industry player to move everyone into a global game, much along the lines we have seen in industries such as white goods with Electrolux, or the airline industry based upon early alliance moves by British Airways. When the competition acts in an under-globalized fashion against the rest of the global opportunity, competitive reaction is likely to follow and change the nature of the competitive game.

> ... changes in the industry that lead to a substantial change in the global industry logic or the critical mass logic are powerful indicators that future further globalization will follow.

Another dimension to watch out for is the global purchasing logic. This captures, as we explained, the purchasing behavior of industry customers. To the extent that they are acting ahead of industry competitors (their suppliers in this case), a signal is sent to all industry participants that they themselves are not acting on the full global imperative.

Finally, changes in the industry that lead to a substantial change in the global industry logic or the critical mass logic are powerful indicators that future further globalization will follow. Such changes might be the result of technological breakthroughs leading to a higher critical mass requirement which in turn leads to greater volume needs driving companies into multiple markets.

The appropriate spiderweb analysis will thus include both a present and future type of analysis, combined with a future trend picture. Since changes in a firm's global logic pressure are very important and take time to internalize, companies are well advised to make their plans on the future, not past or present global logic pressure.

> Since changes in a firm's global logic pressure are very important and take time to internalize, companies are well advised to make their plans on the future, not past or present global logic pressure.

Single versus multiple spiderwebs

An issue that frequently comes up in analyzing global logic is the unit of analysis. As we pointed out earlier, global logic is inherent in an industry and is not company specific. However, some industries are very broad and are made up of a number of sectors, or segments. As the global logic is reviewed, companies will need to be sensitive to any differences by segment or sector. In essence, the question of the number of logics is to be appreciated. For industries with multiple sets of key success factors (KSFs), the experience indicates that a different set of global logic might apply to each segment.

> **The presence of multiple global logic spiderwebs is a challenge for most companies.**

The presence of multiple global logic spiderwebs is a challenge for most companies. There is a direct relation between the chosen generic global strategy and the particular spiderweb global logic pattern identified for an industry. If multiple patterns existed, multiple generic global strategies would have to be accommodated in parallel. This is a major source of the challenge faced by multi-product or multi-segment companies as they roll out their globalization.

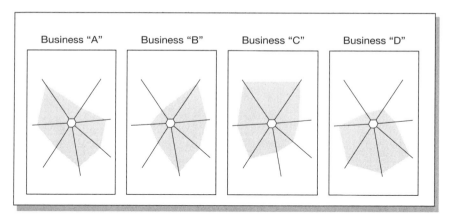

Business "A"   Business "B"   Business "C"   Business "D"

Fig 6.8   Multiple spiderweb patterns

Actual industry versus perceived company global logic patterns

Global logic measures the pressure present in a firm's industry. In that sense, the global logic spiderweb would be identical for all directly competing firms. All competitors would need to make a accommodation to the global logic pressure.

However, we can also depict the situation within a firm by judging the extent to which the global logic pressure is followed. Each company operates on a certain view of the global market. Rather than probing for the factual view, or true state of the global logic pressure within a given industry, we can also draw a pattern of how a firm acts. This would tell us to what extent the company was operating on a over- or under-globalized view. Companies operating under a

Checking perceived against actual global logic can serve as a strong indicator of a company's globalization gap.

perception of less global logic then objectively identified would be operating in a state of under-globalization. The opposite is true for firms who perceive the industry to be having a higher global logic than objectively validated. Checking perceived against actual global logic can serve as a strong indicator of a company's globalization gap.

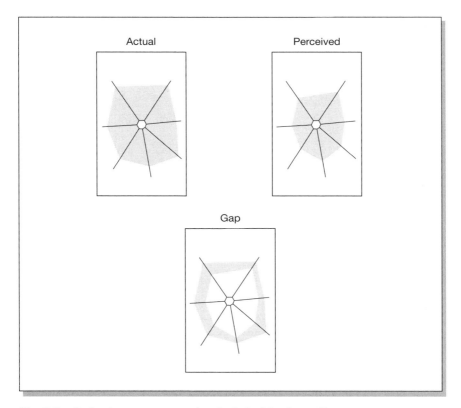

Fig 6.9   Actual versus perceived global logic patterns

⮑ Implications for global strategies

Throughout this chapter, we have emphasized the role of global logic analysis. This type of diagnostic will become the centerpiece of following sections, where we build extensively on those spiderwebs. Because of their central importance to understanding globalization and the global imperative for any firm, it is necessary once more to caution readers in their application. All too often, companies and executives tend to take a tool and apply it without care and insight, filling in the blanks in a way they might fill out a mere form letter. I hope the reader has gained sufficient background into this analysis to appreciate that it must be conducted with considerable thought and requires the application of deep industry experience. Only then can we be confident that the output of this analysis will be of sufficient quality to base further global strategies on it.

Notes

1. See *Economist*, numerous editions.
2. Levitt, Ted, "The Globalization of markets", *Harvard Business Review*, May–June 1983, pp 92–102.

Section 3

Global market assessment

The previous section focused largely on understanding the dynamics caused by finding global logic in a company's business, customer base, or industry. Just as the global logic assessment is unique to managers engaging in global battles, so is the need for analyzing markets on a global basis. Traditional market analysis and discussions about markets tend to focus on individual markets. But if we are to make an argument for the difference between a global mindset and the international or multinational mindset, we should be able to demonstrate specific types of market assessment or analysis that separate the global mindset from other types of mindset.

Although analyzing market opportunities with a global mindset requires the use of many traditional types of analysis, an examination of these will not be undertaken. Of course the global mindset requires a customer orientation and detailed understanding of customer processes, just as is required for managers who operate in single-country operations. Likewise, included in the global mindset skills are basic competitive understanding, and the standard macro data sets managers have become accustomed to when making market decisions.

The types of analyses offered in this section help the manager understand the entire global market opportunity. Many of these are relatively new, and practice of them is still in its infancy at many firms. It can be expected that, as the business community's experience with global business progresses, additional types of analyses will be encountered in the future. The ones selected here center around global chessboard analysis and the capabilities to evaluate the value of a country or territory as part of an overall global market. The second set of concepts deals with the innovation pattern across the world and trend analysis in the form of lead markets and ripple effects. What is true for all of these concepts is the need to keep a large number of markets in view at all times.

Understanding the global chessboard

I have come to appreciate the power of multi-country market analysis when imagining the world as a chessboard.[1] However, the world is different from the traditional chessboard with its 64 squares of equal size, arranged in a neat 8 × 8 square. First, the global chessboard is a set of market opportunities where each country is represented as a square. At present time, and depending on whom we want to base our analysis, there are some 175–200 country squares represented on the board. As the reader might expect, this board has very different sizes of square, depending on the economic importance of each country. And finally, the shape of the board is in constant flux in line with the economic fortunes of each of the countries.

Analyzing the global chessboard with a global mindset thus requires a type of understanding of the importance of each of the chessboard pieces. Just like the chess player in the real game, the manager playing global chess cannot occupy all of the spaces on the board. Managers, and their companies, need to pick those "squares" that are of critical importance while leaving other positions to avoid a dilution of resources.

> **Just like the chess player in the real game, the manager playing global chess cannot occupy all of the spaces on the board. Managers, and their companies, need to pick those "squares" that are of critical importance while leaving other positions to avoid a dilution of resources.**

How a company depicts its own market opportunities on its own global chessboard is the next issue we need to tackle.

Mapping out the global chessboard

Let us first look at the "master" global chessboard including all country markets. When we look at a typical geographic map, we are conditioned to view countries by their shapes and in line with the relative land mass. Building a global chessboard useful for global analysis requires the use of a different metric. It is most helpful to map each country by the size of its economy, or GNP/GDP.[2] The relevant size of each country's square is thus determined by the percentage of its own GNP in relation to world GNP. Large economies, such

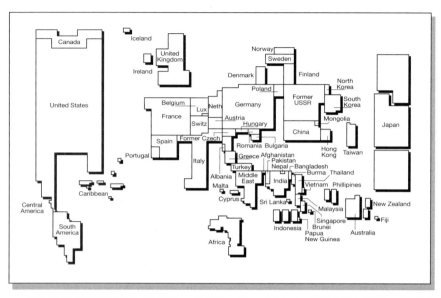

Source: The New State of the World Atlas, 4th Edition, Simon & Schuster 1991 © Myriad Editions Limited

Fig 7.1   The global chessboard: distribution of world GNP

as the USA, would occupy about 20 percent of the world map. Other countries with much smaller economies are represented correspondingly by only very small spaces.

There is one other aspect that needs to be considered. Now that we have all countries represented by the relative size of their economy, we still need to determine if all these countries are part of the global chessboard. So what conditions must a country meet before it can claim to be part of the global chessboard? Clearly, as we indicated in the introductory chapter, the country must be linked economically into the globalizing world economy. For this to occur, there needs to be sufficient freedom of movement for investments, products, manpower, and ideas in and out of the country. This movement allows leverage across many countries, or the use of a position in one country to obtain better market position somewhere else. A country, therefore, that is economically "landlocked", as was the case with many economies in the third world or the former Soviet Union, could never play the role of a relevant piece on the chessboard and was thus detached from consideration for global strategies.

In this context, it may be helpful to think about the evolution of the global chessboard over the past 20 years. For much of the 1970s and early 1980s, the relevant global chessboard consisted of Western Europe, North America (USA and Canada), and Japan with a few other countries of the Pacific Rim. For most of those countries, there was relative freedom of movement for investments, products, services, and key human resources, although it should not be viewed as absolute. Many of our experienced readers would be able to cite numerous experiences where local regulations or laws prevented them from full freedom of movement.

The 1980s brought a substantial change in the global chessboard. Mid-decade, China, through its trade liberalization policy, made freedom of movement of investments, products, and even people much more possible than ever before. By creating the ability to place production there in the first wave of development and to source products for global markets out of China, the country placed itself in a situation where China became a relevant piece of the global chessboard, thus attaching itself to the rest of the economically linked world (see Figure 7.2).

At the end of the 1980s, the world experienced the disappearance of the Soviet Union and the opening of Eastern Europe and much of the former Soviet Union to world trade. Suddenly it became possible to export products with greater freedom to those countries. Companies were in a position to either acquire companies there or make their own greenfield investments. Foreign staff could be sent to those areas, and increasingly, capital returns repatriated. As a result, we can now say that much of this world has joined the global chessboard. The relevance of these countries still remain negligible due the size of their markets compared to the rest of the world as measured in GNP.

At the end of the 1980s and the beginning of the 1990s, the trend to liberalize economies, to privatize government-owned operations, and to open up to international trade swept through Latin America. In Latin America, Mexico "joined" the chessboard through its NAFTA agreement with the USA and Canada. Brazil and Argentina, two countries that had traditionally controlled foreign trade and erected significant barriers to the free flow of products, engaged in significant market opening. Chile had gone through this process earlier. The net effect is the same, however, with most countries in Latin America now part of the global chessboard.

In Asia, we have experienced equally sweeping changes. The move towards trade liberation underway in India has the effect of tying this large population with its economy to the global chessboard. Similar developments are underway in countries such as Indonesia. But the most striking example of this time is Vietnam. Following the unification of North and South Vietnam in the 1970s, the country had detached itself from the global chessboard and was no longer an accessible market for global companies. With the political changes taking place around the world, Vietnam's leadership pursued a course of trade liberalization. This policy opened up the local economy, both as a market for imported products and as a base for exports. As many international companies "discovered" Vietnam, they quickly moved in as it was seen as a vital piece in the ever expanding global economy.

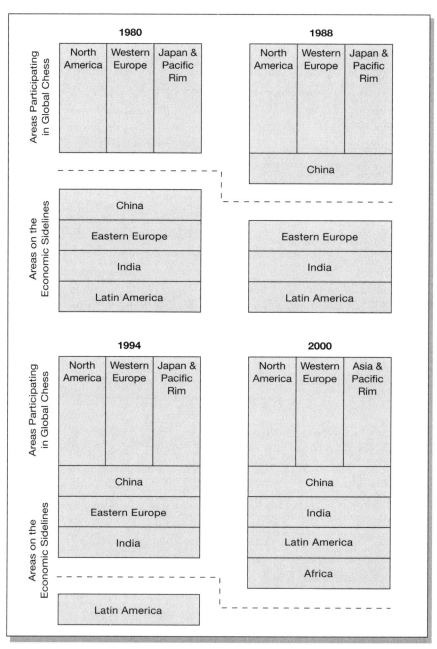

Source: Global Marketing Strategies, 4th edn, Jean-Pierre Jeannet and H. David Hennessey, Houghton Mifflin, Boston, MA , c. 1998, p. 252

Fig 7.2 Changes in the global chessboard

Building chessboards by industry/company

So far, we have spoken of the global chessboard strictly in terms of a depiction of the distribution of world GNP. While GNP data are relevant as an indication of market size, most firms work with much more specific data that determine the drivers in their industry. This indicates that the underlying metric, or appropriate measurement, may be quite different from industry to industry. Needless to say, the global chessboard needs to be drawn with the specific metric in mind.

A company such as Microsoft might be more interested in the population of PCs in each country, thus mapping out its global chessboard on that basis. The supplier of telecommunications equipment might select installed phone lines per country as the metric for market size. Automotive parts suppliers will have to look at the production capacity installed, which tends to be concentrated on a few countries, whereas the supplier of replacement parts will need to understand the installed base, or size of motor fleet, per country. Consequently, each industry has its own very particular chessboard. And firms operating in several different market segments on a worldwide basis might have different chessboards for each customer or industry segment.

> What is important is that each company be completely clear on the nature of its own chessboard which helps define geographic priorities for global strategies.

As we build chessboards to particular segment or industry specifications, some countries might loom large in some fields and be small for others. What is important is that each company be completely clear on the nature of its own chessboard which helps define geographic priorities for global strategies.

Selecting the relevant set of pieces

Determining the relevant global chessboard is a truly global market assessment. What is equally important, however, is the selection of markets needed for a global strategy. "Do I have to be in all markets on the global chessboard?" is a question frequently posed by managers struggling with issues on global strategy.

> Ohmae contends that a global company has to have a strong market position in at least two of three Triad regions (western Europe, USA, and Japan) with a minor position in the third region.

It was the Japanese consultant Kenichi Ohmae who coined the now widely known term *Triad Strategy*. Ohmae contends that a global company has to have a strong market position in at least two of three Triad regions (western Europe, USA, and Japan) with a minor position in the third region. The Triad Strategy was based upon the fact that some 75 percent of the world GNP was accounted for by western Europe, the USA, and Japan. It already implied that large "pieces" on the board were of importance. Ohmae's "2 + 1" strategy was a reflection of a global chessboard that was focused on the industrialized nations. Large areas of the world with huge population masses were still "off the board" and irrelevant for global chess.

The concept of the Triad Strategy nevertheless emphasizes that it is important to understand the major markets from a global point of view, and that a company needs to develop positions in these key markets. We are moving towards an understanding of interrelated competitive positions rather than a set of discrete choices where companies make decisions on whether or not to enter a given country, one country at a time. This discrete set of decisions is clearly coming to an end and managers with a global mindset will have to pick markets with a much more integrative point of view. To pick the right markets also forces management to think about the potential value, or contribution, a given market might make towards the overall market position.

Another thought of value is the consideration of competitive position. Leadership in one single market, or region, is found to be wanting. A company, such as GE's Major Home Appliances Division, was once the largest company in home appliances on the basis of market leadership in the USA where the share had reached some 30 percent. However, GE had few relevant positions outside of the USA. When Electrolux expanded in Europe and the USA, GE lost its overall lead worldwide, but remained first in the USA. Even when Whirlpool, with the acquisition of the Philips business in Europe, eclipsed both GE and Electrolux as the global leader, GE remained the US market leader. The difficulty of the lead position, which is one in a single region or country, is given by the fact that with a smart global company,

Leadership in one single market, or region, is found to be wanting.

the competitive position is not simply a fact of the locally present resources, but a collection of the resources of the entire worldwide network. We are therefore looking to select a number of markets with a view towards global leadership in mind.

⮞ Appreciating the value of a single-country market

The executive looking at one single country only does not have to answer for the value of that country in the overall global strategy of a firm. For global strategists, however, this is an important question. The global chessboard already gives a first indication as to market size. Why should sheer size be of such importance? Many companies know that global leadership in their chosen sectors or markets is of great importance. Typically, such global leadership is measured in terms of worldwide share of market. Companies that are well positioned in large markets do well in the global leadership game since their overall volume is helped by this particular geographic spread. This was the reason for Ohmae's Triad Strategy, and hence the value for large markets.

In most firms the value of a given country is still determined by its profit contribution. The difficulty with this view, however, stems from the fact that profit contribution is valuing the country or territory strictly in financial terms, which is different from strategic terms. Let us look at two examples.

A few years ago, some Apple executives were evaluating the entry of Apple into India. At that time, India was a difficult market, and Apple computers could not be simply imported into the country. To earn the funds to import some method had to be found to source components, or plastic resins, in India and get credit for them to obtain the right to import finished products. This would of course be difficult to achieve and require the collaboration of production, purchasing, engineering, and sales to obtain market entry. Why bother then? What attracted Apple to India was the possibility of selling some 200,000 machines, which on its own would not been very profitable due to the regular restrictions. But if added to its already existing worldwide volume, Apple's importance in the league tables of operating systems would have risen, and more software firms would be interested in writing for Apple. This was a very different view of the value of the "square" India as located on Apple's global chessboard.[3]

The second example is based on the experience of the Brazilian country manager for Siemens Automotive Systems.[4] Siemens had a small and non-profitable business in Brazil, and the question of its fit with the global strategy for the automotive systems division was raised. Because Siemens pursued a strategy of serving the largest automotive companies globally, and thus was interested in obtaining business for them anywhere, the local management realized that major firms were located in Brazil, and adding to those sales was in its parent company's interest. The key was to increase volume with, say GM, and that could be done in any country, even in Brazil, which would lead to a higher standing as a supplier for Siemens AT. The economic benefit might be reaped anywhere, not necessarily in Brazil.

Naturally, as experienced readers will realize, the value of a particular country to the entire global system of a firm cannot neglect that profitability must at some point be achieved. But profits might accrue in some other unit and does not have to be earned equally in all units, country after country.

Projecting the chessboard into the future

So far we have described the process as a rather static one, poring over the global chessboard for maximum advantage. What we need to consider now, however, is that our chessboard is not static like the regular chessboard. Not only do we have squares of different size, but the entire board changes over time. The main factors that make the board change are the economic and political developments that impact on the relative importance of a market.

In the first half of the 1990s, many of the economies of the Asia/Pacific area experienced a phase of tremendous growth. Economic GNP growth ranged around 10 percent for some of those countries, compared to 1 or 2 percent for mature industrialized nations of western Europe.[5] The impact of such disparate growth rates led to radically different market sizes over time, such as the next five to ten years. Markets that were ranked outside the top 20 may become part of the top 20, or even 10. China, for one, is already expected to become one of the major markets in the world, and for some products, such as telecommunications, China might well become the largest market.[6] Other markets that will become much more important are Korea, India, Indonesia, Thailand, Taiwan, Malaysia, Pakistan, and the Philippines.

Some of these markets are already much more important than presently assumed. Earlier we spoke of the possibility to plot the global chessboard along the lines of country GNP as a percent of world GNP. These measurements, as many economists have pointed out, do not adequately reflect purchasing power of a country as we are measuring GNP in real (US$) terms. To be correct, all GNP data would have to be adjusted to reflect purchasing power parity, and then we would see a substantial change in the rank order of markets.

While some markets move more into center stage, others will become marginalized. Among the top 20 markets for most products are smaller countries from Europe that right now still rank as important markets, but in the next decades will no longer be center stage for global strategy. Included here are the markets of Scandinavia, Finland, Switzerland, Austria, the Netherlands, and Belgium. This marginalization must also be considered in terms of investments.

While some markets move more into center stage, others will become marginalized.

Global companies will therefore have to keep in mind that when investments are made, they are made into a constantly changing global chessboard. With major investments made over a time horizon of several years, decision makers need to keep these changes in mind. Playing global chessboard is a difficult game: the board changes while you are moving your chess figures, and you have to plan to put your figure down (in the form of investments) into an anticipated chessboard, and not the present chessboard. Clearly, this is a major challenge for global mindsets.

⮕ Recent upheavals in the global chessboard

The fundamental economic changes that have swept many markets since the second half of 1997, beginning in Thailand and later engulfing Malaysia, Indonesia, Korea, and many other emerging markets, may make readers rethink the opportunity for globalization. These changes, often driven by stock market crashes and major bank failures based upon unsound credit extension in those markets, have an impact first and foremost on the globalization of financial markets. Financial markets, in order to reach a high degree of globalization, depend to a large extent on the free movement of capital for either direct foreign investment or in the form of risk capital for enterprises. The rapid growth of stock values in both the industrialized world and in developing or emerging economies created new wealth which fueled extensive growth for products or services. The rapid decline of those financial markets will invariably reduce such growth, and in some instances, such as for Indonesia, reduce the inherent value of those countries as part of a global strategy.

> ... changes, often driven by stock market crashes and major bank failures based upon unsound credit extension in those markets, have an impact first and foremost on the globalization of financial markets.

Under more extreme circumstances, we might witness that some countries will try to stem the flow of capital by literally detaching themselves from the global chessboard. This might take the form of capital restrictions, or currency boards as was discussed for Indonesia and Malaysia. All of this could result in a substantial restructuring of the global chessboard faced by firms in many industries.

Would such a development call the entire idea of globalization and the pursuit of global strategies into question? First, there is the threat of a mass detachment of countries which, to protect their own financial markets, might find it desirable to cut themselves off from the global chessboard. We need to understand that countries, such as Indonesia or Malaysia, which have been considering or might consider such steps, have done so primarily with respect to their capital markets. The free movements of products, components, people, or funds to purchase goods and services remains largely intact. Those aspects are of greater significance when it comes to judge whether a given country ought to be considered as part of the global chessboard. Capital control might slow down, or temporarily reduce the demand or consumption in some markets, but it would not fundamentally alter the nature of their belonging to the global chessboard.

Even if some countries decided to take themselves off the chessboard, this would not invalidate the nature of the global imperative, and the types of strategies discussed in this book. The idea of globalization, its concepts and its generic strategies as described in the next sections, do not depend on any given number of countries as part of the global chessboard. Although we are currently enjoying a chessboard with a maximum number of participating countries and territories (in

> None of the recent changes in the financial markets, nor their ripple effect through the Asian and Eastern European emerging markets, has reduced the power of the global imperative on firms in any given industry.

excess of 200 by some estimates), the conceptual constructs have validity for a much smaller group of countries. The idea of globalization, as we conceive it in this book, does not depend on a chessboard with a large number of countries. The ideas are valid for a handful of relevant countries, if the circumstances demand it.

... if the global chessboard were reduced due to economic and political decisions that would result in some retrenching from the past years of expansive trade and global economic expansion, the remaining global imperative would create an even greater challenge for firms to enhance competitiveness through focus on the remaining markets.

Finally, we need to reflect on the concept of global logic detailed earlier. There we defined global logic as the principal source of the global imperative demanding that a company pursue some form of global strategy. None of the recent changes in the financial markets, nor their ripple effect through the Asian and Eastern European emerging markets, has reduced the power of the global imperative on firms in any given industry. Actually, even if the global chessboard were reduced due to economic and political decisions that would result in some retrenching from the past years of expansive trade and global economic expansion, the remaining global imperative would create an even greater challenge for firms to enhance competitiveness through focus on the remaining markets.

⮕ The concept of a "must win" market

A thorough analysis of the global chessboard invariably raises the question of the number of countries, or markets, needed for an effective global strategy. Rather than chasing some magic number, we are proposing a different approach to the issue of country or market selection. Companies should concentrate more on the value of each market, and eventually drive their plans toward "must win" markets. These markets are representing countries that play a pivotal role in a particular global industry. This could stem either from their size or volume, or from their technological development.

Companies should concentrate more on the value on each market and eventually drive their plans toward "must win" markets ... representing countries that play a pivotal role in a particular global industry.

"Must win" markets would be countries that any firm in a given industry would have to win if the company aspired to global market leadership. Usually, large markets provide sufficient volume to claim the requirements for scale and often fit the description for that reason. A firm, or managers aspiring to a global mindset must be able to spot and select "must win" markets, and focus resources on them. The "must win" situations can be expected to differ by industries, and we should not expect that for each industry the same priorities would apply. Large pieces on the global chessboard are always indications for a "must win" status.

Summary

In this chapter we have described the global chessboard as an analytic concept global mindsets need to master. The ability to make choices against an ever changing global chessboard is essential for making global strategic decisions.

On an individual level, the understanding of the global chessboard concept is important for any manager with global responsibility in some form. On a company level, firms have to assure that they are adequately represented in key markets.

What sets the global mindset apart from other managerial mindsets is the capability to keep the entire worldwide business opportunity in mind. From that blueprint, the global mindset is able to select the strategically necessary markets ("must win" markets) in order to maximize the competitive impact for the firm. The set of "must win" markets is likely to differ by industry or sector, thus making it imperative for firms to get to know the relevant global chessboard they face as a background for making strategic choices.

> In the absence of a reduction of the global pressure on companies, the drive to accommodate globalization and thus adopt a global mindset continues unabated.

This global behavior is entirely driven by the global logic present in an industry and the type of global chessboard. Economic changes, such as those rippling through the financial markets since mid-1997, although of great magnitude, have done little to affect global logic. In the absence of a reduction of the global pressure on companies, the drive to accommodate globalization and thus adopt a global mindset continues unabated. If the global opportunity were to shrink in the not so distant future, it would even enlarge the global imperative operating on firms, not reduce it.

Notes

1. I am indebted to my colleague, Stephen Allen, at Babson College, for the term global chessboard.

2. The New State of the World Atlas, 4th edn, Simon & Schuster, 1991.

3. Information provided to author during one of the global seminars taught at Babson College.

4. Jean-Pierre Jeannet, "Siemens Automotive Systems: Brazil Strategy", Case Study, IMD Institute, Lausanne, 1993.

5. "Far Eastern markets in the Context of Global Marketing," Jean-Pierre Jeannet, *Thexis* (Fachzeitschrift für Marketing), St. Gall University, St. Gall, No. 2/1995, pp. 5–10.

6. "The job of wiring China sets off a wild scramble by the telecoms giants", *Wall Street Journal*, 5 April, 1994, p. 1.

8

Spotting global trends

While an understanding of global chessboards will give the strategist the basis for planning the appropriate moves, it remains a static view of the world. It remains a challenge to understand the interrelationships between markets, and in particular, the patterns of innovations across a multitude of country-based markets. The question to be answered here is: "Where does a particular trend typically start?" or "Will this new development actually become an isolated event or is it going to be typical for other markets?". Only with answers to these questions can the moves on the global chessboard be appropriately understood.

To help in the analyses of global trends, the concept of lead market was developed.[1] Under lead market we understand a particular country, or region, that is ahead in its development of the rest of the world and where initial new developments tend to set a trend for other markets to follow. The lead market thus serves the function of a bellwether.[2]

Detecting lead markets

The detection and identification of lead markets is a necessary exercise in today's globalizing economy. In the time period following World War II, the USA served as a lead market for most industries. It was relatively simple to follow up trends there and apply them to other regions. Entrepreneurs in many parts of the world created large companies by emulating US examples even before they arrived on their shores in the form of US-owned subsidiaries. This was the case in industries such as retailing, publishing, television broadcasting, and others. Although those entrepreneurs did not actively undertake a formal lead market analysis, they innately understood that copying new developments from the most developed part of the world and re-creating the same business in their own countries would lead to success.

> **Entrepreneurs in many parts of the world created large companies by emulating US examples even before they arrived on their shores in the form of US-owned subsidiaries.**

As the economies of other parts of the world developed, the USA lost its monopoly position on lead markets. Many other countries, for some industries or sectors, became the lead market, making tracking more difficult. Furthermore, lead markets migrate and are not for ever going to stay in the same country. Technological developments, or breakthroughs, can create a lead market in another area.

When analyzing lead markets, it has become clear that several categories of leadership exist. First, there is the issue of the location of a company's most innovative customers which we would find in the customer-based lead market. Second, we have the separate issue of the most advanced products that are produced for a given industry, or product-based lead markets. Technology-based lead markets harbor the most advanced technologies. There is also something in the form of lead practice in operation or management which we term management practice-based lead markets. Since it is not typical to assume that all lead market types are located in the same area of the world, it is necessary to understand the implications of each of them.

Customer-based lead markets

Any company must constantly pose itself the question "Where in the world are my (or our industry's) most innovative customers located?" Customer-based lead markets contain the customers that consistently apply new products or processes first, and whose activities set a trend for customers elsewhere in the world. A company interested in marketing telecommunications networks needs to know where the most innovative operating companies are. For a company involved in medical implants, the location of the most innovative surgeons is of importance. In such a way, every industry has its own lead market, and depending on the particular industry or sector, these lead markets are likely to be in any of some 20 or so major economies.

> **Customer-based lead markets contain the customers that consistently apply new products or processes first, and whose activities set a trend for customers elsewhere in the world.**

The value of understanding the customer-based lead market allows firms a constant analysis of future trends. Many companies have made it to the top of their industry listings by unintentionally exploiting the fact that they were located in a lead market and thus had access to cutting edge clients who made them perform to a new world standard. However, with customer-based lead markets migrating across the world, companies find themselves frequently outside a given lead market and in a struggle to keep up with developments from the customer-based lead market. Leaving this game up to chance becomes equal to waiting in your home market for new ideas to arrive, often in the

> **... with customer-based lead markets migrating across the world, companies find themselves frequently outside a given lead market and in a struggle to keep up with developments from the customer-based lead market.**

form of new competition, when in fact some activities could have been undertaken in advance to anticipate new trends.

Product-based lead markets

Product-based lead markets deal with leadership embodied into new products and answer to the question: "Where in the world are the most sophisticated products in your industry produced?" While the focus of the customer-based lead market is on the location of most advance users, the product-based lead market is focused on producers, or marketers, and their concentration. Essentially, we are dealing with a firm's competitors. Separating competitors from users is important because in many industries, the two types of lead markets are not in the same country.

> **Understanding product-based lead markets gives a company a clear sense of where innovation tends to come from first.**

Understanding product-based lead markets gives a company a clear sense of where innovation tends to come from first. Exposure to such innovation, or ability to compete with these companies, is paramount as it allows the global firm to "meet" such innovators before they reach its own markets.

Operations-based lead markets

Operations leadership essentially deals with production efficiency. The focus of the analysis here is finding the most efficient members of a given firm's industry so as to understand potential cost pressures that might come from them. Operations-based lead markets might be created around cost-efficient countries and in many industries are migrating towards Asia. In the fine chemicals industry, for example, that is largely dominated by players from Europe and the USA, efficient small operators are merging in India and China. They compete effectively on cost efficiency or price, rather than on innovation. Clearly, they are creating new lead markets based on operations despite the fact

> **Operations-based lead markets might be created around cost-efficient countries and in many industries are migrating towards Asia.**

that neither China nor India houses the lead customers and neither is the product-based lead market.

Lead markets based on management practice or systems

For any industry, companies will need to appreciate the country where the relevant industry practice is superior, or leading. Management practice might consist of a number of relevant areas or activities. For a distribution firm, logistics practices might apply. For a producer of electronic elements, this might be the country where the modern electronic design techniques are used. For each business, the relevant areas might differ, but managers who claim to have a global mindset should be in a position to point out the lead market in those areas. Eventually, a company can benchmark its own practices against them and learn for eventual adoption. Since we are dealing with lead markets on a global scale, we are interested in benchmarking world-class firms, or practices.

Accurate benchmarking and learning from management-based lead markets, however, allows a company to learn beyond the capabilities of its own domestic environment.

Lead markets for many management practices and concepts have tended to be the USA. Japan has offered us many new concepts in production, and for many industries Japan, or other Asian countries, have become lead markets. Management-based lead markets are subject to less frequent migration patterns than other types. Accurate benchmarking and learning from management-based lead markets, however, allows a company to learn beyond the capabilities of its own domestic environment.

⮑ Industries and lead markets

We now turn to a brief examination of four industries in relation to lead markets.

Lead markets and the watch industry

The watch industry offers us an excellent example of the development and migration of lead markets and their importance to an industry. If we look at the traditional development of the watch industry, Switzerland is generally the accepted lead market. This was certainly the case for products (most precise), if not in management practice (best or leading firms). Customer-based lead markets, or where the most innovative customer were located, were more likely to be in the large European cities and the USA. Trends in usage were set there, but manufacturing was in Switzerland. The change in technology altered many of the traditional relationships. First, the operations-based lead market moved to Japan, or the Far East, where the most efficient component makers resided and gave rise to such firms as Seiko and Citizen. Then, the electronic revolution moved the lead market to the USA (Texas Instruments was a lead player) and Japan (Casio among others), which became leaders of the electronic revolution in the industry.[3] With the advent of the Swatch, Switzerland has regained the lead and the product-based, if not operations -based lead market is in Switzerland.[4] Throughout this period, the USA has probably remained the customer-based lead market generating many of the fashion trends that later became adopted elsewhere.

Lead markets and the automotive industry

The automotive industry had unquestionably most lead markets in the USA for the first two decades after World War II. Then we witnessed a splitting of the lead markets and migration into different countries. Today, the purchasing patterns, or usage patterns, of the USA might still lead that of other countries. This manifests itself in the high per capita ownership of cars, and the trend to be first in the adoption of new types of cars (the mini-van, the off-the-road vehicle, etc.). However, most industry observers would suggest that the operations-based lead market shifted out of the USA into Japan in the 1970s with the efficiency advantage of Japanese competitors. Whether this is still the case today is debatable. In terms of product-based lead market, which is determined by the adoption of the latest technology into automobiles, Europe is generally viewed as leading the USA and Japan. From a management system point of view, Japanese firms (Toyota and Honda in the lead) can still be given the role of benchmark for the industry.

Lead markets and the telecommunications industry

Recent years have seen substantial changes in the telecommunications industry. In one particular sector, namely wireless, the changes have greatly affected communications of millions of people. For any participating firms in this industry the challenge will remain to stay clear of minor changes that will fade away and to concentrate on the big waves that will eventually go around the world. During the early phase of the development of mobile telecommunications, Europe worked with several analog standards (TACS, NMT) whereas the United States enjoyed a single analog standard (AMPS). With the shift towards digital standards, Europe moved towards GSM as its single standard whereas the US adopted several digital systems (TDNA and CDNA, as well as GSM). Overall, GSM proved the most popular system being adopted in more than 100 countries, whereas the US standards are used in about 30 countries only. Throughout this development period, Europe became the lead market for mobile infrastructure systems, allowing European firms such as Ericsson and Nokia to wrestle global leadership away from US firms. In the sector for mobile handheld phones, the lead markets are regional with the United States leading in cost competitiveness, Europe in advanced features, and Japan in the area of miniaturization. Again, Nokia of Finland was able to catapult itself into the lead, surpassing Motorola of the US. The lead market for mobile equipment is therefore found in Europe benefiting those competitors with close ties to those markets.[5]

Lead markets and the financial services industry

In financial services, Wall Street has traditionally been the driver for new types of services and products. For investment banking, leading New York firms have not only created the type of served they provide, but have "exported" it to many other financial markets. Nevertheless, for investment banking services, New York remains the lead market with respect to talent, ideas, and advanced practice, as well as products. Other elements of the financial industry, such as the use of credit cards for household consumers, have been both developed and first popularized in the USA. Many other markets had experienced slow growth.

US-style credit card products, such as those marketed through Visa, Mastercard, or American Express, have been launched around the world. Local versions of those have become commonplace in most countries. Thus the USA has provided lead market status in those areas for others around the world. The USA has the lead market in credit cards usage through the most advanced and extensive use of cards by consumers, the product-based lead market through the most innovative and advanced forms of credit cards, and the operations-based lead market through the efficiency of credit card operators and the spawning of separate firms that specialize in card processing only.

⬎ Implications for global mindsets

The constant migration of lead markets poses major challenges for international firms. Company head offices, however, are much more likely to remain located in a given country. This suggests that many firms will find it difficult to be exposed to the maximum amount of innovative pressures emanating from lead markets. And yet, it is precisely the spotting of trends that will become typical for the rest of the world that determines the outcome of many competitive battles. For firms with global aspirations, it is essential that they clearly understand the respective patterns of their lead markets and find a way to harness those innovative pressures for their own competitive benefit.

The constant migration of lead markets poses major challenges for international firms.

A thorough appreciation of lead markets inevitably drives a number of other decisions. As we have seen, lead markets emit maximum amounts of innovative pressures. This requires a company to audit its "idea input patterns" such as its development or research facilities. Many firms have built up those capabilities in one part of the world, usually near its original head office, and now find that their location is no longer in the lead market. A company might either build new centers in lead markets, or, as others have done, ask its subsidiaries located

For firms with global aspirations, it is essential that they clearly understand the respective patterns of their lead markets and find a way to harness those innovative pressures for their own competitive benefit.

in those markets to assume roles over and above the current one to take care of running business.[6] Other firms have found that the typical pattern of product launch in the head office country, which was part of the original development of many companies, no longer fits the right pattern. New product launches might be more appropriately placed into lead markets first and introduced in other countries only later on.

Implications for global firms

Monitoring lead markets

A minimal effort to be undertaken by any firm is the close monitoring of lead markets. Monitoring requires a formal process by which a company can ascertain the key developments before they turn up in its own existing markets. Many companies have typically sent executives on visits, tracked publications and press reports, and attended exhibits or technical shows. This type of ad hoc monitoring may be the only way a small firm can operate. For companies with truly global aspirations, however, the process needs to go beyond keeping abreast of developments.

> **This type of ad hoc monitoring may be the only way a small firm can operate. For companies with truly global aspirations, however, the process needs to go beyond keeping abreast of developments.**

Monitoring lead customers

For companies that are marketing their products or services in a business-to-business environment, important customers may be geographically dispersed and not be all in one single geographic area. For these firms, a clear understanding of the lead customers is important. Lead customers may be found among those customers who consistently employ new methods first, are typically at the forefront of innovation, and whose operating practices are imitated by other firms. Every company has such leading firms among its customers, defined through their capacity to innovate rather than sheer size.

For competitive reasons, these customers would have to be closely monitored separately. The experience with these firms can then be transmitted through the worldwide system and others may learn. Lego, the Danish toy group, has developed important relationships with Toys-Я-Us, the world's leading toy retailer, based in the USA. Toys-Я-Us had challenged Lego's US operating company to develop new accounting systems. These systems eventually become the model for other Lego customers as well. Although Lego did not have a global account management system at that time, the experience of its US subsidiary was tapped to guide other parts of the company not only in the interface with Toys-Я-Us, but also in developing account management systems in general. In that way Lego was able to distribute the learning across its entire worldwide organization.

E.K.A. Chemicals, a unit of Akzo-Nobel, was a world leader in producing and marketing chemicals used in the pulp and paper-making process. Although new developments in the print and media industry tended to emanate from the USA, the company experienced that it was the European, particularly Finnish and Swedish, pulp and paper companies that tended to innovate first in the corresponding paper processes. It could thus leverage its experience from those lead customers across its entire worldwide system.

> The challenge with learning from lead customers stems from a lack of familiarity of many other units on the nature of the experience.

The challenge with learning from lead customers stems from the lack of familiarity of many other units on the nature of the experience. If a lead customer in Germany is providing early warning signals to the German subsidiary of a US firm, that will be well accepted in the German unit. The acceptance in other company units, which will be less exposed to the lead customer, and thus may have a different operating experience, is frequently reduced.

Placing units

Given the fact that lead markets tell a story of developments that will eventually go around the world, a business clearly needs to be represented in those markets. Full representation requires an operating unit that competes in those markets so that other units of the worldwide system can benefit from the experience. A globally active company may not in fact have to be a leader in the lead market, but should at least have a significant operating experience in that area.

> From a lead market perspective, it is important to recognize the "must win" markets that also function as lead markets, and to operate there not only for market coverage but also for learning.

In the previous chapter the concept of the "must win" market was discussed in the context of the relevant global chessboard for the firm. From a lead market perspective, it is important to recognize the "must win" markets that also function as lead markets, and to operate there not only for market coverage but also learning. As a result, a company needs to be clear as where its lead markets are, and where new ones might evolve.

Placing R&D facilities

The location of research and development facilities deserves a special mention here. These facilities often depend on real market impact and feedback for break-through ideas. Researchers who are far removed from lead market pressures may be less inclined to see new opportunities, or may simply be unaware of them. The global firm will carefully select the locations of its core research and development facilities to ensure sufficient exposure to lead market pressures.

Placing or recruiting human resources

Lead market pressures may also be considered for the recruitment or placement of key executives and staff. The quality of recruiting, and the extent of lead market learning, can be enhanced if talent is drawn from lead markets with the relevant executive experience. Many global firms have actually gone down this path, and recent executive appointments in some European multinationals are good examples. Swissair's new CEO is an American with US airline experience which was deemed relevant to the newly deregulating experience of European airlines.[7] Some of the European banks which have entered investment banking activities have used US-trained executives to build up their new services.[8]

> The quality of recruiting, and the extent of lead market learning, can be enhanced if talent is drawn from lead markets with the relevant executive experience.

Assigning formal responsibilities

To maximize learning from lead markets, some companies have gone so far as assigning responsibility to units or executives in those markets beyond the local market. The operating unit in the lead market may, in some way, be made responsible for more than that particular local market. A secondary role may be a particular segment, or monitoring responsibility that can be formally ascribed. Alternatively, such a formal role may also be assigned to individuals.

⮑ Summary

In this chapter we described the lead market concept as part of the required set of analytic concepts a global mindset is expected to master. Sensitivity to evolving and migrating lead markets is essential for making global strategic decisions. On an individual level, an understanding of lead markets is important for any manager who has, or aspires to, global responsibility. On a company level, firms have to ensure that they have full access to lead markets by participating in them through marketing, venturing, or observing the trends for implementation elsewhere in the systems.

> Sensitivity to evolving and migrating lead markets is essential for making global strategic decisions.

What sets the global mindset apart from other managerial mindsets is the capability to keep the entire evolving worldwide business opportunity in mind. From that "blueprint", the global mindset is able to select the strategically required markets in order to maximize learning for the firm.

Notes

1. Jean-Pierre Jeannet, "Lead Markets: A Concept for Designing Global Business Strategies", Working Paper, IMEDE, May 1986.

2. Jean-Pierre Jeannet and David H. Hennessey, *Global Marketing Strategies: Text and Cases*, Houghton Mifflin, Boston, 4th edn, 1998, p. 254.

3. Jean-Pierre Jeannet, "Tissot: Competing in the World Watch Industry", Case Study, IMD, Lausanne (ECCH), 1985.

4. Jean-Pierre Jeannet, "Swatch Project", Case Study, IMD, Lausanne (ECCH), 1985.

5. "Hold the Phone! Nokia Takes No. 1 Spot in Cellulars," *Herald Tribune*, 24/25 October, 1998, p. 13.

6. Christopher Bartlett, "Tap your Subsidiaries for Global Reach," look for *Harvard Business Review* November–December, 1986, p. 67 where this is described.

7. "US Chief Executive for Swissair," *Financial Times*, 12 March, 1997.

8. "Fund Management: Dwarf by other European Capitals," *Financial Times* Survey, 13 October, 1998, p. 2.

Global strategic skills

In the previous three sections, we laid out the framework for the need of sufficient global mindsets, and developed global logics as a key analytic tool for analyzing global pressure. The review of the global chessboard and lead markets has given us new insights into grasping the complete global opportunity for a firm.

Section 4 is devoted to developing a fuller sense of the global strategic element needed for global mindsets. The basic, fundamental strategic skills needed for managers, or firms, wishing to compete in single, or domestic, markets only are not discussed. Rather, we will concentrate here on the strategic elements that will be needed precisely for global battle.

To that effect, we first develop the various types of generic global strategies that are available to today's modern firm with the intent of clarifying the full set of choices. This is done in indicative form and readers should not limit themselves merely to these generic strategies. Chapter 9 is devoted to showing that firms may take different pathways towards globalization. This will allow the reader to appreciate the different ways in which a firm might "go global." In this chapter we will also introduce the concepts of the purposely versus the accidentally global firm.

In Chapter 10, our focus shifts towards the multitude of generic global strategies that we have discovered. We make the argument that managers who want to adopt a global mindset will need to show a capability for understanding many different forms of global strategies, ranging from less intrusive through fully integrated forms. This discussion with an emphasis on global functional strategies is continued in Chapter 11. There, we also make the connection between previously explained diagnostics and global logic, and demonstrate how companies can use the global logic conceptualization as a guide towards the selection of the appropriate generic global strategy.

Throughout this section, we emphasize the need to appreciate the multitude of generic global strategies and the necessary for management to make the appropriate choices as indicated by the global logic faced by each firm.

Selecting pathways to globalization

When the debate on globalization began in earnest in the early 1980s, most discussion centered around whether or not a company ought to pursue globalization, or "go global" as it was then called.[1] Much of the research in the following years was concentrated on proving or disproving the validity of a global strategy.[2] However, just as we have seen in the previous chapter that global logics come in different intensities, rather than in abstract yes or no answers, so, too, do global strategies. Managers with a global mindset are expected to understand the various levels, or types, of global strategies. The relevant question is no longer "should we?", but rather "Which global strategy is appropriate for our company?"

This chapter will therefore concentrate on describing the various types of global pathways companies may adopt on the way toward a global strategy. Under pathways we understand a general direction, or series of steps, undertaken by a company in the direction of globalization. We confront the reader with different generic pathways, or prototype approaches towards globalization. Contrary to popular opinion, there are several different pathways a company might consider. We distinguish between different internationalization pathways which take a longitudinal view of how firms internationalize, ranging from domestic to international, and on to global strategies. Second, we look at the types of asset commitment strategies companies make and the difference between selecting a strategy that requires a firm to place assets across the globe as opposed to concentrating them in a single geographic area. Depending on the company history, its existing or non-existing international development, different pathways may be adopted.

⋗ Generic internationalization pathways[3]

For many executives, globalization of a firm is a distant goal. It is considered to be the final destination for some firms, and the way to globalization would go through several other development phases. These phases range from a purely domestic firm, through several layers of internationalization, to some level of multinationalization, to eventually lead to global. While appropriate for some firms who grew historically in that way, the pathway for companies today is quite different. Before we look at the various pathways that might eventually lead to globalization, let us first look at the stages on the way.

Domestic strategies

A firm pursuing a domestic strategy, or one geared largely to its home market, is often viewed as a precursor to other approaches to business. Many business strategists describe this approach as a initial, necessary stage for a company until it strengthens its hold on the market, understands its customers, and perfected its technology, or products. The general view goes on to say that this is largely a temporary stage, and that as the firm expands and its market position grows, a natural transition to the next stage of internationalization occurs.

Clearly, if our underlying assumptions on the globalizing economy hold, there is very little room for domestic strategies in many industry sectors. We also need to appreciate that many of the well-known global players in various industries, for example, Nestlé, or Digital Equipment, or even Siemens, began as domestic companies. They internationalized as they grew. While that is true, it is also necessary to point out that at the time of their formation, the "global model" was not known, and companies did what was common practice at that time. As a result of natural market pressures, and to pursue obvious growth in other parts of the world, many domestic firms begin to develop an international strategy.

> **We also need to appreciate that many of the well-known global players in various industries, for example, Nestlé, or Digital Equipment, or even Siemens, began as domestic companies.**

International strategies

International strategies have moved firms beyond a single (domestic market), to pursue business opportunities in many other countries. This may take the form of exports, as well as including the setting up of subsidiary companies in other parts of the world. While it should not be difficult to see the difference between a domestic and an international strategy, we should not assume that international equals global (see Chapter 2).

Typical of companies that pursue an international strategy are efforts that take products from their domestic market, making necessary adjustments, and bringing them in line with market expectations elsewhere. What is still true for most

> **What is still true for most international firms is that they tend to begin with a domestic concept, and then extend it to international markets only in a second phase.**

international firms is that they tend to begin with a domestic concept, and then extend it to international markets only in a second phase.

Multi-domestic strategies

Multi-domestic strategies are typically viewed as a series of local-for-local strategies where a firm sets up integrated operations in a number of markets, each pursuing its own "domestic" strategy. Arguments for this strategy deal with the ability to create tailor-made products, or services, for the various local markets.

Clearly, the multi-domestic strategy is a step beyond an international strategy, and represents a bigger resource commitment. Multi-domestic firms tend to have many production locations. Firms pursuing this strategy are termed multinational companies (MNCs). They are often defined as companies which market and produce in five or more countries.[4] Multi-domestic strategies were practiced by most large international firms and are still today common for some firms such as Nestlé or Unilever. MNCs are viewed as emerging naturally from international firms. But this is not yet a truly global strategy.

Global strategies

When pursuing a global strategy, a company looks at the market opportunity in global terms and integrates its operations across the world. It runs one strategy for its entire global market opportunity. That is radically different from the multi-domestic strategy, where we can encounter a series of separate and different strategies run in parallel in different countries. Again, it differs from international strategies where we typically find domestic and international strategies run in parallel.

> **When pursuing a global strategy, a company looks at the market opportunity in global terms and integrates its operations across the world.**

Global strategies have been known conceptually since the early 1980s. Many MNCs pursuing multi-domestic strategies have been migrating towards global strategies over the past fifteen years. A poll of executives on names of leading global firms would result in mostly the same names that were in the MNC category some decade and a half ago.

⤷ Pathways to global strategies

Conventional wisdom has it that a company will migrate from the domestic to international, to multinational, and eventually to a global strategy. We find that the large global firms of today, such as ABB (a merger between Sweden's Asea and Switzerland's Brown Boveri), particularly during its earlier history as either Asea or Brown Boveri, had gravitated from domestic to international, and eventually to multi-domestic, before joining the ranks of global corporations. Traditional MNCs adopted at each stage the format most appropriate at that time. During their earlier phase of development they had no capabilities, or knowledge, of running "global" strategies. The pathways of old established firms, therefore, represented more a of a pattern of "Let's select the latest type of strategy." What was not known, or understood, could not be "selected". It would therefore be inappropriate to connect the different pathways to globalization for established firms as an indication for required pathways for recently formed companies.

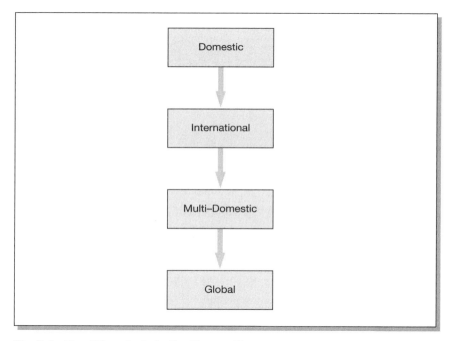

Fig 9.1 Traditional globalization pathway

A different view of the pathways toward globalization is offered by relatively new firms, founded within the past fifteen years, and thus well within the period when the full set of internationalization patterns, or stages, was known. A study of such firms revealed that some recently founded firms which grew to global status did not go through the various steps as quickly as conventional thinking would have it.[5] Rather, some firms adopted a global strategy from inception, and thus avoided all previous steps of domestic to international, and multi-domestic status.

The example of Logitech stands out.[6] This company, founded in 1981 as a partnership between three Italian and Swiss engineers who met in California operated offices in California and Switzerland from the beginning. Pursuing the market of computer input devices (mouse) on both an Original Equipment Manufacturer (OEM) and direct end-user/retail market, Logitech was not only international, but was global from the outset. Much of its product development was carried out in Switzerland, marketing direction came from its California operation, and the major plant was located in Taiwan.

A second example is offered by a small, recently founded company that specializes in the production of user manuals for car companies and similar businesses. The company had its beginning from the need to translate Japanese manuals into various European languages, and quickly expanded to take a major role in the production of user manuals for European cars in Japan. Located in a small Swiss town on the German border, the company has units in several cities and works in a network mode. Again, this company pursued a global strategy from the beginning without taking a step-by-step approach to its internationalization.[7]

Both examples tell us that if a company started over again, or were created today, and operated in an industry that was subject to substantial global logic pressure, a global approach, or strategy would be appropriate from inception. This approach we call intentionally global, because the companies from the outset adopted a deliberate policy of global strategy and, as a result, became global firms. In contrast, many of the firms traditionally referred to as global had no policy to get there, and the impression can be that some business school professor just walked in the door and informed the company that it was in fact global. This sometime appears to come as welcome news to the company and is cause for celebration. These firms I label accidentally global, as they achieved their newly found global status as a result of a series of unplanned steps.

The Alahuhta research[8] was centered on the question of how small units, or independent firms, could grow quickly to become global contenders in their field. One of the important conclusions was the general presence for most successfully growing global business of a deliberate global strategy from the outset, consisting of both a clear sense of the global chessboard and an articulated global vision for the company itself. The results of these clinical studies point towards a policy of adopting a global strategy from the outset, provided a sufficient global logic exists. This is counter-intuitive for many executives. But the myth of the step-by-step migration policy must be eliminated and a deliberate, planned, globalization strategy must be adopted by firms.

The transition towards globalization

As many firms have already experienced, each step on the internationalization path is in itself a difficult process for companies. A company that has constituted itself as domestic will experience the transition into an international firm as a challenge, requiring fundamental changes to its managerial processes. Many of the policies that worked well for the domestic firm will not be appropriate for an international strategy. As a consequence, the transition from domestic to international demands the willful destruction of some procedures and policies that were developed with great effort at one time. The same barriers will have to be crossed for a transition from international to multinational and its related multi-domestic strategy.

> As many firms have already experienced, each step in the internationalization path is in itself a difficult process for companies.

While for internationally experienced firms some of those transitions, and the resulting turbulence, are part and parcel of their history, the transition from multi-domestic, or multinational, into global is one that many executives and companies should still be familiar with. As this volume has already pointed out, "global" is not only a new label but it requires a fundamental change in management practice, corporate and business unit strategies, and organization. These changes are not intuitive, and do not represent a linear extrapolation of "more international." This is because "global" represents not simply more speed in the existing fourth gear (multinational) but the reengineering of the entire gearbox, adding a fifth gear (overdrive), a process that causes many large multi-domestic firms to struggle.

> … "global" represents not simply more speed in the existing fourth gear (multinational) but the reengineering of the entire gearbox, adding a fifth gear (overdrive), a process that causes many large multi-domestic firms to struggle.

Because of this turbulence caused by the transition from one phase of internationalization to another, a company should not have to relearn "business history" experienced by other firms. Rather, firms move directly to the most appropriate one, thus leap-frogging previous stages. Once we have accepted the notion of purposely global strategies, it is only a small step towards directly global, always with the proviso that sufficient global logic exists in that particular industry. A firm might therefore get the "wake-up call" at any time during its internationalization process, although the strategies pursed by selecting a global-type strategy from the various starting points are expected to vary. It also includes the possibility of selecting a global strategy from the outset, which is one of the key points made by Alahuhta.[8]

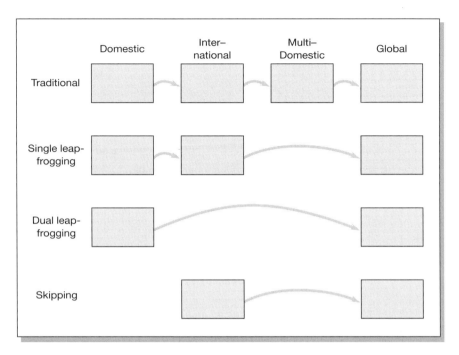

Fig 9.2   Leapfrogging globalization pathways

Different resource commitments for global strategies

I was once visited by the general manager of a division of a large European company. His division had worldwide responsibility for the business which consisted of producing, developing, and marketing chemical dyestuffs for textile firms. With the migration of the textile industry into Asia, the company found itself with a growing clientele far away from its production base in Europe. However, the company had opened technical service centers in the region. Since the parent company of this division had adopted a global strategy, the division manager was confronted with the question: "Can I be called a global business even if all production units are located in my home country only?"

> **Global market strategies are pursued by companies that cover the entire relevant world market and serve their customers well in all relevant squares of the global chessboard.**

Probably the most astute answer to this question is offered by Jolly who has contributed the distinction between asset global versus market global strategies.[9]

Global strategies can fall into two categories by the type of coverage a company aspires to. Global market strategies are pursed by companies that cover the entire relevant world market and serve their customers well in all relevant squares of the global chessboard. Serving those customers does not always require placing vast assets into other countries. Although we can disagree as to what constitutes vast assets, for the purpose of our discussion here we refer to production units and other large fixed assets, but we do not include office space, sales bases, or other customer service units in that category.

Asset global strategies

An asset global strategy implies that the company distributes its assets across the relevant global chessboard. Production may be organized either for each country, or regionalized under a worldwide sourcing system. A company characterized by a global asset strategy would have a significant proportion of its total assets outside its head office country. On the opposite side of the scale would be the domestic strategy whereby all assets are placed in the domestic market.

The interesting aspect of such a conceptualization of global strategies lies in the fact that we have, in its simplified form, four different type of strategies as depicted in Figure 9.2.[10] The underlying assumption of this figure is the separation of asset global and market global into two distinct decisions which yield four different types of strategies. Clearly, the company operating in the domestic market only with all its assets located there is following the classic domestic strategy and is of no particular interest to our discussion. The other three strategies, however, are of interest because they signal different approaches under the global umbrella.

Among the recent technological developments, few can match the impact of the Internet and electronic commerce on the asset global strategies of firms. With the advent of easy electronic commerce accessible to even very small start-up companies, global reach can be achieved without a substantial asset commitment into multiple markets. What would have required the establishment of market companies in previous decades can now be achieved through plugging into the cybernet. In the future, more firms will opt out of asset global strategies and move toward different commitment levels, such as those adopted by firms playing with market global strategies.

> **With the advent of easy electronic commerce accessible to even very small start-up companies, global reach can be achieved without a substantial asset commitment into multiple markets.**

Market global strategies

The company pursuing a market global strategy, and yet placing all of its assets into its domestic, i.e. home country market, is actually adopting a classical exporting strategy. We should point out that this is not the typical exporter, following up on the occasional request for a quote from an international customer. Instead, we would expect this company to have a deliberate market assessment including the entire relevant global chessboard, but to carry this out from it own

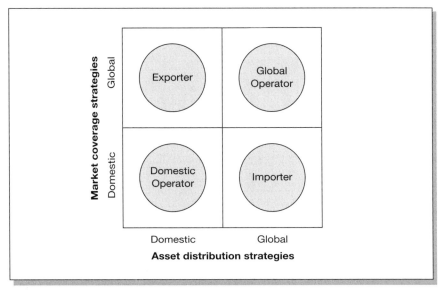

Source: Jean-Pierre Jeannet and H. David Hennessey, Global Marketing Strategies, Houghton-Mifflin, 4th edn., 1998, p. 271

Fig 9.3   Global resource commitment strategies

home base. Companies that largely fit this approach include some large firms in aerospace, such as Boeing of the USA, although that company has begun to work with some overseas suppliers and is moving away from the pure form of market global strategy. Many specialized firms in markets where one single plant is sufficient operate in that mode.

An outstanding example of a market global strategy is undoubtedly Swatch.[11] This brand produced exclusively in Switzerland by SMH (recently renamed Swatch Company), is, since the early 1980s exported to many markets through both distributors and wholly owned sales subsidiaries. The major production assets, however, have remained in Switzerland where a fully automated production plant has been constructed. The relatively high value to weight ratio of the Swatch product allows for such a global exporting strategy.[12]

> **An outstanding example of a market global strategy is undoubtedly Swatch.**

The world of business is full of other examples of export-only companies. Until a few years ago, leading automotive firms such as Daimler (Mercedes-Benz) and BMW were also pursuing only exporting strategies and their asset commitments were largely concentrated on their domestic market in Germany. Their more recent expansionary policies, however, caused both to break out of those strategies. BMW acquired Rover of the UK and built a new car plant in South Carolina (USA).[13] Daimler has opened a car plant in the USA as well and, further, negotiated a merger with Chrysler of the USA.[14]

On the opposite side of the scale we find firms employing a domestic market strategy and simultaneously pursuing global asset deployment. In the extreme, this firm is adopting an importing strategy whereby most producing assets are outside its chosen market. Schwinn Bicycle, a US-based leader in bicycles with sales in excess of $200 million, discontinued its production in the USA over a period of several years and continued as an importer from the Far East.[15] Although the firm did not fully own any of its plants, the pattern of the "global importer" is nevertheless established.

Elsewhere, this type of importing from several sources while concentrating on a local market has been said to create the phenomenon of the "hollow corporation."[16]

The classic global operator is the company pursuing both a market global and asset global strategy. These are the firms that are typically labeled "global," and include some of the large multinational firms such as ABB, Philip Morris, IBM, GM, and Ford. For most of these companies, local markets cannot be held unless supported with sufficient local resources. This may be a function of logistics and shipment costs, or a response towards restrictive local policies.

The third dimension: idea global strategies

Aside from asset or market commitments, companies also make commitments about the sources of ideas. Where should a company look when it comes to new ideas about products or services. Where should a company look when borrowing new and innovative ideas for its operations?

Earlier, we dealt with the concept of lead market and indicated that for a company, or an individual, adopting a global mindset requires being fully informed on the countries where leading ideas might break first, thus becoming trendsetters for the rest of the world. Clearly, if a company were to borrow new ideas abroad, it would have to be from such lead markets.

Along the lines of idea source, we can distinguish two different patterns. Idea local firms are companies which tend to respond to developments only as they arise in their home, or local markets. Idea global firms monitor developments elsewhere and borrow new developments, even when occurring outside their home market, to bring them home and apply them in their home markets. Given the fact that lead markets are increasingly spread across the world's leading economies, it is imperative for firms to turn themselves into idea global even if it is for defensive purposes only.

Some companies, and many leading entrepreneurs, have actually become successful by adopting a idea global posture and combining it with a asset/market global status. Since the USA has spawned many new business models, ranging from different types of retailing to different media, telecommunications companies, and financial services firms, many of these business ideas have been picked up by innovative entrepreneurs elsewhere and applied locally. Although those companies would not qualify as global in either asset or market commitments, they are idea global in nature. Examples include leading media companies such as Marinha's O Globo in Brazil, the Berlusconi companies in Italy, and franchising operations such as 7-Eleven in Japan.

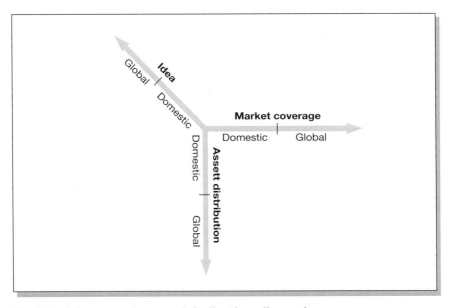

Fig 9.4   Idea sourcing as globalization dimension

⮕ Summary

Let us return to an earlier example. The manager in the example, when confronted with the asset global versus market global pathways, realized that he had pursued a global strategy, but different from the one imagined by his corporate officers. Once he had the full information, he could go back to his head office and discuss the issue on a different level, showing the differences in approaches. I am convinced that many firms are to this date not clear on the differences between those two set of strategies and probably pursue asset global strategies for businesses where market global would be more appropriate.

The importance of analyzing internationalization pathways lies in the multitude of potential global strategies, and in the understanding that there are very different paths to take. In a world where too many executives and companies search for solutions along the lines of the classic global operator, it is reassuring to know that there are in fact many other types of global strategies to adopt. One of the core requirements of global mindsets is a more subtle understanding of the various facets of different pathways toward globalization.

One of the core requirements of global mindsets is a more subtle understanding of the various facets of different pathways toward globalization.

My final comment is reserved for all those managers, or companies, which up to now still argue that the global logic they are facing is insufficient for them to adopt a commitment level that takes them toward either an asset or market global strategy. What I think we will have demonstrated here is that even for such firms, an idea global approach would be advisable. To achieve this, many of the ideas detailed in this book apply as well, particularly those that deal with sizing up the global market in the form of the global chessboard, and the tracking of lead markets around the world. In some ways, it is still a global strategy, but of a different type of resource commitment.

Notes

1. Ted Levitt, "Globalization of Markets," *Harvard Busines Review*, May–June 1983, pp. 92–102; and Thomas M. Hout, Michael E. Porter, and Eileen Rudden, "How Global Companies Win Out," *Harvard Business Review*, September–October 1982, pp. 82–102.

2. Kamran Kashani, "Beware of the Pitfalls of Global Marketing," *Harvard Business Review*, September–October 1989, pp. 91–98 and "Marketers Turn Sour on Global Sales Pitch Harvard Guru Makes," *Wall Street Journal*, 12 May, 1988, p. 1.

3. The idea of globalization pathways was explained by Kenichi Ohmae in "Business Matters" BBC program on globalization, c. 1992.

4. Wilkins, M., "The Marketing of Multinational Enterprise: American Business Abroad from 1914–1970", *Harvard University Press*, 1974.

5. Matti Alahuhta, "Global Growth Strategies for High Technology Challengers", Acta Polytechnica Scandinavia, Electrical Engineering Series No. 66, Finnish Academy of Technology, Espoo, 1990.

6. Vijay Jolly Logitech International SA (A) and (B), case IMD Institute, Lausanne, Switzerland, 1991.

7. "Star AG," *Bilenz Magazine*, February 1995.

8. Vijay Jolly, Matti Alahuhta and Jean-Pierre Jeannet, "Challenging the Incumbents: Lessons from how High Technology Start-ups Compete Globally," *Journal of Strategic Change*, Vol 1, 1992.

9. Vijay Jolly, "Global competitive strategies", in *Strategy, Organizational Design, and Human Resource Management*, Charles C. Snow (ed.), JAI Press, Greenwich, CN, 1989, pp. 55–110.

10. Source: Jeannet and Hennessey, *Global Marketing Strategies*, Houghton Mifflin, 3rd edn, 1995, p. 277.

11. Jean-Pierre Jeannet, Barbara Priovolos and Susan Nye, "Swatch Project", Case Study, IMD, Lausanne

12. "Message and Muscle: An Interview with Swatch Titan Nicolas Hayek," *Harvard Business Review*, March–April 1993, Vol. No. 71, No. 2, pp. 98–110.

13. "BMW to build sports utility vehicle," *Financial Times*, 7 January, 1998; and "BMW buys Rover for £800m from British Aerospace," *Financial Times*, 1 February, 1994.

14. "Daimler and Chrysler near merger," *Financial Times*, 7 May, 1998.

15. Jean-Pierre Jeannet and Robert Howard, "Schwinn Bicycle Company", Case Study, European Case Clearinghouse, 1993.

16. "The Hollow Corporation," *Business Week*, 3 March, 1986, pp. 56–59.

Generic global business strategies

In the previous chapter we focused primarily on different pathways to globalization. This raised the number of options available for management when embarking on the globalization path. With this chapter the focus is on generic global business strategies. This will leave the thoughtful executive with a clearer idea of the many types of global strategies to select from, and that one of the most important choices for a business is the selection of its type of global strategy.

Why focus on business strategies? Although many firms engaging in global strategies tend to be large, we need to realize that such companies are invariably made up of different, distinctly organized businesses. Often labeled strategic business units (SBUs), it is at those levels where some of the most important decisions are taken. GE is a corporation with some one dozen businesses (GE Plastics, GE Capital, etc.), all of which have a global mandate handed down from the corporation. As a corporation, however, GE does not need a detailed global strategy, neither do companies such as Siemens, ABB, ICI, or IBM. Since not all a corporation's business units are likely to face identical "spiderwebs" with identical sets of global logics, it would only be reasonable to expect globalization strategies to differ at the business level.

When making an effort to list generic global business strategies, we intend to give the reader an idea of prototype, or archetypal global strategies. These are intended to be offered in the spirit of examples, and should not be viewed as a finite set of choices. Many intermediate types may exist, and the individual company or executive might even create other alternatives of their own.

Superficial global business strategies

Global reach strategies

"How many countries does a company have to enter to be called a global company?" is a frequently asked question. In boardrooms around the globe, many executives seem still to be under the impression that a company needs to be in "many" or "most countries" to deserve the term "global." At a time when we are undergoing tremendous change in the global chessboard with some countries subdividing themselves into many separate and individual markets (the former Soviet Union and the former Yugoslavia are the two most apparent examples), we are clearly offering great opportunities to firms looking to maximize the number of countries with market representation. Companies who maintain a long semi-circular driveway lined with flags of all countries where they do business have enjoyed flag-raising events on a regular basis. But does maximizing a firm's global reach equate to a global strategy?

Our previous discussion on market global strategies (Chapter 9) would indicate that some form of global reach is itself a valid global strategy. However, as we saw earlier, strategies developed with a global mindset require a thorough understanding of a business's global chessboard with all the market opportunities represented. Companies do not need to select all markets, or countries, on the chessboard to deserve the label "global." Instead, companies should look at the relevant global markets and those that actually need to be won in order to achieve a leadership position. Flags must be raised for "must win," or truly strategic, countries.

> Companies do need to select all markets, or countries, on the chessboard to deserve the label "global."

Two things stand out from this discussion: first, the number of relevant markets is probably a small set of all countries; second, the list of relevant markets is likely to differ by industry, or sector, although similarities are expected. Covering the top 75 to 80 percent of any industry worldwide typically can be reached with the top 20 markets, or fewer. In some highly selective industries, this might be far less. In industries where end-users, or individual consumers, are the relevant customers, experience would indicate that there is less concentration and more markets would be needed compared to a highly concentrated industrial market where a company sold equipment or instrumentation to a select few customers located, or clustered, in few countries.

Even if a company had selected its relevant key markets and concentrated its efforts there, no assurance could be granted that we could call the company's strategy global, for the term global connotes a coordinated and integrated strategy against the global market opportunity. A firm represented in all relevant markets might still operate under many different strategies, adopting a multi-domestic approach. Relevant global reach for a given industry is a necessary element for a global strategy, but in itself it is not yet a singularly sufficient condition to be met.

> ... the term global connotes a coordinated and integrated strategy against the global market opportunity.

Global budget strategies

In the course of research and consulting experience, I have come across a different type of global strategy that, similar to the global reach approach, is superficial in nature and not indicative of a true, integrated global strategy. I call this the global budget strategy because it is reflected in the annual budgeting process of those firms.

There are companies where the annual budgeting process begins at country level, or local market operations. Detailed budgets are worked out, discussed within each country, and then passed onto regional management, such as for Asia or Europe. At regional level, the budget information from the individual markets gets combined into a larger, let us say Asian or European budget. The numbers are larger (many countries now involved) and the consolidated regional budget is sent onto head office. At head office, a large staff of financial specialists collect the various regional budgets, feed them into a still larger computer than those used locally or regionally, and at the end of the budget process, a global budget covering all operations worldwide is produced. Since it covers all aspects of the company, the numbers are large, impressive, and everyone is patting themselves on the back. Does this process deserve to be called "global"?

> There are companies where the annual budgeting process begins at country level, or local market operations.

These types of firms do not necessarily follow a global strategy. The nature of the budgeting process, particularly if started locally, or bottom-up, implies that each country organization makes its own strategy. Large companies, with large budget figures, may look impressive, but a global strategy is not predicated on size alone, rather on the nature and extent of integration of the company strategy.

> Managers or firms with global mindsets are expected to be able to differentiate between truly integrated and superficial global strategies.

Global reach and global budget strategies have some elements in common. Both are, on their own, not sufficient indicators of true global strategies. In many ways, they are superficial and might provide management, or companies, an erroneous impression of "globality." Managers or firms with global mindsets are expected to be able to differentiate between truly integrated and superficial global strategies.

Integrated global business strategies

Now that we have decided to focus on the strategy of individual businesses, SBUs, or divisions, when can we attest them a global strategy? This is a question often posed by senior managers. Instead of debating the pros and contras of a global business strategy, let us first look at the core elements that would have to be present. Whether, or if such an approach were in fact appropriate for a given business, that debate we leave for later.

A business purporting to have a global strategy would have one single strategy for the world market. Emphasis is on one, and not several different interpretations of a global strategy. All units of the business would have adopted that strategy. The strategy would be based on a coherent and enlightened view of the total global market opportunity faced by a business, such as a forward-looking view of its relevant global chessboard. In particular, core decisions, such as segment choice, product line, positioning, research and development projects, and sourcing concepts, would be made from a coordinated and integrated point of view.

Functional strategies, to the extent that they exist, would also be of a global nature. Each organizational unit, or international subsidiary, would be responsible for delivery the global strategy in its assigned market space. The strategy-making process would have its starting point in a complete, or holistic view of the business and would not be primarily driven by bottom-up decisions only.

While one approach is to describe the presence, or signs, of a global business strategy, it is also possible to describe elements indicating an absence of a global business strategy. If a business had adopted different country, or even regional strategies, targeted different segments in different markets, had its product lines uncoordinated globally, and showed little evidence of either leveraging resources across a network of units or learning from a common business approach, it is unlikely to qualify for the label "global business strategy." This is the familiar "I cannot describe it to you, but I can certainly tell you when I see it."

> **Opportunities for completely integrated global business strategies are few and would predicate a constellation of global logics of equal but extensive development.**

I have purposely painted an extreme picture for situations deserving of the name "global business strategy." Opportunities for completely integrated global business strategies are few and would predicate a constellation of global logics of equal but extensive development. Experience at many firms shows that such constellations rarely exist. This is a critical point in the globalization debate, and some executives have interpreted the absence of such a constellation as indicating that no globalization path should be pursued at all. In the rest of the chapter, we make the point that for most firms partial globalization strategies are more appropriate. The insight into the existence of partial global business strategies moves the globalization debate away from the unproductive yes–no argumentation into the direction of articulating areas where partial

> **The insight into the existence of partial global business strategies moves the globalization debate away from the unproductive yes–no argumentation into the direction of articulating areas where partial globalization is beneficial.**

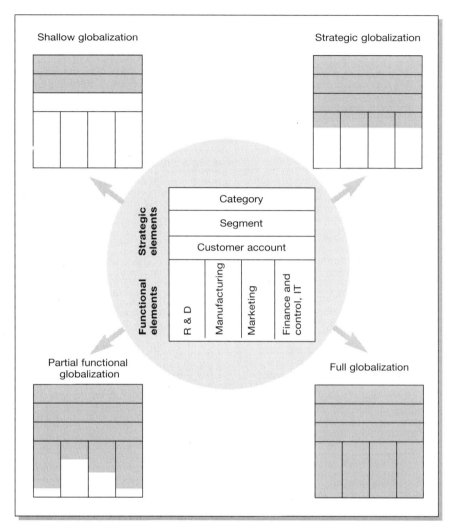

Fig 10.1   Partial versus full globalization

globalization is beneficial. Rather than asking "Should we adopted a global strategy?" companies should ask themselves "Which global strategy is best for us?".

◉ Partially global business strategies

Now we understand that global business strategies can occur in partially global and partially local formats, the question centers on which elements should become global and which elements should remain local.

Global category strategy

Rather than globalizing an entire business strategy, a company might find itself faced with a multitude of operating environments with substantial differences from one country to another. As a result, many of the business's operating parameters need to be governed by local demands. However, there are some similarities in the nature of the business, such as KSFs for operating in a particular industry. With similarities in KSFs, an opportunity exists to leverage such experience and to learn across many markets. This is the opportunity of a global category strategy which represents probably one of the less integrated of the many partial global business strategies.

Rather than globalizing an entire business strategy, a company might find itself faced with a multitude of operating environments with substantial differences from one country to another.

Examples from category opportunities can be found among some primary industries, such as cement, basic chemicals, and the building industry. Many of these industries confront fragmented market opportunities across the globe and companies need to place assets in many markets to be represented, thus adopting market and asset global strategies. With local management in charge to maximize return on a firm's assets, there are realities surrounding "a cement plant is a cement plant," allowing for sharing best practice in operations.

A global category strategy would maximize sharing of best practice by making sure each local operation did not stray outside the business category. Local freedom would be granted for such decisions as segment choice, product line, branding, human resource polices, even pricing. While present in many markets, the company would essentially show a different "face" in each country and come close to a multi-domestic strategy. However, the major difference compared to multi-domestic approaches would be a strong effort, and resulting procedures, for sharing best practice, and a clear sign that on the learning side the company operated in an integrated fashion.

A global category strategy would maximize sharing of best practice by making sure each local operation did not stray outside the business category.

Global category management was practiced for many years at ICI Paints.[1] At that time, ICI Paints was the world's largest paint company with operations in many countries. The company had its organization structured along partially regional lines and also focused its leading management team, the International Business Team (IBT) on key sectors: decorative paints, can coating, automotive refinish paints, automotive Original Equipment Manufacturer (OEM), etc. For each of these sectors, a leader was appointed and regular meetings took place among key executives from various local markets with activity in that sector. By working the coordination across the sectors, ICI Paints effectively adopted a global category management approach and attempted to leverage best practice from one country to another. As the company reduced its operations to fewer segments in the mid-1990s, more integrative coordination became possible.

Nestlé, the large global food company headquartered in Switzerland, had long operated on a global category management. Local operating companies enjoyed considerable freedom of operation in many elements of their business. At head office, "category desks" existed, such as for culinary, instant coffee, chocolate, etc., where a small group of executives was monitoring international markets and passing best practice from one country to another. With product formulation, production, and branding handled locally, Nestlé operated for many years with a low level of global integration.[2]

Novartis Consumer Health, a unit of Novartis, a leading company in the health industry, adopted a category focus for its Over-the-Counter (OTC) business, With market differences globally and operating companies marketing a large number of often different brands, the company saw its major global strategy in coordinating across a limited number of global OTC categories and niches. Global category coordination would come out of the unit's global head office and would affect research, marketing strategies, and other elements. There remained a large number of decisions still to be taken at local operating level.[3]

Although many multinational companies have moved toward global category strategies, the extent of global coordination, or leverage, that can be obtained from this is limited. If the coordinating function leaves considerable leeway for local operating managers to decide, companies often find that there is no one ready to "learn" the best practice examples. Typically, coordinators operate in a staff function only, or, as is the case in some companies, operate under loose temporary or permanent task forces that meet intermittently. Due to the fact that task force leaders can usually not make any binding recommendations for local operating managers, the global category model may be appropriate for those firms only where the global commonality is rather shallow.

> **Due to the fact that task force leaders can usually not make any binding recommendations for local operating managers, the global category model may be appropriate for those firms only where the global commonality is rather shallow.**

Global segment strategies

Due to the limited leveraging opportunities for global category strategies, many firms are in the process of moving into global segment strategies. Companies have realized that, while the starting point is technologically the same, they are meeting different type of customer groups, or segments, with worldwide similarity. Global segment strategies work for companies where the upstream parts of the business, such as production, purchasing, and basic technology are relatively similar, but real differences exist in the downstream parts where the firm interacts with customers. Several global segments can thus be supplied by the same global production system, and the downstream parts may be split among segments depending on the industry requirements.

Due to the limited leverage opportunities for global category strategies, many firms are in the process of moving into global segment strategies.

ICI Polyurethane, a world leader in supplying polyurethane chemicals to several different industry segments, is pursuing such a strategy on the basis that some of its distinct segments, such as footwear, white goods, or automotive, are relatively homogeneous worldwide, but differ substantially from other segments. All segments require essentially similar base products which can be produced in large regional manufacturing units. Global segments exist for major industry groups that require tailor-made sales approaches and detailed industry knowledge. The global footwear segment includes major clients such as Adidas. The global white goods segment consists of large clients that produce refrigerators. And the automotive segment includes all manufacturers of products, such as car seats, supplying the automotive industry. Although the company maintains an essentially regional structure, global segment managers have some influence over the respective marketing and sales efforts across all regions.

Companies pursuing global segment strategies are typically working from the same technological base. Production of polyurethane is similar regardless of the end-user segment, although different grades may be used. Real differences are encountered in the nature of the end-use segment, the understanding of that segment, and thus the need to have executives focus on those. Learning and experience sharing takes place within the segment, and less so across segments. To be successful, global segment strategies require a worldwide segment management team so that leverage can be enhanced.

Global segment strategies differ from global business strategies in as much as core functions, such as purchasing of materials, production, and much of the technology base, are managed as one business, whereas the marketing function is separated by segment with worldwide responsibility. To be consistent, each segment would have its own identifiable resources for marketing in key markets, whereas the other functions might be combined leading to global sourcing strategies under one global manufacturing organization. Global segment strategies do not require that all business assets be dedicated by segment, otherwise we would end up with different businesses, not segments.

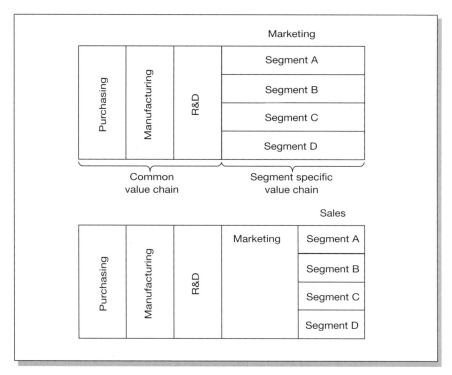

Fig 10.2 Global segment organizations

Global account strategies

Companies which focus their business around key customers worldwide are pursuing a global account strategy. The core aspect of this approach is the concentration on certain accounts on a worldwide basis. This strategy is selected where a large international customer requires full concentration of service delivery to many different locations on a worldwide basis.

Such strategies are often adopted by service firms, such as large, internationally-active advertising agencies serving global accounts. Other services firms, such as large corporate banks, or international accounting firms, have adopted similar strategies. Among those, Deloitte Touche Tohmatsu (DTT), one of the world's leading professional services firms, serves as an example. Large clients who require a multi-country service team are managed by a lead client service partner (LCSP) who is typically located close to the head office of the client. As the client requires, service partners are appointed in the various countries where DTT needs to provide service. Specialist may also be appointed for different services lines. In the case of Merrill Lynch, one of the major clients of DTT, the LCSP is supported by specialists in audit, tax, and consulting services, all with global responsibility for that particular aspect for the client. On one single engagement such as Merrill Lynch, as many as 30 or more partners may participate, all coordinated from a single point. Similar global client-centered strategies have been adopted by large international advertising agencies, such as Grey or Saatchi & Saatchi, which need to focus on few, but significant, account relationships.[4]

Among manufacturing firms, Siemens Automotive Technology Division is an example of the pursuit of global account strategies.[5] That company's main customers include the top ten car manufacturing companies which have assembly plants in various parts of the world. Siemens maintains account teams for each of its large customers, usually located near the customer's head office. and makes account managers responsible for that business worldwide with the assigned client.

Global account strategies are most useful when a company faces a customer with integrated operations on a worldwide basis and a high degree of purchasing centralization. Many global consumer goods companies, desiring to concentrate their advertising business with fewer advertising agencies, want those agencies to deliver integrated campaigns on a worldwide basis. This is a challenge for agencies which must not only maintain relationships with the agency service "buyers," i.e. the central marketing arm of the company, but must also operate dozens of local purchase or service delivery points as they deliver their worldwide campaign service. This strategy tends to work

Global account strategies are most useful when a company faces a customer with integrated operations on a worldwide basis and a high degree of purchasing centralization.

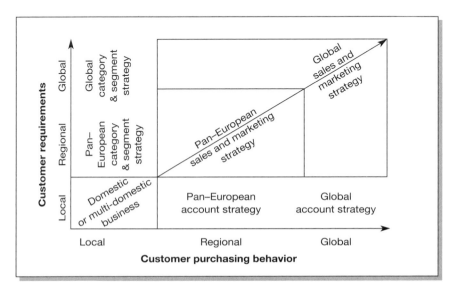

Fig 10.3   Global segment versus global account strategies

best for firms who have a few, worldwide operating customers, whereas firms who have many similar, but different customers spread across the world are better served with a global segment strategy where learning is accumulated across the segment, and not across the client's organization.

Global functional strategies

So far, we have explored generic global strategies that impact on some aspects of a firm's business strategy. However, we can also differentiate among different types of global functional strategy. A company pursuing a global strategy in one of its business functions would in essence globalize that particular function and might leave other functions subject to local control. Different types of global functional strategies can be observed. For our purposes we concentrate on global strategies for the production, finance, research and development, and marketing functions. Needless to say, others might apply, such as the IT, human resources, purchasing, or logistic functions.

Global manufacturing strategies

A company globalizing its manufacturing function would coordinate production in a global, coherent, and consistent way and most likely have a single executive in charge. Subject to global coordination would be all production assets, such as plants, logistics centers, storage and warehousing, etc. With the pressure for improved performance mounting, many firms have moved toward the concepts of focused factories where, in a region such as Europe, a few factories produce a limited range of products. Making this move from a completely local production concept, where all factories produce the total range of products marketed in a given territory, to where certain plants are given regional or global mandates, requires a coherent and centralized manufacturing function.[6]

The economics of a given company's manufacturing will determine how far globalization can go. For companies where the minimum scale plant required for efficiency does not allow for multiple plant sites, a global manufacturing strategy is advisable. Furthermore, a company might find that, although it is engaged in operating multiple plants around the world, the manufacturing process is identical. Under those circumstances, process globalization would allow for better learning and higher performance as the processes are standardized and deployed worldwide.

Traditionally, large companies assigned production assets to local operating companies and therefore often did not provide for central coordination. When production assets are controlled locally, frequently producing a wide set of products for a single market, global scale efficiencies are harder to achieve. Pushing into the direction of global manufacturing strategy, however, requires executive assignments with clear global responsibility in a line function, and thus elevates the manufacturing function from a traditional staff or coordinating role to a full-time function.

Global R&D strategies

The research and development function can also be analyzed from a global point of view. Traditionally, as firms grew, they developed an R&D expertise near to their main or head office operation typically located in the company's home or domestic market. With increased internationalization, firms tended to transfer technology, and R&D results, from their home-based R&D centers to international markets.[7] As international presence grew, and as more and different requirements had to be met, many companies began to set up regional, or market-specific, R&D centers. Many of these centers, however, had the principal tasks of adapting home-market research to local specifications. With more experience, local R&D centers also developed expertise that might be transferred back to the headquarters country. This was the approach adopted by many companies as they moved from a domestic to international and eventually multinational status.

When considering how far to globalize its R&D function, a company needs to determine if R&D is to be carried out on a global, regional, or local level. Increasingly, companies view the local-for-local R&D activities as a "sin of the past" and difficult to justify economically. As the minimum scale of effective R&D units increases, the global logic of organizing R&D on a global scale overwhelms dispersed R&D activities on a local-for-local basis. To deal with this situation, two patterns emerge.

> As the minimum scale of effective R&D units increases, the global logic of organizing R&D on a global scale overwhelms dispersed R&D activities on a local-for-local basis.

First, the established international or multinational firms with long histories of multi-domestic strategies found themselves with numerous R&D units across the world. For these companies, increasing the scope, or activity range of R&D units was the primary focus. This called for dedicating units to single, or limited, focus, but accomplishing it on a global scale. Second, companies reduced local R&D staff and returned to a more centralized function in line with assigning global responsibility to that function.

When, or under what circumstances, can a company assign expressed global responsibility to a R&D unit? First, a review of the global logic, particularly as it relates to customer-oriented logic(s), would determine the extent of similarity in customer requirements. For firms with substantial differences in customer requirements across geographies, a strong argument to tailor product solutions close to markets will prevail. For firms, and this is primarily the case in technology-based industries, with a high degree of homogeneity in their customer base, a global solution is possible.

Different strategies may also be adopted for either basic research or more applied, development or market-specific forms of research. If a company is able to run its research program off a single basic body of knowledge with similar applications around the world, the basic research may be subjected to globalization. If many country- or market-specific adaptions were needed, the second phase, or the D of R&D, might be dispersed and not run on a global basis.

Siemens of Germany, with its private communication network division, serves as an example of the challenge of globalized research and product devel-

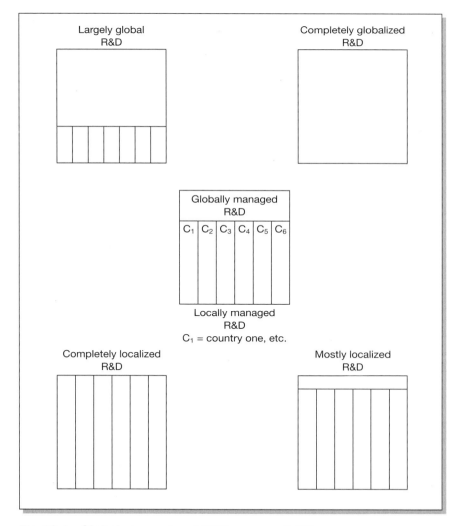

Fig 10.4   Global versus local R&D responsibilities

opment. Originally started in Munich and serving European clients with Private Business Exchange (PBX) and similar telephone equipment, Siemens expanded overseas partly through the acquisition of GPT of the UK and Rolm of the USA (from IBM). Both companies had their own system configurations and through their own research efforts developed new generations of products. Given the economics of developing private network systems, Siemens needed to avoid duplication and concentrate certain task in certain location. The Munich group took responsibility for the hardware development whereas Rolm, with its location in the USA, was given primary development for the development of software application products, such as voice mail, which were more advanced in the USA. Each of the units did, however, engage in research that was meant to be used by the others, thus were handed global responsbilities for R&D.

New companies have the opportunity of not only globalizing their R&D function more readily than established companies with assets in place, they also get to deal with the issue of research location. Elsewhere in this volume we discuss the concept of lead markets. If a company were to place its research capabilities freely, with regard to past practice or head office location, lead market locations would be preferred as they would generate the best pressure for new developments. Access to sufficient research resources, such as trained manpower, would be another reason for locating units in given markets. However, with research mandates globalized, wherever the unit was located, R&D, or some elements of it, would be managed globally. The opportunity to do so is largely driven by the extent of similarity of the underlying research and concept knowledge, and the need to keep R&D units of sufficient size so that fertilization and specialization can occur.

Global finance strategies

The finance function of a firm may also be subject to globalization. For the purpose of our analysis, we are considering the finance and control functions in their broadest sense, including information technology. We would thus group under finance information technology, treasury, controlling, financial accounting and reporting.

The extent of globalization desired, or achievable, depends to some extent on these finance elements. In many firms, corporate treasury operations already exist that centrally manage such elements as cash management and foreign exchange management. Technology is sufficiently advanced that globally active firms can easily globalize that function. Furthermore, evidence suggests that the cash management function may best be maximized by netting transactions on a global scale. On the other side of the continuum, financial accounting and, in many firms, IT, were functions largely left to local organizations. Financial accounting, due to local reporting requirements and regulations, often called for local solutions. IT was also frequently managed locally.

A firm may therefore not have a truly global finance strategy. Instead it may run a global treasury strategy while running a local financial reporting strategy in parallel. A company thus needs to review the nature of its requirement and may, depending on circumstances, globalize all, part, or only certain elements of the total finance and control function. Worldwide, many companies have come to voluntarily adopt a single global standard, such as the one required for listing shares on the New York Stock Exchange. By selecting a global shareholder or investor strategy,

> **A company needs to review the nature of its requirement and may, depending on circumstances, globalize all, part, or only certain elements of the total finance and control function.**

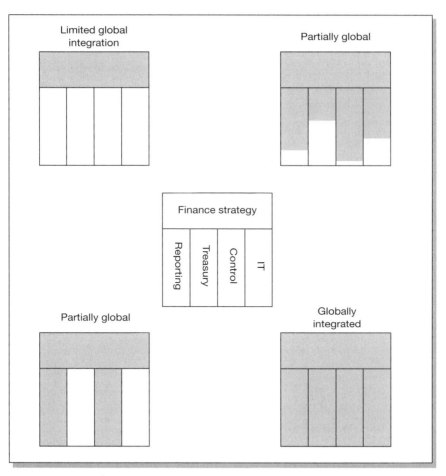

Fig 10.5   Global finance strategies

significant elements of the total finance and control function, as well as the reporting systems, will have to become globalized.

The same might apply to information technology. Here, the implications are even more pervasive. Traditionally, most firms maintained highly localized IT infrastructures. Networks tended to be developed by office, or subsidiary, and rarely from a overall worldwide enterprise point of view. This has left many firms with decisions to make *vis-à-vis* the nature of the IT platform. Should the infrastructure and communications network be structured globally, and if so, where should the local responsibility start? Firms which have conceived their IT network globally find it easier to transmit messages, exchange e-mail, and engage in other document or data transfers that are not available if each unit builds systems on a local basis.

⮕ Summary

In this chapter we have further refined the concept of a generic global business strategy. It is more useful, at this stage of the game, to think in terms of global strategies for businesses, rather than in corporate terms. Different generic global business strategies were defined, ranging from superficial ones to integrated strategies. For managers, it is important to recognize that a large number of different generic global business strategies exist, and that the approach to partial globalization is most likely a better route to success and more relevant to most firms.

Aside from business strategies, there are also a large number of functional strategies that need to be reviewed in terms of globalization. As we outline, for each of the major business functions, ranging from manufacturing to R&D and finance and IT, separate and specific decisions as to the level of required globalization need to be made. There is one function that we have not touched on, namely marketing. We deal with the required, or partial globalization strategies for marketing in the next chapter.

Notes

1. Jean-Pierre Jeannet, "ICI Paints (A)," Case Study, IMD, 1990. "ICI Paints (B)," Case Study, IMD, 1993.

2. John Quelch, *Nestlé S.A.: International Marketing (A)*, Case Study, Harvard Business School, 1984.

3. Jean-Pierre Jeannet, *Note on the World Over-the-Counter (OTC) Drug Industry*, IMD, 1996; *Note on Competitors in the OTC Drug Industry*, IMD, 1996; *Note on OTC Brands*, IMD, 1996.

4. Robert Collins and Jean-Pierre Jeannet, "Deloite, Touche Tohmatsu: Understanding

Global Client Needs", Case Study, IMD, 1998.

5. "Siemens Automotive Technology: Brazil Strategy", Jean-Pierre Jeannet, Case Study, IMD, 1993.

6. Robert Collins, Roger Schmenner, Clay Whybark, "Pan-European Manufacturing: the road to 1992," *European Business Journal*, Vol. 1, Issue 4, 1989, p. 43–51. Robert Collins, Roger Schmenner, "Taking Manufacturing Advantage of Europe's Single Market," *European Management Journal*, Vol. 13, No. 3, September 1995, pp. 257–268.

7. Jean-Pierre Jeannet, *Transfer of Technology within Multinational Corporations*, Arno Press, New York, 1980.

Adopting generic global business strategies

First, we tackle the last of the remaining generic global functional strategies, namely the ones concerning the marketing function. As we did in the previous chapter with other partial global strategies, we demonstrate that even in a function such as marketing, widely different patterns of globalization may be appropriate depending on the circumstances faced by the firm in a given industry. We conclude the generic global strategies chapter with the description of the global focus, or niche strategy.

The main focus of this chapter is the need to select the appropriate globalization strategy for a business. Given the myriad choices, it will become essential for managers to make the choice that best fits the global logics present in a company's business. In order to guide companies through the appropriate choices, we will revisit the global logic concept from previous chapters and combine it with the most suitable form of generic global strategy.

Generic global marketing strategies[1]

When the debate on global marketing started in the early 1980s triggered by a seminal article by Levitt, the debate early on split profession and management practitioners into two principal camps.[2] The first camp included the proponents of global marketing who argued that consumers worldwide were becoming more homogenous, thus a global marketing strategy was desirable. The second camp included the opponents who argued that due to the still significant differences registered across markets, global marketing was not advisable. In particular, they disliked the approach of using the same product or service, promoted in the same way, to customers all over the world, as something not in line with marketing principles. This debate created the impression that global marketing was a choice of all or nothing, and companies needed to decide if they had a global marketing strategy, or if they rejected adopting one.

Over the past years, we have come to realize that the stark either–or decision depicted in the initial debates on global marketing missed the rich opportunities for partial global marketing strategies. It is those partial global marketing strategies that we would like to explore in the next section of this chapter.

Global product strategies

Global product strategies offer a particular challenge to companies since they require firms to offer largely similar products across the world. For a global product strategy to work, a company's customer base would have to be using the product, or service, under essentially similar circumstances demanding similar, or even identical, functional properties. The global product, if suitable, allows a company to source across different locations, and to transship products from different plants as logistics, or inventory situations demand it. A company with country-specific products would not be able to suddenly transship from another sourcing point just because capacity allows for it.

> **Global product strategies offer a particular challenge to companies since they require firms to offer largely similar products across the world.**

Global product offerings also demand largely standardized plant configurations, something not many firms have achieved.

Few companies find themselves in a position where they can actually do so because of different use conditions, or customers that require different functionalities in some countries. However, the fact that some adjustments are required misses the point. Many companies, if pushed, do recognize that, aside from some differences, their product or services offerings are partially similar, or partially global.

If we can accept the fact that a global product strategy does not consist of exactly identical products offered worldwide, we gain some additional flexibility as we can explore partial globalization, or modularity. For some firms, core elements of a product might be identical, such as for PC companies. This standardized core might be as much as encompassing most of the designs, or it might consist of only a small part. Nevertheless, economies of scale can be obtained for the core elements.

Other firms might think in terms of different modules consisting of many different components. A classic example is offered by the Danish toy company Lego, which produces a relatively small number of basic product shapes. However, these shapes can be combined in a vast number of different configurations. On a per component basis, we may achieve economies of scale while keeping flexibility for different requirements through different modular, core component, combinations. The global firm is challenged in the same way, accepting that complete standardized global products are rare opportunities, but that real advantage might be gained by smarter modular configurations, resulting in "Legoization" of the product or service lines.

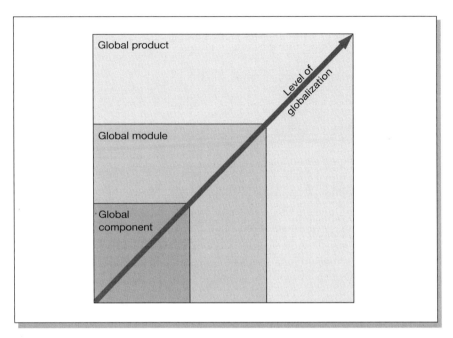

Fig 11.1   Global product strategies

Global communications strategies

Few elements of global marketing have been debated more intensively than the communications strategy, encompassing advertising and other forms of business communications. A company pursues a global strategy in its communications if the essential elements used worldwide are largely similar. The key elements we are interested in are the advertising strategy, consisting both of the positioning and the advertising theme, as well as the audience strategy dealing with the target audience. Finally, we include branding under the communications umbrella. The principal understanding companies have to gain is to appreciate that the communications strategy contains several different elements.

Traditionally, global communications had been perceived as a strategy that only be employed if identical messages could be utilized around the world. Naturally, with differences common across key markets, many companies abstained from globalizing communications due to the difficulties in finding suitable messages for global appeal. If we consider, however, that a company may globalize only some of the communications elements, and continue to keep local strategies for others, additional opportunities arise. Utilizing some form of global communications does not require that an entire communications program be completely standardized. Rather, companies should explore the suitability of doing so with some parts of the program, avoiding globalization in others. Let us first proceed to review the various elements individually.

Global advertising strategies

Companies pursuing global advertising strategies are essentially globalizing their positioning strategy and/or their advertising themes. If a firm were to utilize essentially the same positioning platform across its key markets, the positioning would be globalized. It is frequently mentioned by executives that the business environment is often too different for advertising to be globalized, or standardized around the world. While this may be very much the truth, it also needs to be mentioned that again we should not look at this from an all-or-nothing point of view.

> **Companies pursuing global advertising strategies are essentially globalizing their positioning strategy and/or their advertising themes.**

Instead, just as is the case with other communications elements, partial global strategies apply here as well and may be more appropriate than full global advertising strategies. A company may view the advertising copy as global or local. Separately, the advertising theme selected may be globalized or adapted locally. Equally, the core visuals may be global or local. Once again, the relevant question is less one of determining if we should run a global advertising strategy for a company or business but of coming to an agreement as to which elements can be globalized, and which ones we leave more usefully to local initiative.

Global branding strategies

Branding, although often folded into the communications strategy, is again a decision area that is frequently debated by globally active firms. If a firm decides to systematically use the same name across many countries, the firm were to pursue a global branding strategy. Companies pursuing this are such well-known firms as Nike, Coca-Cola, Microsoft, Adidas, Sony, Heineken, and Lego. These companies spend considerable effort maintaining their brand names worldwide, usually combined with a common logo for immediate, worldwide recognition. There are other firms, however, who use local brand names, or regional ones. Nestlé, the large consumer goods firm, does not use identical brand names everywhere, although some are carried over into multiple markets. Procter & Gamble of the USA also uses different brand names in some categories, such as detergents, whereas Pampers for reusable diapers is a global name. Clearly, the decision to brand globally, or locally, is one that needs to be debated.

What is even more important is the need to see that advertising, positioning, and branding may very well be independent decisions, and may be carried out with different levels of globalization. A firm may use a global brand name, but use different advertising themes by country or region. Unbundling brand name from advertising can be a helpful element in the often divisive globalization debates that surround communications decisions, and can add a new level of sophistication into understanding how far a company, or business, might drive globalization in advertising.

> ... advertising, positioning and branding may very well be independent decisions ...

Global audience strategies

A final component that could be analyzed separately is the nature of the communications audience a company faces. Local audiences are groups of customers who would be exposed to communications messages within a local market only. Regional, or global audiences are characterized by international groups who are simultaneously exposed to communications messages. Global audiences can occur around the use of certain media, be they print or electronic, or around events that attract viewers or spectators from many markets.

The Soccer World Cup held in France in 1998 is just such a global audience opportunity. With millions of viewers from many different countries tuned into the same game, an opportunity exists for a firms to play up against such a global audience by exposing it simultaneously. However, this only works if the same brand name were to be used so that a large audience were exposed to it. Companies marketing their products or services to large audiences that occasionally turn "virtual" in the sense of watching the same event, can move towards a global audience strategy. This largely shapes the outcome of the global advertising debate and may be one of the determinants for using a globalized approach.

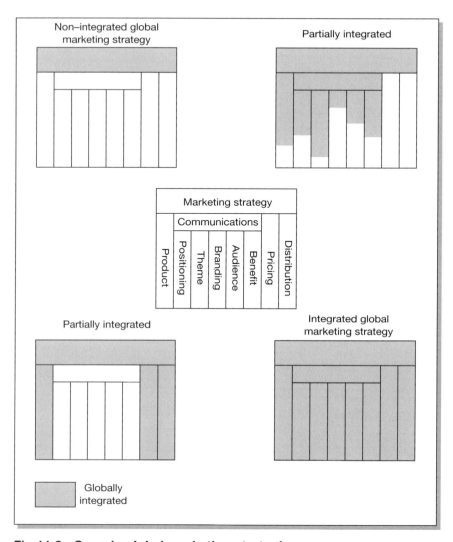

Fig 11.2 Generic global marketing strategies

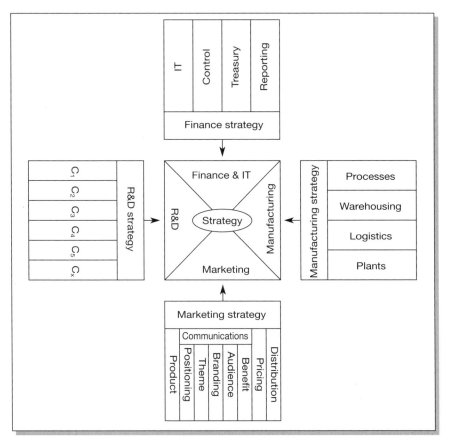

Fig 11.3 Functional global strategy fit

⮕ Fitting generic global strategy options

The previous chapter and earlier parts of this chapter have given us a chance to review globalization across the various functions. We indicated from the outset that it would not be possible to go into more than four major functions. For each of those, however, we have been able to demonstrate that a major improvement in our globalization debate can derive from understanding that this is not an issue where we must choose between all global or zero global, but that instead sophisticated, and well-thought-out debates need to be undertaken to move us into the direction of "How far should we globalize each function," rather than whether we should or should not. The often fruitless debate between all or nothing does not get us into the direction where a company, or business, must carefully select the areas to be globalized and separate them out from those better left to local initiative.

Every business needs to carry out this debate where the line between "play into globalization" is reviewed versus "relegating for localization." The key judgment companies need to make now is the extent of their globalization versus localization. In line with our previous discussion, it is important to recognize that different levels of globalization may be selected for each function, and that this process is not a matter between totally globally or totally local.

The key judgment companies need to make now is the extent of their globalization versus localization.

Once companies can move their discussions to the issue of "appropriate levels" as opposed to either–or, substantial progress in the globalization debate can be made and the discussion can be focused on the truly important issues.

At this point, it is important to stress that global

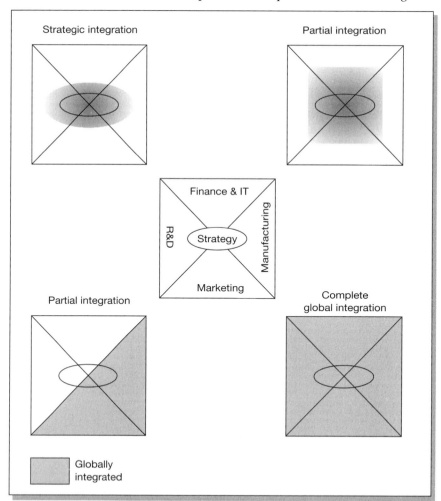

Fig 11.4   Global integration of functional strategies

managers should appreciate the fact that not all globalization strategies need to be balanced, or of equal depth across all functions. As we have demonstrated, companies need to review each function as part of a bigger puzzle, and determine for each of the pieces its proper level of globalization. In our experience, this understanding will frequently open up debates across hardened lines, or in all-or-nothing situations.

Crafting generic global strategies

Naturally, a new challenge now arises. If each function, or part of the business, has to have a differentiated approach, we need to be able to help managers to resolve the issue as to how far they should go with globalization. What analytical tools can they use to have an informed, insightful, and sophisticated debate on the elements that need to be subject to globalization, and identify others that better be left to regional or local control?

To help in this situation, we want to return to an earlier section where we developed the concept of global logics in detail. In Chapter 5 we reviewed the concept in the industry and the competitive environment, as well as among the customer base. Each one of the global logics, if present, we identified as a necessary pressure to globalize that a company needed to accommodate. If no accommodation took place, the company would risk competitiveness. This is how we defined global logics.

First, however, we should investigate the relationship between a given global logic and the suggested generic global strategy to be employed. We are returning here to Chapter 10 where we described the various generic global strategies. These strategies, although related, are nevertheless distinctly different. Executives need to be able to relate the need to apply one or the other strategy to a given configuration of global logics.

Accommodating global customer logic

Strong global customer logic indicates that customers desire consistently similar products from a functionality point of view, and that customers tend to satisfy similar desires and search for similar benefits. First, a company needs to adopt a market global approach to its business strategy since its customers operate on a strong similarity of needs worldwide. Beyond that, a company faced with such customer logics would naturally follow both global product strategies and global benefit strategies, as well as applying a global segment

> **Strong global customer logic indicates that customers desire consistently similar products from a functionality point of view, and that customers tend to satisfy similar desires and search for similar benefits.**

strategy. Global segment strategies would be indicated because of the similarity of the customers and the requirements, country after country. The global product strategy would aim at a globalized product concept, offering similar configurations around the world. Evidence of strong global customer logic tends to drive a highly visible globalization as any actions that affect products or benefits, and thus the communications strategy, are strategy elements with high visibility towards the market.

Accommodating global purchasing logic

The presence of a strong purchasing logic indicates that customers have moved from operating strictly on a local purchasing radius towards regional and global purchasing. As we pointed out earlier, such a move may occur at several levels, such as end-users, retailers, distributors, or wholesalers, and the global purchasing logic may not be of equal extent for all the various purchasing actors. However, the implications for the choice of generic global strategy are quite similar.

> **The presence of a strong purchasing logic indicates that customers have moved from operating strictly on a local purchasing radius towards regional and global purchasing.**

In the broadest sense, a market global approach is again appropriate since the various customers pursuing global purchasing strategies will invariably drive companies toward covering the relevant global markets. More specifically, a company facing strong global purchasing logic will want to approach its customers with global account management strategies. These generic strategies will allow for capturing the wide purchasing range of firms and can accommodate the need to offer a single face towards companies whose purchasing approaches are coordinated globally.

Finally, the very nature of the global search practiced by customers and users alike, and the fact that they tend to "travel the purchasing space extensively" will open up the opportunity for global branding. We particularly differentiate global branding driven by global purchasing logic from global customer logic. When a company's customers scour the globe for products or services, it will be paramount to be present worldwide with the same brand to assist customer identification. For customers, as far as some products are concerned, such as luxury watches (Rolex comes to mind), initial learning about the brand may take place in Hong Kong and yet the purchase might take place in Geneva or New York. Such moving targets are clear indications of the benefit of global branding.

> **... the very nature of the global search practices by customers and users alike, and the fact that they tend "to travel the purchasing space extensively" will open up the opportunity for global branding.**

Inherent in the global purchasing radius of the customers, global pricing strategies are typically required. Since customers scan the globe for superior offers, they are usually well informed about price differences and can easily engage in parallel imports if gaps develop. Companies are thus well advised to exert considerable pricing control inevitably leading to a global pricing strategy. This is particularly important if the products are relatively homogeneous, as driven by the previously discussed global customer logic. However, where customers are not requiring similar solutions around the world, product differentiation might be a sufficient barrier to parallel imports. Finally, global distribution policies are often required to deal with global purchasing logic involving globally coordinated logistics systems and distribution strategies involving wholesalers, distributors, or retailers.

Accommodating global information logic

Earlier in this volume we identified the nature of global information/audience logic as a condition where a firm's customers search for product information globally. When strong global information/audience logic is present, a company is well advised to accommodate it by reaching out globally for target customers. The evidence of such strong logic might come from the reading of common literature and attending the same trade fairs. In either situation, the company experiencing this logic would need to employ global branding again as this is the only approach that ensures that the firm takes maximum advantage of the information acquisition routine of its customers.

Even in the situation of the global event, such as sports events watched by large audiences in many countries, the benefit of using global branding strategy is clear. In the case of the soccer world championship, whose games are watched by millions in dozens of countries, companies can become sponsors with their names displayed around the stadium. Only companies with global branding strategies will obtain the full benefit of this sponsoring activity.

Additional global strategies, particularly those related to marketing and marketing communications, are advised. Global themes in a company's advertising strategy become possible when the intended audience is exposed in multiple geographies to a company's product, or service. Medical professionals, for example, attend conferences in many different countries and attendance at these conferences is typically international. The opportunity thus exists for a coherent theme into different markets reinforced as target customers travel from airport to airport. Global positioning is advised when the customer group is exposed to a consistent set of alternative products thus allowing the firm to position its products in a similar competitive space. Finally, the use of global visuals, or symbols is directly related to the extent of global information acquisition logic present in the market. The use of such global visuals allows for the reinforcement of a message that might be delivered to customers traveling in different countries or cities around the globe, building into a coherent, strong campaign that would become diluted if delivered locally in different formats.

Accommodating global industry logic

The strong presence of global industry logic indicates that an industry operates under similar imperatives, or sets of KSFs, around the globe. As we go from country to country, we observe that essentially the same approaches to the industry lead to success. Three of our earlier described generic global strategies stand out when this condition is satisfied.

Strong industry logic at a minimum favors the generic form of global category strategy. A company, as in some homogenous industries such as cement manufacturing, basic chemicals, energy, and others, can easily leverage its experience in one geographic area to others since the requirements for success are similar. The key is to remain within the same category of activity. If a global cement manufacturer were to open up operations in a new country, considerable operating experience would be leverage from previous locations. Since the customer base, or local market structure might not be similar, the company may have to adapt marketing, use different brand names, and target different segments. The essential category strategy, however, would still apply due to the strong commonality of the industry KSFs. Companies that operate under strong global industry logic would become more competitive if they were to leverage their experience, and those that remained local, or regional, would forgo the benefits of such leverage. The result would be a asset global strategy with assets present in multiple markets.

As the KSFs become more functionally specific, a company may elect to adopt a global functional strategy concentrating its leverage on the key function that comes from the understanding of the industry KSFs. For an industry where the KSFs are heavily oriented towards the marketing function, the marketing operation would be subject to global leverage. Such leverage, or global functional strategy, may not include brand names, positioning, and other specific marketing outputs. Instead, it might be the general way of approaching marketing, and leverage would apply to the operational and process experience. The food industry, with its many differences on a country-by-country basis comes to mind. Firms such as Nestlé still leave their operating managers substantial leeway on specific marketing decisions, including brand, advertising, positioning, and pricing. However, Nestlé and other such firms have experienced a common approach to marketing that can be transferred from one operating firm to another. Such

> **As the KSFs become more functionally specific, a company may elect to adopt a global functional strategy concentrating its leverage on the key function that comes from an understanding of the industry KSFs.**

experience is transferable even when customers are different and even when otherwise no visible global strategy exists.

Other global functional strategies that might be adopted are in the areas of manufacturing operations, research, logistics, IT, finance, etc.

Accommodating critical mass logic

As we pointed out earlier, global critical mass logic is a particularly important driver towards globalization that is closely related to the global industry logic. It helps, however, for our purposes, to view it separately, due to its implications for the choice of generic global strategy.

The strong presence of global critical mass logic invariably forces companies into a wider choice of markets to write off ever growing initial commitments, be they of a research or operational nature, against a growing market territory. Consequently, the typical outcome is the pursuit of a global reach strategy that maximizes the market coverage. The global reach strategy needs to be targeted against the most important markets, the "must win" markets, and needs to be driven by a sophisticated understanding of the global opportunity, discussed in earlier chapters when the concept of the global chessboard was introduced.

> **The strong presence of global critical mass logic invariably forces companies into a wider choice of markets to write off ever growing initial commitments … against a growing market territory.**

This imperative of global reach, or into multiple, key markets, can be so strong that it supersedes weaker global logics, such as in the customer or purchasing dimension. We are thus facing in extreme conditions the need to push for global coverage against the presence of differentiated demand. Under those circumstances, companies may have to reduce the global offering to a modular design and be extremely judicious in determining the exact elements subject to global reach. In the case of machinery it may only be a cored driver element, with the rest not subject and therefore driven by local demands. In the pharmaceuticals industry, the core element might be the initial molecule, but different forms of the product (liquid, pills, patch, etc.) may be needed to fit into local market demands.

Since building a multi-country presence to accommodate the logic typically consumes considerable resources, companies may have to limit themselves to fewer initiatives, product lines, or segments. Such a trade-off against more limiting resources is described in more detail when introducing the global niche or focus strategy in Chapter 12.

Accommodating global competitive logic

Firms which are facing strong global competitive logic will experience a need to coordinate their actions on a worldwide basis. The capability to play tic-tac-toe on the global chessboard, to retaliate against competitive action in, for example, the UK, with counteraction in Germany or Japan, places special demands on any business organization. Although a variety of generic global strategies may apply, three stand out:

● a global category strategy;

● a global segment strategy;

● an integrated global strategy.

Global category strategy

A global category strategy that emphasizes the leverage function in a given sector, or category, on a worldwide basis, would appear to be the minimum. To square off against competitors which put in place a coordinated global strategy demands that the company be able to learn globally, act on information in one country and pass it on to others as need arises, a firm would need at least the coordinating power of the global category strategy. Under these circumstances, a central unit would be in charge of coordinating input from around the world and passing it on to other operating units. Global category strategies would still allow for distinctive, local responses, and would not mandate any operating units to engage in global marketing or other, more limiting, generic strategies. If a firm did not get to the point of enabling a least a global category coordination, significant competitive disadvantage would result from being outmaneuvered by better integrated and coordinated global firms.

Global segment strategy

A more structured response to meeting global competitive logic is the adoption of a global segment strategy. Less driven by the need of similarity among the customer base, the global segment strategy nevertheless allows for close and well-coordinated response to a small set of similar, but highly coordinated set of competitors, particularly where they may fall into a clearly specified segment. When the global category strategy becomes too unwieldy, or unfocused, grouping activities along several global segments will allow for enhanced global coordination and monitoring of competitors.

Integrated global strategy

Global firms such as Nestlé or Procter & Gamble, use the category management structure to pass on key learning from one unit to another. The inherent weakness of category management, however, is the fact that much of the information, or advanced practice, passed on rests with local management for voluntary implementation. The only approach that will allow for mandated learning of competitive developments is a move towards the integrated global strategy. Under this strategy, the decision-making power is centralized and units are organized in such a way that the same decision, or strategy, can be put in place in a multitude of geographies. If the company experiences global competitive logic only, the integration may be restricted to strategic parameters of the business. To the extent that other, more market-related global logics also exist, the integration could extend to functions and thus include many more business parameters.

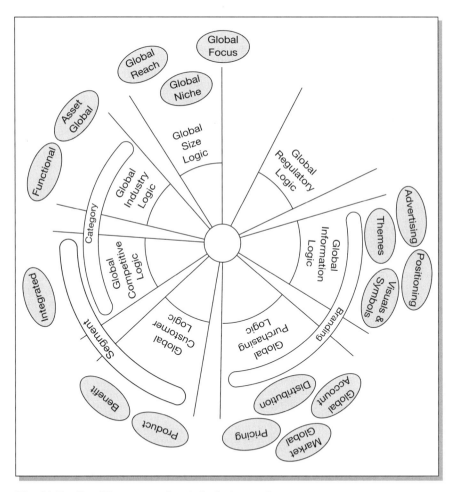

Fig 11.5   Crafting generic global strategies

Notes

1. Adapted from Jean-Pierre Jeannet and David H. Hennessey, *Global Marketing Strategies*, Houghton Mifflin, 4th edn, 1998, p. 291–95.

2. Theodore Levitt, "The Globalization of Markets," *Harvard Business Review* May–June 1983, pp. 92–102.

12

Prioritizing generic global strategies

Previous chapters have left us with a multitude of generic global strategies that may be employed under a given global logic set. As can be seen in Figure 12.1, each global logic dimension tends to generate its own set of distinctive generic global strategies. Clearly,

> ... each global logic dimension tends to generate its own set of distinctive generic global strategies.

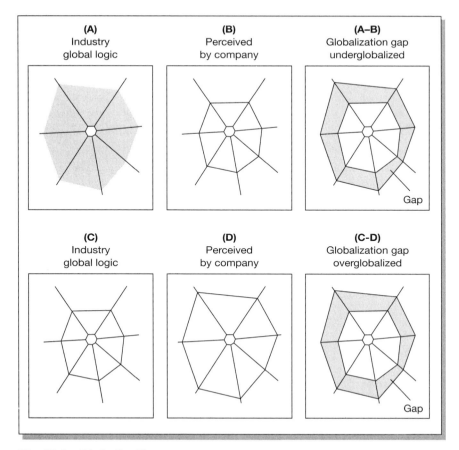

Fig 12.1 Globalization gaps

managers will now be confronted with an assessment as to which of these sometimes conflicting generic strategies may apply.

As our analysis of the global logics asked for prioritization, or identification of the relevant strength of the global logic, we now have a clear idea as to which global logics are relatively stronger. If a business cannot prioritize the global logic pressures, it will be forced into pursuing a multitude of simultaneous global strategies, or, in the end, to pursue ultimate global strategy which calls for total integration. (That could, however, be "overkill" compared to the opportunity presented.)

A firm pursuing a global strategy that went beyond the indicated opportunity or generic global strategy would, by inference "overglobalize" and thus pay a penalty for the incurred integration and coordination costs. A firm that, in contrast, does not go as far as the logics suggest might, through a process of "underglobalization", miss substantial opportunities arising from appropriate coordination and integration. Clearly, the most judicious result would occur if a company were to find the ideal point where both the existing globalization pressure as evidenced from the global logic analysis would meet the chosen generic global strategy's integration need.

⋗ Identifying the globalization gap

The global logic analysis, combined with the generic strategy selection, can also be used to identify the appropriate gap a company faces. Although the spider-web chart is intended to depict the actual situation a company might face in a given industry, it can also be used to demonstrate the perceived situation in a company. Once the actual and the future, expected, global logic pressures are charted, a similar set of questions might apply to the company's perceived behavior. We could assume that we wanted to depict how the company acts, on what basis it appears to set its globalization course. Using this approach, we might detect if the firm over- or underglobalizes its strategy.

In Figure 12.1, two hypothetical examples are depicted. In both situations, the actual industry global pressure are identical. In Figure 12.1(b) the perceived global logic pressure (or the combined action of the firm) is shown as less extensive than the actual situation. This would indicate that the firm acts less globally than realities would indicate, and that a gap exists that the company might want to close. In Figure 12.1(b), we show a company where the company-perceived globalization, as based and interpreted on its actions, is actually beyond the existing global logic. Clearly, under these circumstances of overglobalization, the gap consists of overachieving globalization and the company should consider a reduction in its globalization integration or effort.

➔ Facing multiple spiderwebs

So far we have been analyzing markets for global logics with the assumption that one single global logic set would explain the entire market, category, or segment. In Chapter 6, however, we accepted the notion that spiderweb configurations can be very specific, and an industry or category might in fact contain several of these configurations, with the global logic pattern showing different strengths.

In Chapter 11, we demonstrated that the generic global strategy should be matched up with the appropriate global logic configuration, or spiderweb. If we accept that we should properly match up global logic with appropriate generic global strategy, it follows logically that each identified spiderweb would require its own selected generic global strategy. Conceivably, a company might run several different global strategies in parallel. This latter notion is not as far-fetched as might at first appear. Experience has shown that companies, even competing in one large industry only, might find different sets of KSFs for each sub-sector, or segment.

The real challenge for companies competing globally stems from the requirement that different global strategies have to be accommodated under one single organizational roof. How does a firm accept, and organize, for the fact that one of its industry segments best be globalized using a category strategy, while a second one may be better off with a global brand strategy? Clearly, large corporations with multiple businesses need to accept that it is highly likely that several different generic global strategies will have to be accommodated. From an organizational point of view, that present a particular challenge.

> **The real challenge for companies competing globally stems from the requirement that different global strategies have to be accommodated under one single organizational roof.**

➔ Playing the resource game: global focus or niche strategies

So far, a clear picture has been painted of the type of different generic global strategies a company might select, and how those strategies need to fit the particular global logic pattern faced by a firm. The analysis of most firms in terms of "globalization gaps" tends to result in a verdict of "underglobalized", which means that, in our experience, the vast majority of companies have not yet gone far enough in their globalization drives as indicated by a thorough logic demand analysis. To make matters worse, it is more than likely that firms will find that their market coverage is not yet fully in line with the current, never mind emerging, global chessboard. The rest of the chapter is devoted to this particular challenge, and how companies can focus resources to achieve strategic imperatives imposed by the global nature of their industry and customer context.

Challenge of meeting global logic imperatives

Following through on the demands imposed by a firm's global logic and the ever changing, global chessboard typically imposes considerable demands on a company's resources. Starting from the experience that most firms suffer from "underglobalization", their response tends to pull them in two directions. First, they find themselves with a generic global strategy that offers less leverage than it should, given their global logic spiderweb patterns. As a company moves up in terms of globalization level, added strains are placed on the organization. Committing larger parts, more functions, or more decision-making processes to global coordination, such as moving from a global category to a global segment strategy, demands an organizational and mindset change that is difficult to achieve and will take time. We focus on the organizational implications in a later chapter, but for now we can at least mention that this rewiring of the company would require substantial managerial effort, commitment, and investment into a different type of manager, namely managers with global mindsets and organizations which can act likewise.

The other side of meeting the global imperatives is the challenge to adequately compete across the relevant global chessboard. Few companies are positioned to take advantage of the full global opportunities. "Filling in the blanks," or building a presence in key markets con-

The other side of meeting the global imperatives is the challenge to adequately compete across the relevant global chessboard.

sumes large resources and takes time. Firms which are able to pursue a market global strategy have an advantage as their network creation is less capital intensive and restricted to marketing, sales, and customer service organizations. More difficult is the situation for companies requiring asset global strategies which will then find that occupying each of the key markets can absorb substantial financial resources, often outstripping what such companies can do on their own.

The financial constraints of a globalization effort that compensates for the gap both in terms of generic strategy and deployment across the global chessboard are best described in the context of the firm's funds flow cycle[1] which results in a given sustainable growth rate.[2] If a company goes beyond that critical point, growth can only be achieved if more capital were added, or if the capital intensity of the operation were reduced. Typically, the sustainable growth percentage of a firm might be sufficient to allow for growth within existing markets. Closing substantial gaps, however, often outstrips those limits. With the more recent emphasis on shareholder value, companies are placed under additional demands to generate positive free cash flow as a basis for shareholder value creation.[3] This discipline, imposed by the capital markets, acts as an additional constraint. How can companies meet their global logic demands while staying within their limited resources?

How can companies meet their global logic demands while staying within their limited resources?

Resource web

As a first step, the company's full set of opportunities can be depicted as a web with each possible improvement direction represented by separate rays. The analysis would start with an examination of status quo and systematically find the different growth options, all of which might be different approaches to bring the company from a state of underglobalization to one of "appropriate globalization". The term appropriate level of globalization, or generic global strategy, implies a strategy consistent with the global logic pattern of the company's industry.

Figure 12.2 depicts the resource allocation of a biotechnology firm that finds itself pulled into developing several new segments while navigating a substantial change in technology from older forms of production to the new type of biotech reactors. The company, if it wants to exploit its resources, is confronted with substantial capital needs to expand production technologies, to support R&D for new products, to build new customer franchises into new therapeutic areas, and finally to expand its drive into the world's relevant key markets. Figure 12.2(a) contains the neutral web with the potential avenues for growth. Figure 12.2(b) shows the existing resource commitment across these various avenues. Finally, Figure 12.2 (c) shows the desired position.

This multitude of opportunities, sometime referred to as a veritable "crisis of opportunity", needs to be confronted with internal resource generation by the existing business and new capital infusions. Any move along one of the depicted rays of potential growth creates new resource demands. When faced with choices, companies will need to decide along which axes they intend to go "long", to invest additional resources, and along which other axes they will have to pull back, essentially reducing resources. This resource trade-off is often played out in a debate between more global reach for the business versus more breadth (segments, etc.). A look at recent developments with many multinational firms gives us some insight into how this resource constraint is resolved and how it has affected strategy making in many boardrooms.

Global logic and the dismemberment of the traditional multinational firm

In Chapter 3 we characterized the key elements of the multinational company

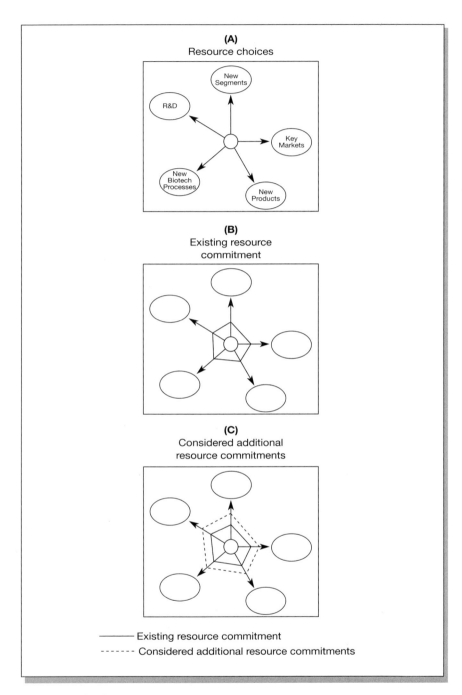

Fig 12.2   Global resource web

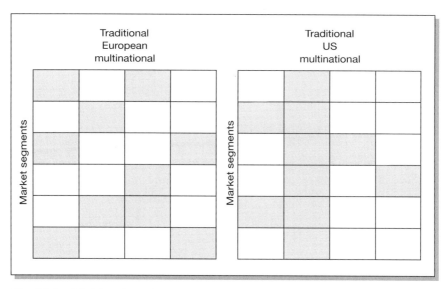

Fig 12.3 Multinational geographic coverage

following the multi-domestic mindset. Just ten or fifteen years ago, the industrial landscape was dominated by such firms, of both North American and European origin. The typical multinational was a company with wide-ranging interests, such as many different lines of business, and covering a good part of the then available global chessboard.

European firms, characterized by such long-standing multinationals as Siemens of Germany, Nestlé of Switzerland, and ICI of the UK, found themselves in a large number of different business, although they tended to be related to a core industry. Nestlé operated largely in the food industry, but its range of food categories was broad, ranging from drinks to confectionery, dietetics, dairy, and culinary products (dried soups, bouillon, etc.). Siemens, although restricted to the electrical and electronic industry, occupied a wide competitive space with businesses ranging from power engineering to electrical distribution, telecommunications, and medical equipment. ICI was traditionally a broad-based chemicals industry spanning both the life sciences with pharmaceuticals, agrochemical, as well as many industrial chemical products. For any of those three firms we could find a number of similarly structured European competitors.

The geographic expansion of these firms took different directions. While Nestlé had operations in many different countries, the distribution of businesses was not consistent. Not all countries offered the full product line, and the geographic spread in extent and strength of strategic position varied greatly. Similar pictures emerged from the other multinational firms. At first glance it appeared that all relevant markets were covered, but they were not consistently covered for all lines of business. The merging pattern was a "checkered" position with widely dispersed resources.

US multinationals were typified by a different pattern. Although achieving already considerable global reach by the early 1980s, they were still dominated by a largely domestic business, or mindset. Although large in size, few US multinationals could claim to have more than half of their business abroad, and most had considerably less. They were, much like their European competitors, broad-based companies with many business lines. The challenge for US companies consisted in how to break out of the chokehold of the US market and move to becoming truly global. This was usually accomplished by building large international divisions that combined all the company's businesses internationally.

In the mid-1980s, a new type of globally active company emerged. These firms operated in relatively few business lines but instead preferred to stake out a global position. Their strategy was to become a global leader in a narrow, specific field. Examples of such firms abound, but one of the best known is Nokia of Finland. Originally a diverse group of companies with interests ranging from paper production to chemicals, electronics, consumer electronics, to telecommunications, Nokia began to narrow its focus in the late 1980s and to move towards a global niche strategy in telecommunications. Eventually, the company narrowed its focus even further in telecommunications, specializing in wireless, or mobile phone applications, both for mobile infrastructure and for the handsets. Rapidly expanding its mobile telecommunications business around the globe, the company succeeded in building a leading position in the field on a global basis.

Horizontal tigers versus vertical dragons

Companies that follow a global niche strategy consisting of a narrow business focus but practicing extensive global reach across the entire relevant global chessboard have achieved significant strategic advantages over other firms which have a broad business focus but have narrowed their geographic spread to a region or single market.

Companies that follow a global niche strategy consisting of a narrow business focus but practicing extensive global reach across the entire relevant global chessboard have achieved significant strategic advantages over other firms which have a broad business focus but have narrowed their geographic spread to a region or single market. Companies adopting a global focus or niche strategy can be referred to as the new horizontal tigers, reflecting their strategic position of multiple geographies but few or single businesses. These firms, Nokia among them, have been aggressively scoring strategic points against the older, more traditional vertical dragons, which are those firms that follow a

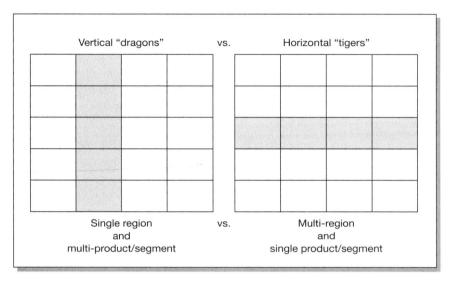

Fig 12.4 Global business focus

multiple business line strategy combined with a narrow regional focus. Horizontal tigers, as has been demonstrated many times, can focus their energy on a single or limited business and typically beat vertical dragon firms where they meet. Most old-line European and US-based multinationals are examples of vertical dragons.

The lessons of the horizontal tigers have not been lost on the vertical dragons. Much of the wholesale restructuring witnessed across Europe and North America is driven by this realization. Increasingly, vertical dragons desire to build global businesses on their own, thus strengthening their strategic position. The difficulty for them lies in their limited resources, as the process of globalizing many businesses simultaneously consumes considerable resources. How then can vertical dragons become global firms under stringent resource constraints?

Since building a global position in any business absorbs substantial financial and managerial resources, even large vertical dragon firms will have to act selectively. In essence, they need to select some businesses where they want to build global positions while at the same time exiting from other businesses where that option is not available. Checking the developments particularly among European multinational firms over the past ten years has shown how many companies, in order to end up with a string of pearls around the world, will make substantial resource commitments to some businesses while divesting others.

Resource commitments in building a global string of pearls may consist of acquisitions to plug geographic holes in some parts of the global chessboard. Alternatively, a company may engage in alliances, although this is less likely to result in a truly integrated global business with the required leveraging opportunities. Resources can be obtained through the sale of other businesses that might make a better match in some other company's collection of pearls, thus yielding better prices for sold operations. In some instances, this might even result in the swapping of businesses among two firms.

Resource commitments in building a global string of pearls may consist of acquisitions to plug geographic holes in some parts of the global chessboard.

One of the most telling examples of this practice aimed at building global business units that resemble our horizontal tigers is the simultaneous purchase and sales of two businesses between DuPont of the USA and ICI of the UK. DuPont acquired from ICI the man-made fibers business which had a major strength in Europe whereas DuPont was strong in the USA and Asia. For DuPont, it represented a quick approach towards completing the global tiger in fibers, and to accomplish this strategic position more rapidly than building the European business on its own. In return, DuPont divested its acrylics business which was strong in the USA but had not yet obtained strong beachheads in Europe and Asia. In contrast, ICI operated its own acrylics business with a major strength in Europe and Asia. The acquisition of DuPont's acrylics business allowed ICI to build a horizontal tiger in acrylics faster than it could have managed it on its own.

More recently, many companies have begun to divest some of their businesses which have become global business in their own right. Ciba and Sandoz, merging into Novartis, have decided to focus on life sciences, resulting in a demerger of the specialty chemicals business of both companies. They now operate under the name of Ciba Specialty Chemicals and Clarient. Similar narrowing of focus is under way among many other chemicals companies, such as Rhône-Poulenc of France, Hoechst of Germany, and ICI, the latter having demerged into two separate firms.

Narrowing the focus of the business system

So far we have spoken of narrowing the business line to achieve focus. However, there are also opportunities to narrow the focus of business activities from a business system point of view. Such focusing would again be used to achieve greater coverage of the relevant global chessboard.

Few companies offer such an illustrative glimpse into the trade-off between geographic coverage and business focus as the cola industry. Coca-Cola and Pepsi, locked into a global fight for years, have chosen two different strategies of resource allocation.[4] Pepsi has typically chosen to select independent bottlers as partners and to acquire as much as 50 percent or more of the partner's equity. Pepsi argued that the company needed such heavy stakes to effectively control the bottling business, an important aspect in the soft drinks industry. In contrast, Coca-Cola has opted for a different form of bottler. Coke typically selected large anchor bottlers which controlled entire regions, often across several countries. The company took relatively small equity positions in those business, preferring to control bottlers through the power of the brand. This meant that Coke had its business model arranged so that it required a smaller investment amount for each dollar sales growth than Pepsi, allowing it to grow faster, covering more markets and countries more quickly. In essence, Coke had focused its business more specifically on fewer valued-added steps, which allowed it to be more aggressive in either spending on brand building or on geographic expansion.[5]

Few companies offer such an illustrative glimpse into the trade-off between geographic coverage and business focus as the cola industry.

Operating under a less resource-intensive strategy can be of decisive impact, and Pepsi, after many years of trying to keep up with Coke, finally changed course. The company announced that it would divest its fast food restaurant business, which on its own required considerable capital to fully globalize, in order to concentrate on the soft drink and snack food business. Furthermore, the company also indicated that it would follow a bottling strategy that more closely resembled Coke's.

The role of the global dimension

The lessons from Nokia and the Cola Wars are important in understanding the value of focus when facing strong global logic. Both companies, for different reasons, were faced with strong global logics which required them to pursue all relevant, large, parts of their respective global chessboards. For Nokia, this meant key markets such as China, now its largest market. For Coke and Pepsi, the road led to all major markets with large populations, such as China and India. Building a beachhead in most markets demands considerable financial and managerial resources. Both Nokia and Coke leverage their limited resources by narrowing the business focus and yet maximizing the coverage of the international markets. That is an important lesson for aspiring global mindsets to learn: to make limited resources stretch around the globe, companies may have to concentrate on fewer businesses, or only one, but then to expand that business into all relevant parts of the global chessboard. The geographic dimension may thus be the one along which companies should not focus in a limited way, rather

The lessons from Nokia and the Cola Wars are important in understanding the value of focus when facing strong global logic.

... to make limited resources stretch around the globe, companies may have to concentrate on fewer businesses, or only one, but then to expand that business into all relevant parts of the global chessboard.

they should marshal all available resources and go long on the geographic dimension.

Building global strategies thus requires a company to be clear on the required geographies, as determined by the global chessboard the company faces. This analysis will result in the required global coverage. The coverage needs to be reached as the imperative of globalization, or the global logic, will dictate that the company first satisfy necessary global reach before expanding into other types of businesses. Larger firms therefore may be able to fund and grow several such horizontal tigers, whereas smaller firms may be required to limit themselves to few, or possibly only one.

Regional strategies versus global strategies

So far our discussions have dealt with global strategies only. The question is often raised by managers who wonder if there is a difference between global and regional strategies, such as those often referred to as pan-European. The conceptual framework we have developed in these chapters, ranging from understanding global logics, global chessboards, and generic global strategies, can easily be adapted to the context of a pan-European strategy. The conceptual thinking of a manager who needs to focus on the top global markets is identical to the thinking of plotting strategies across the top European markets. In the pan-European context, the global logics become pan-European logics, the global chessboard transforms into a pan-European chessboard, and the global generic global strategies become generic pan-European strategies. While the scale and context change, the conceptual thinking is unchanged. Global strategic thinking is identical to European strategic thinking.

Once we have established the similarity between pan-European and global thinking, we can go a step further. Regional strategies of any kind are based on the same conceptual framework as global strategies. This means that strategies across North America, pan-Americas strategies across both North and Latin America, pan-Asian strategies in the Asia Pacific area, Atlantic strategies for both North America and Europe, trans-Pacific strategies for both North America and Asia, or Euro-Asian strategies involving both Europe and Asia, are all based on the same conceptual frameworks. For those managers whose responsibility is limited to regional theaters, a careful reading of this book will equally well prepare them for their business strategy requirements as those who are already planning and acting on a global scale.

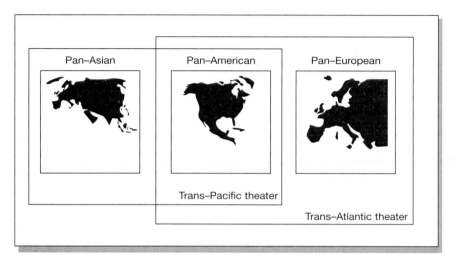

Fig 12.5   Regional competitive theaters

Notes

1. Robert C. Higgins, *Analysis for Financial Management*, 5th Edition, Irwin McGraw-Hill, 1998.

2. Michael E. Porter, *Competitive Strategy*, The Free Press, 1980, p. 66.

3. A. Rappaport, "Creating Shareholder Value," The Free Press, 1986.

4. David Yoffie, and Richard Seet, "Internationalizing the Cola Wars (A): The Battle for China and Asian Markets," Harvard Business School Case Collection, 1995.

5. "If you can't beat them, copy them", *Business Week*, 17 November, 1997, p. 50.

Implementing global mindsets

The previous sections have dealt with new analytic concepts and strategic concepts for managers and companies which aspire to a global mindset. As practicing managers everywhere will know, the idea of strategic direction alone does not guarantee successful implementation. With this realization, this section is dedicated to implementation issues at the organizational, personal, and company levels.

Organization issues with be covered in Chapter 13. In particular, we introduce the idea of a global mandate for both businesses, organizational units, and individuals. Secondly, we give some coverage to organizational design issues that closely parallel the pursuit of global strategies. Finally, we will deal with the processes companies have to go through if they want to extend the learning organization globally.

Chapter 14 deals with the individual manager. In particular, we address behavioral requirements, skill levels, and knowledge requirements for a manager who aspires to run a business with a global mindset. This concludes in an agenda for personal growth and will be useful to both practicing and aspiring global managers.

Chapter 15 concentrates on the company, and how to grow or implement global mindsets in firms. This builds on some of the organizational issues of Chapter 13 and suggests actions companies can take to develop more managers along the dimension described in Chapter 14. Suggestions are made as to what companies can do to foster global mindsets across entire companies, or businesses. Growing global mindsets is a major managerial challenge that, if addressed, has a chance to create lasting competitive advantage for companies.

Chapter 16 suggests a step-by-step approach on how to apply the global mindset described in this book.

Organizational concepts for global mindsets

If companies are to realize their chosen global generic strategy, unless it is adapted, the organization is likely to get in the way. This is based on the understanding that with a global strategy needs to go a new form of global responsibility, and that most firms do not traditionally approach the global strategy paradigm with a organization that fits earlier paradigms, either of the international or multi-domestic variant. In this chapter, we take a closer look at the required organizational adaptations, and at new approaches to parcel out responsibility and accountability that will support various types of global strategies.

Defining geographic organizational mandates

Inherent in any type of international activity is the range of responsibility a company allows for individual managers and business units. For many business today, if you were to check a mission statement or job description, you would find it full of functional details but often lacking the specific geographic territory for which the management responsibility applies. For international subsidiaries, or market companies, the limited geographic responsibility was usually included. But it is not uncommon for a business unit, or a group of managers, to search their mission statements in vain for any definition of the range of responsibility or limits to their mandates.

For businesses implementing any form of global strategy, it is of crucial importance to have a proper mandate that is in accordance with the chosen generic global strategy. The geographic mandate is an expressed description of the responsibility assigned to a business unit or individual executive. The mandate is considered global when the responsibilities assigned imply decision-making or coordinating functions across the globe, or specifically, across the markets where the business is operating.

> **For businesses implementing any form of global strategy, it is of crucial importance to have a proper mandate that is in accordance with the chosen generic global strategy.**

The value of global mandates

To whom should we hand a global mandate? This question is often heard among corporate management. Since the term global is relatively new to the business community, in regular use since only the early 1980s, many companies still tend to think in terms of international mandates. However, there is a difference between an international mandate and the more sweeping, global one. International mandates tend to be assigned to executives with responsibility outside the domestic, or home market, and is very typical for US companies. In essence, the responsibility pertains to everything but the domestic market. Now, as is inherent in the understanding of global, it requires the combination of both international and domestic responsibility.

Some years ago, when we first embarked on research for supporting programs on globalization, we made the rounds among some US-based international firms. We approached a well-known US-based computer firm for interviews with managers with global responsibility. After some hesitation, it turned out that there was but one single executive with such responsibility, namely the CEO. All other responsibility was divided along geographic lines right to the top level. When all managers but the CEO have geographic limited responsibility, it is difficult to execute on a global strategy. The entire integration task, the pulling for an overall global strategy, and the global thinking behind it is left in the hands of a single leader, much too much for assured success. Assigning a global mandate will help move an organization toward global integration, and the more numerous the mandates, the stronger the pull in the global direction. Conversely, the more prevalent a geographic division in a business, and the higher level at which this split occurs, the more difficult the implementation of a strategy is likely to be. This is due to the fact that a number of executives with geographically limited mandates tend to act and think in limited, not global terms, since both responsibility and reward systems tend to support this limited mindset.

> **Assigning a global mandate will help move an organization toward global integration, and the more numerous the mandates, the stronger the pull in the global direction.**

In 1998 Procter & Gamble, the leading US consumer goods company, offered us a telling example of the changing directions among established global firms.[1] Long having exposed management along geographic territories, P&G had major responsibility placed into four regional operating units, each with its head reporting to the CEO. Recognizing that it became increasingly difficult to compete globally across a broad product range, Procter & Gamble announced a reorganization that would regroup its business into seven globally-defined product units such as baby care, beauty, fabric, and home care. Each of these units would have formal global mandates with P&L responsibility and an executive reporting directly to the CEO.

The trigger for the new P&G organization was a new fabric care product, Febreze, launched and developed in the US market with expected sales of $150 to $200 million. P&G believed that if the product could have been launched by a fabric care unit operating under a global mandate, it would have been able to launch in many markets simultaneously and achieve initial volume of $500 million. Under the present (old) structure, other countries will follow as they see fit, thus leaving some potential untouched. [2]

Different forms of global mandates

Global mandates can be assigned at all levels of an organization, and need not only take the form of a CEO at the corporate level. While global responsibility is inherent in the executive responsibility, we need to understand where else in the hierarchy global mandates can occur.

At a small business unit (SBU) or division level, global mandates have begun to occur more frequently. As many international firms have restructured along business lines, it has become common to assign formal global mandates to executives in charge. Typically, these executives tend to be clustered around the head office and run their units with a full staff complement.

As companies have restructured for global responsibility, they have endowed other positions with global mandates. Companies may run global segments, each segment headed by a coordinating executive with global responsibility. Other firms have appointed global sector, or category heads, again assigning formal global mandates to them. Finally, firms have also globalized their staff where direct reporting staff, by implication, have been assigned global mandates for staff functions such as IT, human resources, legal, or other coordinating functions.

Less common, but increasingly coming into vogue, are global responsibilities for functional executives. Functions such as marketing, finance Chief Financial Officer (CFO), research and development, and increasingly manufacturing or sourcing, have all in some circumstances been given global mandates. This is particularly common where a business is operating largely on a functional level, with functional heads reporting to an executive with a global mandate.

All of these types of global mandate come in a formal, permanent form. Since they are captured in the organization, we can track them through organizational charts. Most companies, however, have a different form of organizational layer comprising a series of task forces, experience sharing groups, or other group efforts that may or may not warrant global mandates. When a company pushes for a global launch of a new product, a temporary task force may be created to accompany the event. Once completed, the task force dissolves. For other purposes, a company may maintain a set of semi-permanent task

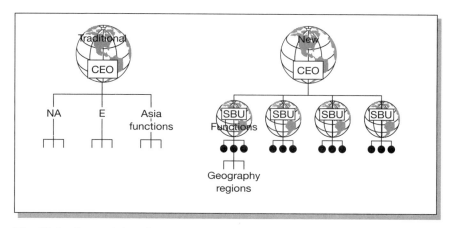

Fig 13.1 Organizing for global mandates

forces that meet on a regular basis. In both instances, global mandates may be bestowed to those task forces and its members.

Having expanded our understanding of global mandates both hierarchically, and in terms of permanent versus temporary, we can now pose the question: Who should have a global mandate? Percy Barnevik, when CEO at ABB, and one of the foremost global managers, expressed in an interview the idea that a company such as ABB did not need a large cadre of global managers. Rather, some 500 global managers, or executives with global mandates, would suffice to run a company such as ABB.[3] While this number might be considered large for some companies, it is rather small for a company the size of ABB. Consider yourself in the shoes of any one of the 500 global managers, running a business, segment, or sector somewhere in the ABB organization. Each one of these managers will have to rely on a group of direct reports to deliver on the global mandates. To accomplish this task, these directly reporting managers will need either to have their own global mandates, or to be at least able to work at a global level, that is, they must possess a global mindset. If this were missing, ABB's small cadre of global managers would have an impossible task to accomplish.

Assigning global mandates to business units

Just as we can assign global mandates to individual executives, we may also look at the global mandates assigned to business units, divisions, or other independent organizational units. The nature of the global mandate is relatively recent, and corporations have traditionally not expressed any geographic range in the mission statements of their units. Assigning a global mandate formally to a business unit implies a need to develop a formal global strategy on the part of the business unit management. Corporations who assign such global mandates do so when they believe that a global position is a competitive requirement for the business. Increasingly, business are asked to be among the top group in a certain category, and companies actively collect "firsts", or global top rankings, for their businesses.

Clearly, corporations need to assign global mandates to units that face strong global logic. This would make the requirement to find a global response explicit, and allows corporations to track the progress of the unit over time. What needs to be avoided is the artificial creation of global positions that are intended only to make a business look good, but that ultimately are of no consequence. Assigning global mandates is more than insisting on "Being Number One" since that could be accomplished more simply with large volume in one large market. Many US companies have achieved global "leadership" as measured in size or volume on the basis of competing in the largest market. A *true* global mandate requires the building of a consistent global strategy across the entire relevant global chessboard. A relevant distribution of a firm's revenue reflecting the true global opportunity is a better indicator of a firm's global competitiveness than sales volume leadership, however concentrated.

> ... corporations need to assign global mandates to units that face strong global logic.

A second concern to recognize is the definition of the business, or industry. This is a long-standing issue, and has been hotly debated for many years.[4] With pressure on publicly listed corporations to show consistent improvements in performance and shareholder value, companies sometimes resort to bundling units into categories that are of no strategic importance but are more useful in camouflaging results of ailing, or sub-par units.

> A relevant distribution of a firm's revenue reflecting the true global opportunity is a better indicator of a firm's global competitiveness than sales volume leadership, however concentrated.

Finally, the erroneous assignment of global rankings should remind us of our discussions surrounding global logic and relevant competitive theaters. By combining several business into one overall category, a company may obtain bragging rights of being Number One or Two, but the relevant competitiveness may be more a function of the strength of some sub-units, segments, or sectors. The key test would be the global spiderweb, or global logic chart. Corporations need to make sure that they assign a global mandate for each global logic set, or spiderweb. Thus testing for the presence of one or more spiderwebs, and asking "How many Spiderwebs do you see?" when analyzing a certain sector, becomes of crucial importance in guiding companies in the assignment of relevant global mandates.

To follow up on our discussion on regional versus global logic, it may be appropriate to assign regional mandates to some businesses, such as for Europe, North America, etc. In many international firms, regionally-defined organizational units abound. The danger of the regional mandate is its potential conflict with the execution of a true global strategy. However, for areas where the global logic is weak, or regional at best, it does not add any value to assign a global mandate to the business.

Expressed versus implied global mandates

If a business faces significant global logic in its industry, it is necessary to make the global mandate public and communicate to all concerned the need to craft a global response. The expressed, articulated, and well-communicated global mandate ensures that the management team is responding to the strategic necessity and at the same time allows the corporate team to monitor progress. It is also true, and can be observed under many other circumstances, that formally expressing a mandate affects those charged with executing it. The other side of the coin is to leave it dormant, and to let businesses, or executives, respond as they see fit. In our experience, there are many executives and businesses which operate under a creeping global mandate that is implied but not formalized, and yet the strategy and policies chosen reflect a domestic or at best regional approach. The mere discipline of formally expressing the global mandates, of noticing them in either mission statements for businesses or job descriptions for executives, is a healthy endeavor that has a beneficial impact on the strategic behavior of businesses.

> The expressed, articulated, and well-communicated global mandate ensures that the management team is responding to the strategic necessity and at the same time allows the corporate team to monitor progress.

Globalizing the organizational charter

Assigning expressed global mandates is placing the responsibility in the right hands, and communicating them appropriately. Clearly, this is not the only element of globalizing the organization. What needs to follow is to write the organizational charter in such a way that requisite authority flows with formalized responsibility. In business terms, this requires a company to review the decision-making authority for key business areas and to come to agreement on terms as to what the company would consider a local, regional, or global parameter.

Parameters in a business are key decisions areas relevant for the particular industry. Choice of segments served, research and development, pricing decisions, IT systems, are all parameters that each business needs to assess as to where to place the appropriate responsibility. Typically, these parameters might be categorized into those of a more strategic nature and others of a more operational nature. We should keep in mind that the type of parameters following into either category may differ by business or industry.

The locus of decision making represents the other part of the matrix. Decisions may be made at the local, or subsidiary level. In some companies, regional operating units, such as those for Europe, may play another role calling for regional parameters. Finally, global parameters include decision areas to be made from a global strategic point of view. Reviewing the matrix, the issue faced by companies is to place the appropriate decision-making authority in the hands of the appropriate executives, and to equip the global mandates with the proper amount of authority.

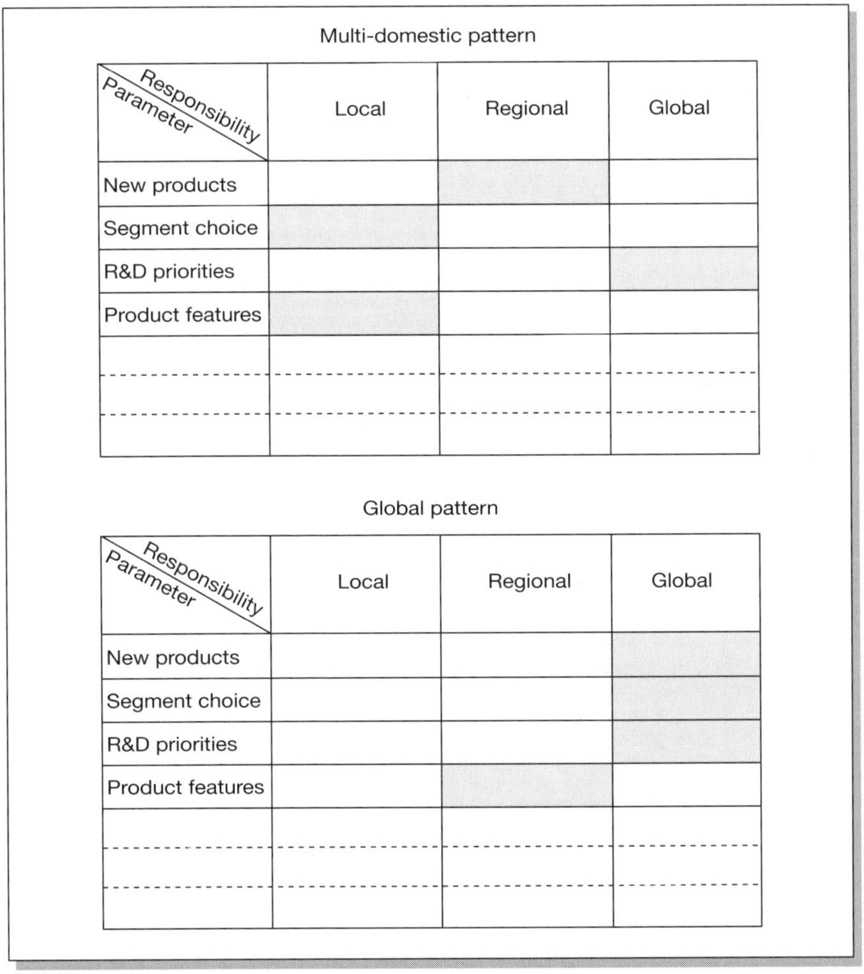

Multi-domestic pattern

Parameter / Responsibility	Local	Regional	Global
New products			
Segment choice			
R&D priorities			
Product features			

Global pattern

Parameter / Responsibility	Local	Regional	Global
New products			
Segment choice			
R&D priorities			
Product features			

Fig 13.2 Local versus global management parameters

Approaching the decision of apportioning the parameters, a review of the company's spiderweb, or global logics, will be of utmost importance. As we have determined earlier, the spiderweb picture will help in figuring out the most important sources of global pressure. These sources, or key logic areas, should be properly represented in the decision matrix. Clearly, areas with strong, or dominating global logic, need to be reflected in the "global parameter" part of the company charter. If that were not so, it would become very difficult for a firm to capitalize on the necessary leverage possibilities if decision-making authority were diluted particularly in those areas. Conversely, areas with low global pressure might be relegated to the status of regional or local parameter.

Lego, the Danish toy manufacturer, had long viewed distribution and pricing sales as a local parameter, whereas branding (its Lego brands) were held to be globally controlled parameters. Changes in the global logic, however, resulting from a change in the purchasing policies of some retailers and the global emergence of Toys-Я-Us as a global powerhouse, have forced the company to review its account management. As a result, merchandising and price coordination have moved up in terms of control, changing from purely local to joint local/regional, and even global parameters. Just as we have observed that changes in the spiderweb are important precursors for changes in the generic global strategy, so too they are indicators of impending changes in the company charter.

Equally important is the relationship between chosen generic global strategy and the organizational charter. Any selected generic strategy requires some key strategic parameters to be global, and companies need to ensure that those required global parameters are in fact in the "global column" when it comes to assigning global mandates and responsibilities. A company selecting a global branding strategy needs to make sure that branding, segmentation, and positioning would be global parameters, otherwise the organizational design would be implicitly rigged against the intended strategy.

Observing the assignment of authority and responsibility in many multinational firms, our experience has indicated that companies tend to place fairly strict controls over operating procedures, such as finance, accounting, human resource policies, IT, and many other procedures that reflect a "company culture" but on their own are not very strategic. Conversely, we have observed that companies have left to their own local organizations considerable degrees of freedom on issues such as launch dates for new products, launch decisions for new products, segments chosen and served, as well as in areas of marketing with respect to positioning, branding, etc. This is in fact opposite to what would be called for,

> Many companies ... need to review their organizational charters and to redistribute responsibility in line with global competitive realities.

given most companies' global logic realities. Many companies therefore need to review their organizational charters and to redistribute responsibility in line with global competitive realities.

Maximizing global leverage

One of the most enduring concepts surrounding globalization and global organizations is the notion of added leverage. Many of today's mergers and reorganizations are built on that notion. Many companies and executives have great difficulties making the leverage concept tangible, and more importantly, many firms indicate pain in finding appropriate leverage points and enhancing their business as a result. Before we discuss ways of finding leverage opportunities for global firms, let us first look at the principle of leverage.

The principle of leverage is based on an understanding that a company can either get more benefits out of critical resources, such as research and development, by expanding globally, or alternatively, two or more organizational units may share critical resources, thus lessening the burden on either unit. Specifically, if a company operates a research and development program for a particular product line, it often finds that those expenditures represent a fixed cost level if a world-class standard is to be reached. This is in line with our critical mass logic (Chapter 5). By expanding into additional markets, this fixed burden is not necessarily increased, but the company can lower it as a percentage of its operating costs. A company can then either lower its cost burden or, in an aggressive case, spend more in absolute terms while keeping the relative burden, thus adding to its competitiveness.

The other approach to leverage is best illustrated when comparing merger benefits. (See figure 13.3.) A German company with a sales volume of $100 million purchases a same size US company. If both firms have equal profitability, the new firm does not manage a higher level of performance for the combined unit unless some common elements between the two are shared. Two approaches can be identified. First, some companies have pursued the path of combined effort by paring the overall expenses in for example, R&D, back to the level of one company. If the acquiring firm had a R&D budget of 10 percent ($10 million), and the acquired firm as well, leverage could be pursued by eliminating one of the R&D units and keeping overall expenditure to the original amount, but reducing the percentage burden. The second path would attempt to combine the two efforts into a single one and make each company compete on the basis of the combination, or $20 million in R&D. If so, each operating unit would experience a benefit equal to a doubling of its R&D resources, effectively doubling its competitiveness, and a substantial business expansion could be expected. These two types of leverage are fundamentally different, and firms

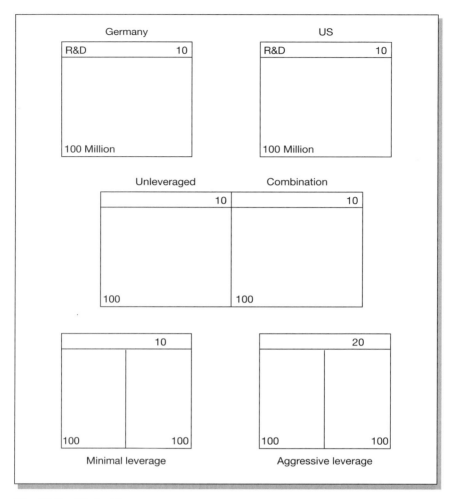

Fig 13.3 Global leverage

will use either one depending on the nature of the situation. In either situation, however, leverage can only occur if the commonality in the business of the operating units is such that they extend to the key operating functions: namely, what cannot be shared or used in multiple geographic territories cannot be leveraged. Finding those commonalities, therefore, is a key element in approaching this task with a global mindset.

The process of locating leverage points for global businesses has its starting points in assessing the common elements versus the local/regional elements of a firm's business. This discussion could possibly be represented by a series of graphs where the common part of a business is depicted on the top part of the chart and the regional, or country-

... what cannot be shared or used in multiple geographic territories cannot be leveraged.

specific parts on the bottom. (See figure 13.4.) The extent of commonality is an assessment to be made by any business team, and it should be clear to the reader that an unlimited amount of options exist. How high, or low, to draw the line that depicts the commonality barrier is a important part of sizing up the global business. In discussions with global business teams in the past, we have used a prototype chart and, through discussions, had the business team assess the commonality by visually lowering or raising the bar.

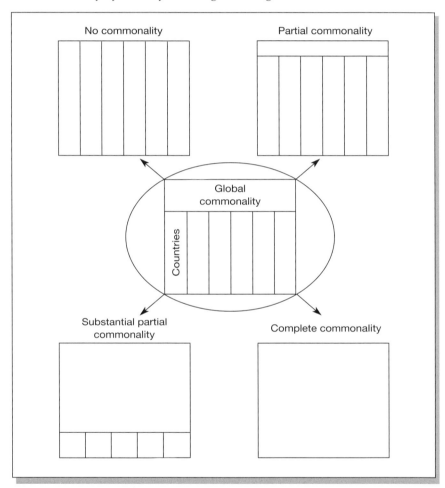

Fig 13.4 Global commonalities

Once the relative amount of commonality versus differences has been addressed, analysis and discussion should now move toward the determination of the elements that go above or below the bar. Here, we can reflect back on our earlier discussion on global versus local parameters, which should represent a helpful start in this discussion. Equally important is the need to review the global logic chart which will also indicate areas that might be leveraged globally.

Global leverage may occur around items that represent major spending activities, programs, business functions, or processes. The connection to major expense items is easier to understand. However, in cases where global logic is more centered on industry KSFs leading to category-type global strategies, leverage is often along processes rather than visible products. A company needs to decide it wants to leverage its brand worldwide, or if it prefers to leverage the process of branding, which is the managerial activity to achieve brand dominance regardless of the brand name used. Alternatively, a company might leverage a given R&D result or the process by which problems are resolved for customers. In general, firms with a high degree of customer related-global logics will be finding more opportunities to leverage "finished products" or decisions, whereas firms facing more of the hidden type of industrial global logics will find it easier to leverage processes.

> **Global leverage may occur around items that represent major spending activities, programs, business functions, or processes.**

Global integration versus global standardization

The benefits of achieving leverage globally are substantial. Although the financial impact via cost savings are often cited as the most important ones, in reality the potential from resource sharing and making individual units compete with the total group resource is more far-reaching. This stems from the fact that there is a fundamental difference between global integration to achieve leverage and the more commonly viewed attempt to standardize to achieve cost savings (figure 13.5).

Global standardization strategies are efforts to simultaneously conduct a given activity in the same way, regardless of country or region.[5] The result is a clearly visible level of standardization where a large number of operating units engage in the same activity in the same way. In the extreme, a company might clone similar operating companies around the world engaging in business the same way. As we have seen from earlier descriptions, leverage implies the concept of operating units around the world sharing a critical resolve whereby either one unit does something for all the others, or all units jointly share in one single activity. Standardization can occur, in the extreme, without sharing, and results in duplicative operations, each on their own, each engaging in business in the same way. Leverage or sharing always implies that some activity is done for all and not duplicated necessarily in each business location around the world.

The challenge for global companies today is to move beyond the concept of global standardization. Standardization is a heritage from the multi-domestic mindset whereby companies opened many similar operating units to be independent: companies went around the world and cloned mini-firms that had the full complement of activities. They were identical to the parent firm, or very nearly identical. This fostered standardization in business practices and processes, but was difficult to convert into a enterprise where, through leverage, multiple units tapped into a global network to avoid duplication of expensive resources. The latter process we have called leverage. Most firms we have come

The challenge for global companies today is to move beyond the concept of global standardization.

across in our research can be described as over-standardized and under-leveraged, a situation which suggests there exists a still considerable number of opportunities to make global firms more efficient and competitive.

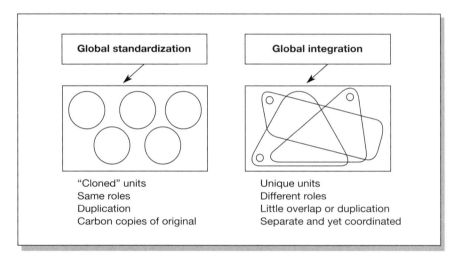

Global standardization	Global integration
"Cloned" units	Unique units
Same roles	Different roles
Duplication	Little overlap or duplication
Carbon copies of original	Separate and yet coordinated

Fig 13.5   Standardization versus integration

In line with global mandates, globalized organizational charters, and a need to maximize global leverage, the organizational forms of companies desiring to compete with a global mindset will require adjustment. With the divisional organizations so typical of the multi-domestic or multinational mindset, we cannot fight the global competitive battles of tomorrow. In the context of this chapter, we will only be able to provide a glimpse of some of these new archetypal organizational forms.

First, the time of the "cloned" organization, with similar fully-fledged units in multiple markets, has ended. Companies need to move to a more dedicated format where individual functions, or activities, will be placed in the best

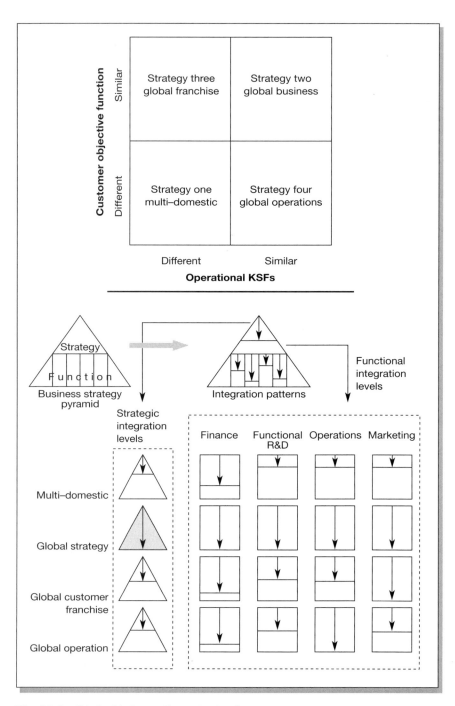

Fig 13.6   Global integration strategies

possible country. This results in a function-specific investment policy where the new global company will scan the world opportunity for locating specific activities. Research units may be placed near the best available research talent pool anywhere in the world. Production units can be situated in areas where the most efficient production unit costs can be assured. Finance will be near the most sophisticated financial centers, and marketing may be near the most advanced customers as dictated by the market.

A look at the first few years of Logitech, a Swiss/US maker of computer input devices, such as the mouse, is probably a harbinger of this type of strategy.[6] In the early 1980s, the company had hardware research and finance mainly driven from Switzerland, software and marketing strategy from California, and production was located in Taiwan. Even the head office, legally maintained in Switzerland, was viewed as "up in the air" as the company's founders and main executives shuttled between its Swiss and California bases. What was unusual about the early operation of Logitech was the presence of functionally oriented centers, focused on a limited set of activities, while dotting the landscape with sales offices for many markets.

Logitech, as many readers will correctly point out, was a start-up firm without prior company history and thus able to make choices a long-established multinational firm could not make. Observing the behavior of existing multinationals, both US- and Europe-based, indicates, however, that even firms with long histories of full-fledged operating subsidiaries are moving towards the Logitech model. As part of moving towards pan-European strategies, established firms have begun to review the organizational charters of their European operating companies. Many companies have instituted pan-European manufacturing approaches whereby local manufacturing operations are folded into a regional function with its own leadership no longer under the control of the local country head. The same has been the case of research activities where many small markets maintained sub-critical operations that needed to be folded into an integrated and coordinated pan-European research thrust. Again, local operating heads lost control over those units, although they may not have been moved and often remained in their previous facilities. In line with this trend, marketing strategy, often developed and delivered on a per-country basis, is also folded into a regional unit with pan-European marketing operations taking hold.

One of the most recent developments can be observed in administrative functions such as finance, accounting, and control. Dow Chemical, operating traditionally dispersed units in each country, moved towards consolidation whereby parts of the activities became concentrated in certain countries, different from operating the full accounting and control function in each subsidiary. In the next phase, many of these activities dispersed across Europe can be folded into a single "accounting factory" that could be placed anywhere in Europe where the infrastructure is supportive.

The specter of pan-European consolidation can be observed on a global basis as well. The process of concentration across twelve or fifteen main European markets does not substantially differ from a process of concentrating key activities into a dozen leading world markets as dictated by a companies global chessboard. Local country management has continued to lose some degree of freedom, shrinking the charter of the local unit more and more into a function-specific business unit dedicated to sales and local market support. Key functions will be placed with specific considerations into most suitable parts of the world, thus changing the role of local management and strengthening the role of newly appointed global heads in functions such as manufacturing, research, IT, and others, all areas that used to be organized on a staff reporting basis, and not with line responsibility over people in many different locations.

While this type of concentration might be viewed as a process to increase head office control over local units, it needs to be pointed out the head office is itself being reconfigured. Our view of head office as a fixed location with large offices and the circular driveway with the proverbial number of flag poles representing global reach may be a thing of the past. For many business units with global mandates, head office is where the group of key executives happen to be, and this might be at a place other than where the administrative head office is located. Just as in a navy fleet the chosen position of the admiral connotes the flagship, and thus the point from where the battle is to be directed, so do present-day business unit teams select their position for "residence" by picking one of its operating units as the base as the global competitive battle requires it. For companies such as Siemens and ABB, many of the operating units with global mandates have their head office not only away from corporate headquarters, but also in different countries. Location may be driven by lead markets, as we discussed in Chapter 8, allowing the key executive team to be situated in the market that tends to be ahead of others, thus assuring that the business picks up on the leading trends as early as possible.

⊖ Moving toward a globalized organization

A global, or globalized, strategy needs to go in tandem with a global, or globalized, organization otherwise the best-laid plans will be difficult, if not impossible, to implement.

In this chapter, we wanted to make it clear that managing with a global mindset involved more than setting a strategic course of action. The full unfolding of any global strategy, whatever form it might take, requires a corresponding adjustment in the company's organization. The creation of multiple forms of global mandates, which we have suggested in this chapter, demands that companies follow up with a corresponding move on responsibility assignment that breaks down the barrier of parceling out executive responsibility on a purely geographical basis. The organizational forms of the 1980s will invariably stifle the freedom required to fully develop the global strategies demanded in coming decades. A global, or globalized, strategy needs to go in tandem with a global, or globalized, organization otherwise the best-laid plans will be difficult, if not impossible, to implement.

Notes

1. "P&G will make Jager CEO ahead of schedule", *Wall Street Journal*, 10 September, 1998, p. B1.

2. Ibid., p. B8.

3. "The logic of global business: an interview with ABB's Percy Barnevik", *Harvard Business Review*, March–April 1991, pp. 91–105.

4. Derek F. Abell and John S. Hammond, *Strategic Market Planning*, Prentice-Hall, New Jersey, 1979.

5. Jean-Pierre Jeannet "Global Integration of Business Strategies," *Leadership in Global Markets*, Harvard Business School Publishing Division, Corporate Leaders Forum 1988, pp. 167–174.

6. Vijay Jolly, *Logitech International S.A.*, IMD Case Study, Lausanne, 1991.

Building global minds for individual managers

In the previous chapters, we have made a strong argument for populating globally thinking companies with a sufficient number of managers who execute on global mandates. We have also described the type of strategies they might pursue, and how they might interpret global logics and the global chessboard for guidance in crafting the relevant global strategy for their firm. It is now time to go into more detail on the personal make-up of the global mindset as it affects individual managers.

What does a global mindset have to know, be able to do, and how should it function as distinctly different from the traditional mindset that has governed domestic or multi-domestic business practices?

The global mindset, or the global manager, is often described as a type of executive that can be sent anywhere, travel extensively, and is able to execute his managerial responsibility from any point in the world. At the same time, we hear from companies that, while there is some opportunity for such managers in the modern globalizing firm, only a small cadre of such managers is needed. We have seen in the previous chapter that the need for global mindsets in most companies is far greater and goes beyond those few who might be sent on a constant tour of the world.

This idea of the global mindset as a roving globetrotter is probably overblown, and clearly, managers possessing, or aspiring to a global mindset, need to come equipped with a globalized database, or some factual knowledge that is different from the domestic mindset. Furthermore, they need to be able to view the world differently. And finally, their thinking patterns, responses, and cognitive skills differ sharply from a traditional domestic or even multi-domestic mindset.

Components of the global mindset[1]

Global data bank

Let us start with the factual knowledge of the global mindset. In this day and age where the Internet reigns, and where so much data are available on the World Wide Web for instant consumption, the need to come to global competitive battle equipped with a hard disk with key data is not very fashionable. However, too many managers, although claiming to be able to look up anything they need to know, are more likely than not to proceed to make judgments on what they already know, oblivious to the fact that they may miss crucial data points. So the status of your hard disk containing key, or relevant data, is of importance as it shapes your thinking, analysis, and decisions.

From my experience observing how successful global managers operate, their database differs in as much as they had accumulated necessary facts on the world in different ways, and stored the data in different categories. Traditionally, as we argued in Chapter 3, most managers grew up in a limited cultural experience, attending school and early professional education in the same cultural environment, thus having little exposure to other countries, or regions. Most of the facts accumulated in school concerning history, economic systems, political systems, and business practices tended to be shaped by exposure to a single culture. Clearly, global mindsets have to become exposed to data about the world that are not only country specific, but also global in nature.

⊜ Acquiring key market knowledge

Just as we have expounded in Chapter 7 reviewing the global chessboard that global strategies concentrate on the key markets for a given industry, we should restrict the market or industry knowledge of the global mindset to the top markets as dictated by a given industry. In most situations, this might rarely exceed the top 20 markets. For practical circumstances, let us then reflect on our own businesses and pose some questions:

What are the top 20 markets in our industry?

This question centers around the industry-specific global chessboards, the largest and most important markets, or countries. Of great importance here are the countries that we could classify as "must win" or "must have" to succeed globally. From our own experience, this is not always easy for managers to list since many of them have country-specific responsibility only. Clearly, the global mindset would have a clear picture of the relevant top 20 markets in his or her own industry.

Once we have the list of markets to be understood, there is now a series of questions that can be posed on each of them. So, if you want to demonstrate for yourself that you have the requisite knowledge, continue with the next questions, each of which would have to be posed for each of a firm's top markets.

However, we are not only interested in factual knowledge as expressed in numbers, statistics, or key words. The knowledge we would like to have accumulated would be written down in the form of two or three paragraphs, or in prose form, which is always more difficult than in bullet form, statistics, or names, or other abbreviated facts.[2]

What are a key country's defining historic moments?

Under defining moments we understand those historical developments, actions, or events that shape a country's current behavior, or its soul as it were. This does not consist of a long list of dates, battles, or government leaders. Instead it requires a keen understanding of a country's history and an ability to select the most important developments from a myriad activities. The best place to start might be your own home country, and see if you can settle on the five defining moments (selectivity is key). In a second phase, it would be important to find the equivalent important events in the top 20 markets. These events would then be written down in a prose narrative and connected. This would constitute a first phase of historical understanding.

One of my visits to Finland, a country in which I was fortunate enough to meet many outstanding managers, I was confronted by a group of senior managers from an international company. In my discussions with the CEO of that company, he indicated to me that Finnish managerial behavior could be understood if one learned to appreciate the experience of Finland during World War II when two wars were fought against the then Soviet Union. Clearly, in the minds of those managers, the Finnish-Russian wars of that time were such defining moments that shaped the consciousness of Finnish management to this day. Any foreign manager visiting Finland would have to learn about this event.

Likewise, each country has its own defining moments of history, some more recent, others in the distant past.

What are a key country's defining cultural moments?

Just as there are defining moments in history, so too there are defining moments in culture. Each country has its own cultural heritage, its leading artists, writers, musicians, painters, sculptures, and so on. Defining moments in the cultural development of a country could go back centuries and might be equated with the source of the present language, its writing, its religious background, and possibly even its social background in terms of societal structure. All of these elements combine into a narrative that could be structured around key, or defining, cultural events. The challenge is to summarize those defining cultural moments in a couple of paragraphs on the key countries.

What is the economic system and performance of a key market?

Clearly, as managers, we need to understand the economic system or structure of a given country. This might include knowledge of its key industries, its foreign trade position, particular competitive advantage, and understanding how the business and society function in that country. The role of stock markets, the role of private versus public capital and ownership, and the regulatory environment are part of this understanding. A knowledge of the foreign exchange situation would be part of such an understanding. I am often reminded how difficult it is for certain managers to have discussions around financial data in other than their home currency. Global mindsets can handle multiple currencies!

Apart from the existing structure, we would need to be able to address current issues in the economic system, such as if the country were in expansionary or recessionary mode, if there was an unemployment problem, if consumption was expanding, etc. Such knowledge would allow managers to gain an understanding of the forward movement of an economy beyond this static structure.

What is a key country's political system?

Knowledge should include the existing political structure and decision-making process as well as the government structure. Managers need to know the way a country appointed its key government officials, either by election or by appointment, the role of parliaments, the role of national versus local and regional governments, and the power distribution along judiciary, government, and legislature. Familiarity with major political parties, or philosophies, would be part of such knowledge.

As in the case of a country's economy, knowledge of current political issues and debates are important. The political system of any government is often intertwined with the economic and cultural system, and the astute analyst would need to disentangle the entire "plumbing system" of a country's power structure or decision making.[3] These governance systems differ, and any anticipation of a given country's reactions to future political or economic moves depends on an accurate understanding of those relationships.

What are the relevant business practices in a key country?

This explanation would govern prevalent business culture, or behavior, as relevant to the conduct of business in that country. It would be necessary to know this for interaction with executives from that country, or for active involvement in visits, negotiations, and executing business transactions in that key market.

Although some of this is often reported in rather simplistic forms, it would range from greeting executives to booking appointments and other person-to-person interactions.

At the risk of digressing, I would like to recall a personal experience that might demonstrate to the reader what I mean by this. I frequently make visits to European firms on behalf of Babson College. In many of those visits, or in the context of contacts, I am accompanied by American colleagues. As is customary for them, they quickly switch into a first name situation with the foreign visitor. This is typically not the norm for interaction among Europeans, even if one knows the other party well. This results in the curious situation where I, as the European with the personal contact with the visitor, remain in the more formal address modes, while my American colleagues easily banter on a first name basis. This creates discomfort for our hosts that typically goes unnoticed by the others involved.

What are the major geographic features of the key country?

In many instances executives divulge gross lack of appreciation of the geographies of a country and as a result have to accept a lesser standing in negotiations, or loss of authority. While no one is expected to "know everything that fits a map," it needs to be pointed out that a spatial understanding of countries is needed without constant recourse to a map. This may include the location of major cities, the understanding about the topography of a country, the neighboring countries, and a sense of distance (or should I say flight distance?) between major cities.

Why should a manager with a global mindset know such detailed, or non-strategic facts? This is a question I am often asked. My only response is to revert back to experience and observations of many conversations between international executives. Many times executives make decisions for which there is no opportunity for a fully fledged search of all the facts. In fact, precisely because of a lack of specific knowledge leads to the conclusion that "there is no need to search further" often leads to biased decisions against certain countries, or regions. The argument that, when in need, all relevant facts can be looked up, does not hold because one often only looks up facts one deems relevant for search. Up to that point, executives depend on their own perceptions, or limited knowledge. A limited data bank on the key market, therefore, results in decisions that might be made differently if the full set of circumstances where known.

There is also a difference among managers from different cultures on how to deal with that. American education tends to downplay knowledge acquisition, particularly in the area of history and geography. European educational systems, and the Eastern European ones in particular, favor far greater knowledge in those matters. An American executive encountering a European, or Latin American, while displaying gross lack of such knowledge risks losing credibility, which might result in either a reduced ability to convince the other party of a new plan, or reduced negotiation ability in a transaction. This risk to credibility should not be underestimated.

Understanding the global superstructure

Up to now, we have discussed knowledge that should be present with respect to the leading markets, whether defined in general terms or as it applies to the markets faced by an internationally active firm. For global mindsets, however, there is also a need to understand what we call the global superstructure of the same items, namely history, culture, economy, and political systems defined in global terms. This is relatively new knowledge, and differs from the understanding about countries in the more traditional "domestic" context. In our view, the data bank of the aspiring global mindset is not complete without an analytical and full understanding of those elements.

Global history differs from traditional, single-country history, as it covers historic developments that transcend a single country. Examples of such historic works that cover broad global, or regional trends include Kennedy's *The Rise and Fall of the Great Powers*, Rougemont's *The Idea of Europe*, de Reynold's *Tragic Europe*, or Spenglers *The Decline of the West*.[4] Viewing historic thought in global, or regional, terms is part of gaining a global perspective and will aid in building a perspective that goes beyond the country-specific knowledge discussed earlier.

A global mindset would also need a thorough understanding of the global economic system. This understanding would embrace appreciation for the interconnected economy. The world economy is more than the sum total of the individual country economies as described earlier. It consists of a system that connects the world, covers both trade and finance, the world capital markets, and the major trade areas. It also includes the working of the various international economic and trade bodies, such as the WTO in Geneva, IMF, World Bank, and the many regional bodies, such as the European Union, Nafta, etc. Particularly during late 1997 into 1998, as we have seen major economic crises move through many parts of Asia, Russia, and Latin America, a manager who would like to possess a global mindset would be expected to understand the complexities and ramifications of these trends.

The global political system, which includes global political developments over and beyond political trends in any individual country, is another domain that will challenge the global mindset. Global political trends may be both security based, or contain major trends in philosophy, regional trends such as the events in Europe leading to the European Union (EU), and the sweeping trends concerning the change from state-traded nations to liberalized free-trade economies. These changes that took place in the area previously dominated by the former Soviet Union has created major changes in Europe and elsewhere. Managers with a global mindset would thus be expected to appreciate such developments over and above the specific political developments in key markets.

> **What appears to be important is that the new, global, mindset could not go into competitive battle with a data bank outdated not only in factual content, but in structure as well.**

In the context of this book it would be impossible to do full justice to the complete data bank suggested for a global mindset. What appears to be important is that the new, global, mindset could not go into competitive battle with a data bank outdated not only in factual content, but in structure as well. That new structure would need to encompass an understanding of the world at large in a broader context where knowledge cut across individual countries.

Cross-cultural skills

So far we have emphasized the cognitive skills consisting of the conceptual understanding and the factual knowledge of the world. As many of our readers who have extensive international business experience will appreciate, there are also behavioral skills that involve the interaction between managers from many countries, or cultures. These cross-cultural skills are an essential part of the global mindset. Described in great detail in the works of Trompenaars,[5] cross-cultural skills have to be seen in context. It becomes impossible to train managers for all cultures they might possibly encounter, so it may be that an international manager needs to work with, or face up to, nationalities or cultures for which he or she does not have in-depth training.

One of the most frequently posed question in the context of cross-cultural effectiveness is the notion of foreign language skills. Does a global mindset need to have extensive foreign language skills? This is a difficult issue, and in some parts of the world more emphasis has been placed on acquiring foreign languages than in others. The reality of the global business environment has moved heavily into the direction of English as the lingua franca reducing the incentive to learn other languages for business purposes. Observing discussions among executives in many parts of the world, it is clear that managers select the language where they can talk with the highest common denominator. In practice, it means that a German executive with limited French but good English, meeting a French manager speaking limited German but good English, will opt to engage in a conversation in English, a language foreign to both of them, rather than carry out a discussion in one of the languages spoken possibly haltingly by one of the partners. As English has risen in dominance, becoming the first foreign language in most countries, it has assumed the role of the common language in many international firms, particularly European ones. Companies such as Nestlé (with head office in the French part of Switzerland), or Roche (with head office in the German part of Switzerland), or ABB (joint Swedish-Swiss firm) have easily adopted English as their corporate language. The rise of English as the first foreign language taught in an increasing number of countries has reduced the incentive to learn foreign languages, a trend that is certainly very pronounced in English-speaking countries today. The pervasive use of electronic mail and the World Wide Web, most of it English based, has further contributed to the dominance of English.

I would like to repeat some advice I have often given to aspiring young global managers from many countries. When a company is appointing an executive for a foreign assignment that might take up several years, there is usually an implicit understanding that the candidate acquire a knowledge of the local language. For many of the regular visits, or frequent travel and meetings attended, the mix of nationalities is often so unpredictable that English as the operating language will suffice. I might add here, it should be the type of English that is not too heavily loaded with idioms, which is not easy for either British or American-English speakers.

While this might appear to give native English speakers a free ride, we might want to consider the reason often cited for learning foreign languages. Typically, it is advanced that the learning process generates a deeper understanding of the culture, and that language represents a key to a foreign culture. While this is true, it is also a very time-consuming way to learn a foreign culture. Much can be learned about a foreign country, or culture, by studying materials in one's mother tongue, such as the foreign country's history, cultural background, political and economic systems, as outlined earlier in this chapter. From personal observation of working with executives from many cultures and countries, it has often proved to be more important to discuss the foreign country's environment in English, demonstrating good understanding, than try to ask in a halting way for some basic necessities of life, such as ordering coffee or a drink, in an effort to demonstrate cultural empathy with your hosts. I am fully aware that, at least among those executives that I would characterize as possessing an international, or even multinational mindset (Chapter 3), the reliance on full foreign language capability is much greater.

Cultural roots for global mindsets

Many readers may now have the impression that this new global mindset we are proposing for individual managers would go in the direction of an uprooted individual wandering the world without any deep roots in any part of it. This would be far from the mark. While the global mindset would be able to maintain an equidistance in cultural terms and thus be a manager who might be above the fray, so to speak, there is no doubt that a person needs cultural roots somewhere for personal balance. Gonzague de Reynold,[6] a Swiss historian, wrote eloquently about his relationship to Cressier, his home town, in terms of concentric circles:

> You are the center of my life, the field where my stake is placed, from where I am able to pull on my cord in all directions, all the way to the end of this world, and where my cord will always bring me back. This is the place where I can always find refuge when I have the feeling of being lost, when I am hesitating, or suffering from doubts. In my case, the whole world turns around you.

In similar vein, the global mindset is a manager that is operating from a long rope, or cord, with a large radius, not constrained by ethnocentric views, but grounded in a home country culture for personal balance.

The spirit of generosity

In a recent conference held at IMD, I was discussing global mindsets with a group of experienced managers. One of them pointed out that a quality that often missing was "generosity," which was interpreted as magnanimity. During discussions, meetings, or when disagreements occured, this manager meant that the quality of personal generosity, which allowed for others to proceed even if it was not exactly what was initially requested, went a long way towards a functioning global company.

Notes

1. This section borrows heavily from Chapter 7 in Jean-Pierre Jeannet, and David H. Hennessey, *Global Marketing Strategies*, Houghton Mifflin, 4th edn, 1998.
2. For those readers who would like to go through the key country market data exercise without any affiliation to a given industry, use the list of the top 20 countries by GNP to assess your knowledge accordingly.
3. The notion of "plumbing system" as a metaphor for a country's government structure we owe to Clifton Clarke, a former senior executive at Digital Equipment who had extensive experience in government relations.

4. Paul Kennedy, *The Rise and Fall of the Great Powers*, Random House, New York, 1987; Denis de Rougemont, *The Idea of Europe*, MacMillan, 1966 (translation of the original in French under the title *Les vingt-huit Siècles d'Europe*); Gonzague de Reynold, *L'Europe Tragique*, Spes, Paris, 1935; Oswald Spengler, *The Decline of the West*, (translated by Ch. F. Atkinson), Knopf, New York, 1928.

5. Fons Trompenaars, *Riding the Waves of Culture*, The Economist Book, London, 1993.

6. Gonzague de Reynold, *Cité et Pays Suisse*, Payot, 1948, final version, p. 3.

Implementing corporate global mindsets

Having spent a considerable amount of time defining the contours of the individual global mindset, we need to recognize that companies, through their operating culture, can also be said to possess (or miss) a global mindset of their own. For the purpose of this chapter we shall call this the corporate global mindset to encompass those cultural aspects of a company that define the extent to which the firm has learned to think, behave, and operate in global terms.

The observation that it is not only individuals, but companies as well that need to adopt a global mindset we owe to some feedback on earlier material on behalf of a internationally experienced manager. As we pursued this area in greater depth, partly through discussions, and partly through conferences and lectures, it became clear that at a time when we often discuss intellectual capital, the ability of an entire firm to operate with a global mindset could assume the role of a competitive advantage.

Our understanding of the corporate global mindset is built upon the assumption that even if a company were populated with an adequate pool of managers, each possessing a global mindset, this would be insufficient if the company as a whole, through its structure, processes, and behavior, did not also espouse the same principles.

We begin with a diagnostic that might be used by companies to determine the extent of the global mindset of the firm. Since each of the questions asked in the context of this diagnosis reflects some underlying assumptions, we discuss each of them and explain in

> ... the ability of an entire firm to operate with a global mindset could assume the role of a competitive advantage.

detail how they might be answered. The second part of this chapter will reflect on the actual global logics faced by a firm and review any particular fit needed between the global logic set and the firm's corporate global mindset. Finally, there are some suggestions as to how the corporate global mindset might be expanded to assist in the development of global strategies required by each business.

Diagnosing the corporate global mindset

Needless to say, the questions asked here reflect the preferences and biases of this author. The reader will recognize their conceptual origin from studying previous chapters. The explanation supplied here will thus be short, and in case a given concept is not familiar, the reader is directed to the appropriate chapter of this book.

We have structured the questions into three broad groups. First, we will look at the strategic situation faced by a corporation, or company. The second set of questions deals with the managerial pool of a firm and its global qualities. The third set of questions is aimed at organizational realities. The primary purposes of this material are to enable companies to reflect on the status of their corporate global mindset and to begin moving in a direction that allows for a higher degree of global thinking throughout their organizations.

Although the questions asked are broad, we suggest that they be answered in terms of quartiles, or percentages. It is not necessary to keep precision, but what tends to work best is if a company look at its questions in terms of rough quartiles, such as 0, 25, 50, 75 or 100 percent. A company giving itself a score of 100 percent would be completly fulfilling the content address in that particular question. An answer of zero would indicate total absence of that quality, with answers of 25, 50, or 75 percent placed in between. This judgment results in the perceived level of global mindset. It is only a start, but the answers in other circumstances have proved robust enough that managers are comfortable to work with them.

Looking at the business strategies pursued by the firm

Our first questions are directed at the corporation operating a number of businesses. If a company were relatively focused, this might apply to each segment, SBU, or profit center, however the firm prefers to define the appropriate unit of analysis.

What number of businesses should actually compete on a global scale?

Looking at a company's businesses (as defined in relevant terms for the firm), an assessment needs to be made as to how many should compete on a global scale. If more useful, the unit of analysis might be segments, sectors, or some other way to organize the company's total business into identifiable sub-components. Clearly, the fundamental answer is driven by the extent of global logic present in each firm, and to what extent none, some, or all of these businesses are compelled to pursue a global strategy. In some companies, this might easily amount to 100 percent. It is conceivable, however, that some firms might find only some of its businesses require that approach.

Are there businesses with explicit global mandates?

Using the same unit of analysis as utilized in the previous question, a look at the global mandates would tell us how many of those business actually operate with expressed, or explicit global mandates. Checking their mission statements would indicate the extent to which corporation passed on formal global mandates to each business.

A company with a high degree of corporate global mindset would have all businesses operating under strong global logic running with expressed global mandates. This step, undertaken from a corporate center, is a strong expression of global interest. Rather than letting this decision be taken by operating managers, the company drives the process. Our argument is that such a step is a clear indication of the advanced stage of a global mindset of a company as it gives the company an opportunity to set public goals for each of its businesses. Furthermore, it gives the company a chance to review those goals in a next step, which are expressed global strategies.

How large is the corporate volume generated by businesses operating under expressed global mandates?

We would like to know if the business volume operating under global mandates is a small percentage, moderate, or large percentage of the total business volume. This indicator would prevent a company with a number of small, but global businesses, combined with one or two large but domestic businesses, from giving the false impression of globality.

Companies with a high degree of corporate global mindset are likely to be firms which have a substantial amount of their business volume subject to global, formally expressed mandates. A high percentage in this category could be used as another indicator measuring global thinking in a firm.

How many businesses operate under a formal global strategy?

The focus of the question is not only the global logic and the assignment of expressed global mandates. With this additional step, we would like to learn how many of those business have formalized global strategies. If we review their strategy papers, would we find clearly expressed global strategies covering the relevant part of the world market? Or, alternatively, would we find a series of regional or country strategies that had been pulled together in a single, global budget, without any formal global integration?

A company that operates with a strong global mindset would most likely go beyond assigning global mandates. Having formal strategies, written plans,

Expressed, formal, global strategies allow corporate management to review business performance and to engage in a strategic dialog that influences the execution of the assigned global mandate.

and clearly documented goals that make it clear to all concerned that the business in question operated under some form of global strategy (see Chapter 10, on generic global strategies) would be the strongest indicator that a company had moved beyond superficiality. Expressed, formal, global strategies allow corporate management to review business performance and to engage in a strategic dialog that influences the execution of the assigned global mandate.

Looking at a firm's managerial talent pool

The previous set of questions dealt primarily with the business pressures and the competitive environment faced by a company's businesses. However, as we pointed out in previous chapters, the creation of well-thought-out global plans is likely to fail if a sufficient cadre of individual global mindsets is not present. It is the presence of the individual executive talent pool that is the focus of our next round of questions.

How many managers understand their business in global terms?

Looking at the senior and middle manager pool of executives, we would like to have an assessment of the number of managers that can actually think about their business in global terms. The type of thinking, outlined in detail in Section 1, 2 and 3 of this book, particularly along the lines of global logics, global chessboards, and generic global strategies, should serve as a guidance for the assessment.

This question is based on the assumption that companies need to have their global ambitions supported by a talent pool that is able to think globally. The mere handing out of global mandates and insistence on the development of global strategies alone does not ensure that the firm actually operates with a global mindset. Under the worst case scenario, a company might find itself pushing very hard for global strategies developed by executives who operate under a domestic, or multi-domestic mindset. Only global mandates carried out by the individual who possesses an individual global mindset can be assured of a reasonable chance of success.

How many managers in upper management pool operate under global mandates?

We would like to know the percentage of managers that operate under formalized global mandates. These mandates could be formulated, as we pointed out earlier, for a business, a function, a segment, a sector, or a task force.

Even executives who, as individuals, possess a global mindset, would find it difficult to operate if their firm did not grant them global mandates with the prerequisite authority to cut across geographic lines. A firm that prides itself on a corporate global mandate would thus have to create a pool of global mandates which would supersede many of the traditional local or regional lines of authority. This question would quickly ferret out firms that had not yet put their money where their mouth was, as we so nicely say in the USA.

Looking at a firm's organization

If global mandates measure the amount of cross-border authority assigned to executives in an organization, we can now see clearly that individual global mindsets can be frustrated, or prevented from executing their mandates, if a company's organization is not properly adjusted for the new task. The organizational features have been pointed out extensively in Chapter 13. As a result, the following questions give the reader an opportunity to review a firm's global mindset along organizational capabilities. An inappropriate organization can prevent companies from realizing their global ambitions. A company with a strongly developed global mindset would naturally possess organizational features that would be in line with its global intent.

> … individual global mindsets can be frustrated, or prevented from executing their mandates, if a company's organization is not properly adjusted for the new task.

> An inappropriate organization can prevent companies from realizing their global ambitions.

At which level does the first geographic split in organization occur?
Our first question deals with the presence, or absence of a geographic split in the organization. A company in which the managerial responsibility is divided at the highest levels along geographical lines, such as regional mandates for North America, Europe, or Asia–Pacific regions, would have a much lower level of global mindset than a company where such a split occurs only in the second, third, or even fourth level of management. Since we would have to convert this fact to a ranking along percentage lines, we view a first-level geographic split as the inverse of a high global mindset.

This rating needs some additional explanations. We saw in Chapter 13 that the changing corporate charters commensurate with the pursuit of global strategies require that key strategic parameters are assigned to a

> Extensive regionalization of managerial responsibility is tantamount to building roadblocks to global thinking, thus a company with strong regional organizations would be viewed as one having difficulty applying a global mindset to its thinking, behavior, and actions.

global responsibility. However, if a company were to split its managerial responsibility along geographic lines, it would become very difficult to execute along global mandates. In fact, it can be said that in a company where the a business is organized first along geographic lines, only the CEO possesses a true global mandate. Extensive regionalization of managerial responsibility is tantamount to building roadblocks to global thinking, thus a company with strong regional organizations would be viewed as one having difficulty applying a global mindset to its thinking, behavior, and actions.

How many functional managerial positions operate under global mandates?

This question gets at the number of managers who operate below the level of the senior line managers, namely in functional positions. Functions covered might be R&D, production, marketing, finance, etc. We would like to know how many managers at that level operate under expressed global mandates, which would signify that they act out their responsibilities on a global basis.

Observing global firms with a strong corporate global mindset, we have noticed that for those firms global mandates exist on functional levels. Particularly for businesses that operate under assigned global mandates, the necessity arose to structure functional positions, or some staff positions, with global responsibility. It is obvious that if such global mandates were rare, a company would signal a less developed global mindset.

How many teams or task forces have global mandates?

Most firms operate a large number of task forces on either a permanent or temporary basis. Permanent task forces are groups that carry out standing assignments. Temporary ones might have been created for a single purpose and, when task are completed, might be disbanded. For the purpose of our question, we would like readers to think about the incidence of having such task forces or teams operate with expressed global mandates as opposed to local responsibilities only. A company with a high percentage of teams or task forces operating with global assignments is believed to show more of a global mindset. Conversely, a company where such assignments are rare is believed to demonstrate less of a corporate global mindset.

Companies will invariably need to deal with a number of tasks on a group or task force basis. A firm where all task forces operate only within the assigned country, for example, with US-based managers meeting only among themselves, will have remarkably less of a global mindset than firms where the task force includes managers from not only the USA, but also from other countries. In some situations, these teams may have to function in other ways than meeting formally in the same room or a single location. More often, global teams will be operating virtually using modern communications technology to stay in touch.

Extent of global IT structure?

This question focusses on a firm's information technology infrastructure and assesses the extent to which it has been globalized. A globalized IT infrastructure would allow members of the company, although operating in different countries, to enter the same, or centralized databases. Could sales teams operating on a global account tap into the same database although they are doing it from different countries? Can a manager from any office send electronic mail to others and access the technology regardless of office location? A firm where the total IT infrastructure was globalized would be considered high on the global mindset chart, and a firm where the IT was strictly country based with few connections would be viewed very low.

The rationale for this rating is related to the previous question. To have a global organization requires that each part easily communicate with others. Where this ease of communication is absent, barriers to global communications exist and a corporate global mindset is more difficult to achieve.

Mapping out the corporate global mindset

Having assessed a company's position along these questions, we can now turn our attention to mapping out the extent of a company's corporate global mindset. Employing the same approach as we used in Chapter 6 to assess global logic, we can depict progress along each dimension by moving from the center point of the chart (depicting zero globalization for the particular question) to its perimeter (indicating full globalization according to the question). A corporate footprint thus emerges that allows a firm to assess the extent to which it already satisfies its global capabilities in terms of business strategies, individual and organizational capabilities.

Fit with global logic

Once the corporate global mindset has been assessed, it now remains to interpret the results and to relate them to our earlier diagnostics applied to the global strategy for a given business. We would expect that companies that face substantial global logic pressure would be equipped with extensive corporate global mindsets, indicating an ability to live up to their challenge.

When discussing the relationship between global logic and global mindset, it has been pointed out by experienced managers that the organizational capability should actually be leading the requirements faced in the market, rather

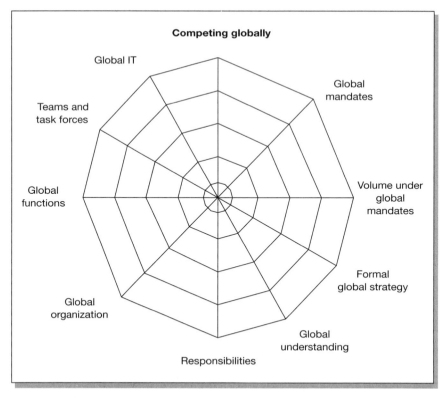

Fig 15.1 Corporate global mindset map

than the other way around. This would lead us to suggest that the corporate global mindset needs to become an enabler for implementing whatever generic global strategy a business has chosen. Leading indicates that the organizational ability to think globally would need to be ahead of the need to pursue a global strategy. Where this is not present, companies would face difficulty in following through with their indicated global strategy needs. As a result, expanding those organizational capabilities, resulting in a more extensive corporate global mindset, would become an important agenda item for firms aspiring to global competitive leadership. The next section of this chapter is devoted to precisely that challenge.

> ... companies that face substantial global logic pressure would be equipped with extensive corporate global mindsets indicating an ability to live up to their challenge.

Expanding and building global corporate mindsets

The development of corporate global mindsets is a relatively new endeavor. We should not expect most companies to find themselves in the comfort zone where the global mindset present in their firms already leads the requirements as outlined by their global logic and chosen global strategy. It is more likely that most firms will find a substantial gap from the desired situation. What actions can a company undertake to expand, or improve, its corporate global mindset such that its desire to compete globally is appropriately supported?

The following section aims at suggesting a series of actions that might be adopted. This is not an exhaustive set of remedial actions; however, we expect that companies will find specific ideas which might be further expanded. Furthermore, it is our hope that this type of conversation is a necessary part of the ensuing global dialog in most firms. The actions described in this text stem from a wealth of experience gained in the author's own work in management and organizational development, as well as from ideas suggested by practicing global managers.

Providing global experiences for individuals: enhancing the talent pool

Probably the most common approach firms undertake is to expand the global mindset of individual managers with the expectation that those globalized managers would impact on the organization at large. Typical among those actions are rotations through a series of international assignments, management development, and through the management selection process at the intake level. Each of those has its own merits and drawbacks.

> **Probably the most common approach firms undertake is to expand the global mindset of individual managers with the expectation that those globalized managers would impact on the organization at large.**

Providing managers with experiences outside their own home turf has been tried by most international firms. In the period of the multinational firm, those were the expatriates that were parachuted in for limited amounts of time. Clearly, such assignments help move a manager with a domestic mindset through to an international mindset, particularly with the first major assignment. But the arrangement of overseas assignments is a time-consuming process, and after a few years at the most only a few areas could have been included. To provide for a true global experience, a executive would have to be rotated a large number of times, something that is not possible if we want to build a critical mass of globalized managers. Aside from time, the second major drawback is the nature of the executive responsibility assigned. As has been pointed out many times by senior managers who themselves have benefitted from this route, their assignments were inherently limited to a certain geography, or country, and did not provide for opportunities for global thought. The evidence suggests that a series of single-country experiences does not necessarily lead to global thinking. What is helpful, though, is the assistance in internationalizing the mindset. But global minds, as we pointed out in Chapter 3, are clearly beyond that.

The second common strategy chosen by companies is to impact on their executive pool by management development. Could we not put them through an international program, expose them to some different environments, and speed up the globalization process? For those of us active in the field of management education, this is a very common request, often coupled with the notion that all of this can happen in a very short period of time.

To the extent that global thinking is a cognitive process, management development can certainly make a greater contribution. In such a setting, we can work through the thinking patterns necessary for a global mindset, expose managers to the concepts described in this book, and let them return to their original world, or positions. It is probably true that the conceptual elements of globalization can be understood in the context of a longer executive seminar just as we expose MBA students to those materials as part of their formal degree programs. The process works when the materials are truly global and the discussions require evidence of global thought, two conditions that are not easily met. As a member of a business school faculty, I probably have more faith in this approach than others might have. Nevertheless, the approach is limited to impact on individuals only and does little to change the environment in the firm.

Directly related to this approach is impacting on a company's hiring processes. Should we not hire young executives with global mindsets? Most executives are not born with global mindsets as their own educational experience is gained within, and defined by, national perspectives which – even when the executives concerned are of high intellect – rarely prepares them for the transition to global thinking. There are indications, however, that some young executives might be more adaptable later than others. In the context of business schools, we have come to define that as international curiosity. Students, or young executives, with a demonstrated high level of international curiosity tend to be better at absorbing the content of the global mindset. Again, we are not suggesting that firms find complete globalists at the hiring point, but ascertain that the preconditions exist that later globalization experiences would be absorbed and internalized quickly. Demonstrated international curiosity is a good proxy for such later globalization capabilities, and can take such simple forms as expressing and having the interest in things foreign, being comfortable around foreigners and having the ability to talk about things foreign in terms other than comparison to home environments, foreign language proficiency, etc.

> There are indications, however, that some young executives might be more adaptable later than others. In the context of business schools, we have come to define that as international curiosity.

The three avenues of building global mindsets through individuals demonstrate that these are necessary, but not sufficient conditions for the functioning of global firms. It is the contention of this author that a number of individual global mindsets alone do not result in an extensive corporate global mindset, and the questions employed to diagnose the corporate mindset have already indicated that more needs to be undertaken.

Building new global processes: providing experience for global thought

Referring back to the traditional method of assigning executives internationally, we said that those types of broadening experiences often did not allow for global thought. A company eager to expand its corporate global mindset needs to have a detailed look at how it is allowing its existing executive pool to think globally. It is very difficult to train global mindsets without giving them some measure of global thinking opportunity. The company must therefore create in a deliberate way opportunities for experiencing global thought which will help shape the individual development. The measures that can be adopted range from impacting on the planning process, the meeting process, to creating assignments specifically designed to create an opportunity for managers to think globally.

In a typical firm's planning cycle, much has been said about the starting point. In many global firms, annual planning still starts at the local level and then

> **Most firms will never quite be able to move totally away from local concerns.**

gets agglomerated to a regional, or global plan. Many discussions and reviews that take place are largely focused on the local planning units, i.e. countries. In such an environment, it is hard to break out of domestic, or multi-domestic thinking. A company aspiring to enlarge its corporate global mindset would have to find ways whereby much of its planning discourse would encompass global issues, such as situations that cut across multiple countries. Most firms will never quite be able to move totally away from the local concerns. Nevertheless, if one were to listen in on the planning and strategy discussions of a firm, the proportion that was devoted to individual country issues needs to become smaller, and the corresponding proportion devoted to global issues needs to increase. Thus helping the nature of the strategy dialog in a firm, or business, creates more opportunities for global thought, and thus has a positive impact on building an executive cadre with, and capable of, global thought.

The structure of a company's meetings is a second area where firms can create deliberate opportunities for adding to their own global mindsets. Maximizing the opportunity for meetings where the composition of attendees is truly international can have a strong impact on expanding the corporate global mindsets. A global company should thus avoid a situation where the head office nationality (or location) is typically chairing meetings to move into a situation where other countries are habitually assuming the role of chairs. This of course takes some doing, and in some instances would involve more travel to bring about the desired breadth of participation. However, current technology, such as video conferencing and electronic mail make participation even on a virtual basis possible. Again, an audit of the meeting process and composition of a firm would quickly indicate any gap present.

Adopting new organizational forms

One of the most potent forms of creating deliberate increased opportunities for global thinking is the company's formal organization. An organization that does not provide such global learning opportunities can encounter barriers in achieving a corporate global mindset. As we pointed out in Chapter 13, the creation of global mandates is potentially one of the most powerful ways to impact both on the individual executives and the company's global discourse.

Creating global mandates

A company should aggressively pursue the creation of formal global mandates at all levels of the organization. Such global mandates could be of a permanent or temporary nature. The intent is to throw executives into purposely designed global roles that would force them out of the domestic thinking into the new world of global thinking. The notion that we can wait until a executive has reached substantial executive experience and then assign a global mandate in the form of a globally structured business unit is missing the point that such managers have, unless given previous global mandates, no preparation for truly global thought.

The form for such global mandates can vary greatly. Opportunities range from assigning a single-country executive an additional, part-time role in the firm of a global segment coordinator, all the way to a full-time role, either on a staff or on a line basis, of a segment, sector, product line, brand, or some other relevant assignment. To be of value, such global mandates need to be formally expressed, communicated, and the holders of the mandates need to know about them. Deliberate global mandates are different from implied, or creeping ones where the job holders do not really understand or know that a global component to the position exists.

As we indicated in our diagnostic earlier in this chapter, the presence of many global mandates at all levels of an organization is one of the strongest indicators of the presence of a strong corporate global mindset. Such assignments would preferably take place in the early phase of a manager's career, and on the way up the hierarchical ladder, it is conceivable that executives might have experienced a series of such assignments.

Monitoring such global mandates, assignments, and progress need to be shared between line management and the human resource function. A truly global firm would maintain records of the nature of global mandates assigned for its high potential managerial talent, thus giving a firm a clear view of the nature of its pipeline and size of globalized executive pool.

Globalizing the IT infrastructure

In today's world where it is becoming increasingly difficult to move executives and their families from one country to another, the presence of global mandates might allow companies to create global learning opportunities without relocation. Companies who desire to keep executives in place and yet assign global mandates will find that this greatly depends on a firm's global IT structure and the ability of executives to communicate with each other across countries. All too often we see firms that have single-country communications solutions whereby easy communications across country operations do not exist. Communicating effectively across an expanse of local operations requires that executives can easily bridge the distance and time gap. The distance gap is closed when the need to physically travel to another location can be avoided. Probably the most effective tool for eliminating travel for meetings is the emergence of video conferencing. It gives companies a chance to include managers from distant locations into their meetings. Equipping all its relevant locations with video conferencing substantially contributes to a corporate global mindset.

Bridging the time gap, created due to the various time zones, is a second requirement of effective IT. Unfortunately, video conferencing requires participants to be present at the same time although in the not too distant future we will probably enter the world of video mail. Until that time, effective use of electronic mail is required. This requires companies to compose global address lists, standardize their e-mail access so that managers can reach everyone else in the world from a given location. While e-mail is present in many companies on a single-country solution, there is still a gap when it comes to truly globalized systems.

Apart from the hardware and technology, the information systems need to become more globalized to support global mandates. By that we mean access to financial, operational, competitive, or transaction data from multiple points. A firm where everyone dials into a single global database acts differently from the firm where everyone works off their local database with only limited connections or comparability. Clearly, by eliminating such technological or systems barriers and adding the technical capabilities a company can enhance its corporate global mindset.

Adjusting the formal organization

Companies have a strong tool in their formal organizational design to influence the creation of enhanced corporate global mindsets. As we indicated earlier, the division of managerial responsibility along geographic lines is a key hindrance in creating a global mindset. Naturally, most companies will find that, at some level, managerial responsibility will have to be assigned on a territorial basis. However, it should not come at the top level to assure the creation of sufficient line positions that offer global mandates. Redesigning the organization itself will therefore offer new opportunities for creating global mandates and should be deliberately used by companies.

> **... the division of managerial responsibility along geographic lines is a key hindrance in creating a global mindset.**

Many opportunities are also available in the active, thoughtful creation of global teams or task forces. Companies often maintain such groups, both on a permanent and a temporary basis. When task forces are created, it is suggested that companies make a deliberate effort to assign a global mandate to the group, and to internationalize its membership. Both strategies are powerful ways to create additional global learning opportunities and contribute to the global mindset of companies, as well as individuals.

> **Redesigning the organization itself will therefore offer new opportunities for creating global mandates and should deliberately be used by companies.**

Creating a global learning organization

"Learning organization" is a frequently used term that has different meanings for different people. The focus here is on the implications for enhancing a firm's global mindset.

If we observe traditional learning in many global or international firms, the earlier mentioned assignment of managerial responsibility along territorial lines inevitably means that managers learn from events that take place in their assigned countries. At the extreme, managers only learn what happens in their own geographic territory, and would even disregard events occurring elsewhere. In such a organization, managers would only process at the speed of learning opportunities produced in their own countries. For managers operating in lead markets with many events, learning might be sufficient to compete. For managers working in secondary, or peripheral markets, events might be so infrequent that learning would take place only sporadically. Worse, each manager would compete only on the basis of learning acquired locally and miss out on the global learning opportunity. Simplified, each manager competes on the basis of his or her own learning curve only.

Contrast this with a true global learning organization. Here, events occurring at different locations throughout the world would be plotted onto a single, global learning curve. Managers would incorporate the learning of all their colleagues, or the entire widespread global organization, for their own activities. A manager in one country would benefit from experience in a distant market as it had occurred locally, though calibrated for any cultural or economic differences. Since many learning events occur on a globally pooled basis, managers can come down their own learning curve more rapidly, thus enhancing their own and the firm's competitiveness. Each local organization, thus organized, would compete on the strength of all the lessons learned, and not simply the local ones. All units would be stronger,

> **Those firms which manage to implement such a corporate global mindset ahead of others will have a clear competitive advantage as they embark upon the 21st century.**

more intelligent, and more competitive than if they were operating on their own. This is the challenge of the global learning organization faced by firms which aspire to achieve a true corporate global mindset. The challenge is clear, and the hurdles to overcome have been described in this chapter. Those firms which manage to implement such a corporate global mindset ahead of others will have a clear competitive advantage as they embark upon the 21st century.

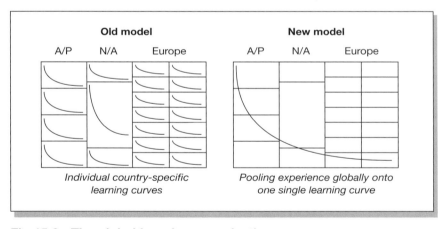

Fig 15.2 The global learning organization

The concept of the globally learning organization has implications beyond competitiveness. Such a firm, anchored in the key markets of the world, is no longer dependent on the competitiveness of its own physical locations, in particular no longer dependent on the head office location. The competitiveness of the global firm with fully deployed corporate global mindset is more than the sum total of the competitiveness of its individual country locations. Instead, the firm, through the adoption of the global mindset, can set itself off and compete on the best of each location, in the end achieving a state of competitiveness that can become location independent. This is the prospect of the global mindset in the 21st century.

Practicing global mindsets

After having absorbed, studied, and internalized the concepts described in the previous chapters, how does a company, or an individual, go about analyzing a business with a global mindset? This is the question we would like to address in this final chapter. This chapter is called 'Practicing global mindsets' because it will involve a sample analysis, covering all our concepts. Before we continue, we need to be clear that we do this in an abstract way not related to a real firm, business, or company. As a result, we can suggest some sequence of analysis that might be changed, or adapted, in a real life situation. It is hoped that the reader will be able to put his or her own business through this type of structured analysis. However, the reader needs to be flexible enough to appreciate the need to innovate or adapt this methodology to a specific case.

I hope that the organization of the following analysis into several clearly identified steps does not lead to an oversimplification of the process. For ease of understanding, I will take the reader through clearly identified sets of analysis that are described in detail in earlier chapters. At each step, sample charts are identified to illustrate the content of the analysis. My concern is that the charts themselves will be seen as the essential elements, and that the explanations that need to accompany each chart, or step, may be lost in the process. Analyzing a global business cannot be relegated to filling in simple forms alone, and the following sets of charts are not meant to be interpreted in that way. It will be the detailed explanation that follows each chart that will carry the full content of our analysis. I hope the reader will understand and appreciate this limitation and the inherent risk in taking what follows too literally.

⊛ Step one: charting the global opportunity

Coming to grips with a company's global opportunity is the first step in practicing global mindsets. Following our description in Chapter 7, the first step consists of understanding the global chessboard faced by any firm. The starting point is the definition of a appropriate metric that describes the global opportunity. Once determined, the world is analyzed along the key metric with a view to identifying major markets. The result might be a world map that depicts each country by its market size.

The translation of the global chessboard into a graphic depicting today's opportunities needs to be combined with the existing or anticipated trends. The next step is to predict tomorrow's global chessboard, and be clear on the changes that will take place over time. The future global chessboard is understood from the existing global opportunity, the metrics as discussed above, and the growth trends that can be anticipated for key markets and regions.

The present and future global chessboard may be contrasted with the company's existing geographic spread. The purpose of this comparison is to visualize the present and future opportunities and potential migration that the company needs to make to capture the full global opportunity some time in the future.

Many companies, or business teams, are responsible for a number of product lines or segments. If the diversity of the business lines is such that a single global chessboard does not meaningfully depict the reality, it is suggested that the business look at several of these chessboards. Each series would be composed with its own metric and be conducted on the basis of past, present, and future company deployment.

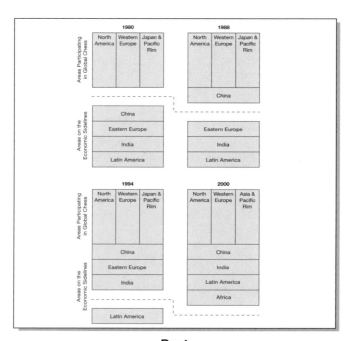

Past

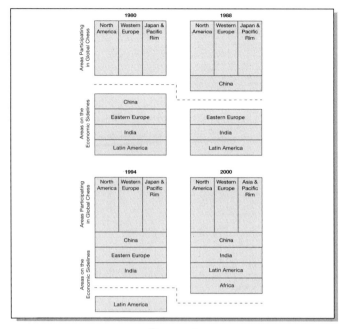

Present

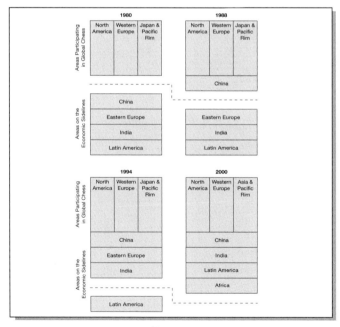

Future

Fig 16.1   Global chessboards

Once the opportunity is defined, the analysis needs to test for dynamics among key markets or regions. This test may be based upon the concept of lead markets, which can come in various categories. As outlined in Chapter 8, there are several lead markets and the analyst needs to determine in each case where the customer-based, the product-based, operations-based, and management practice-based lead markets are.

Reviewing the four different lead markets, and the nature of the forward trends in the markets, leads to an understanding of the must-win markets (see chapter 7). Essentially, no firm can pursue all potential markets. Thus, prioritization needs to be made based on impact on global strategy. This evaluation will lead companies to target large markets with major volume importance and/or markets with bellwether impact, such as in the form of lead markets.

Customer-based

Product-based

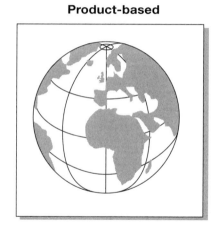

Operations-based

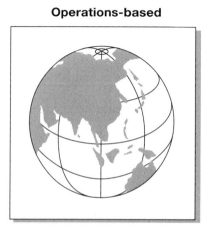

Management practice-based

Fig 16.2   Global lead markets

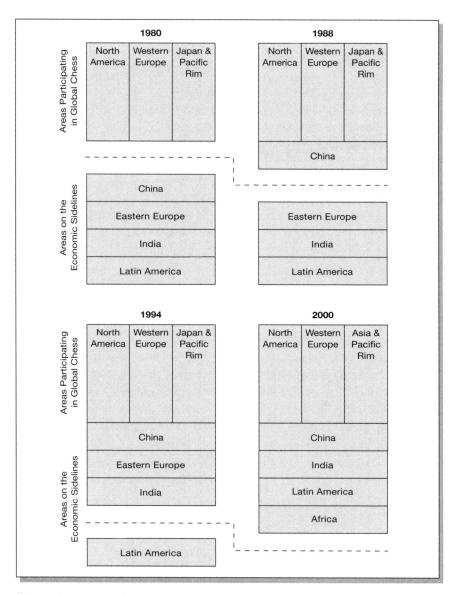

Fig 16.3 Must-win markets

This analysis can again be conducted on the basis of present and future must-win markets (they might change over time due to industry dynamics) and the companies' deployment across these win markets. A gap, if applicable would be readily discerned from the analysis. This analysis would need to be repeated for each set of market opportunities if the company marketed several different products into different markets.

Step two: assessing the global logic pattern

With the global opportunity mapped out in the form of a global chessboard, our next step takes us into the realm of global logics. Here, following our detailed explanations in Chapters 4, 5 and 6, we need to determine the extent of global pressure along each of the global logic segments described. This exercise, however, is not only a matter of committing to some kind of pressure indicator. Just as important is the content on each dimension, which contains the full explanation of the nature of the pressure and the dimension investigated.

The process may begin with mapping out the global logic pressure from the customer base. Asking the series of questions we have detailed in Chapter 4, the analysis leads to a description of the extent of the global logic along the dimensions of customer, purchasing, and information acquisition. Querying the extent to which we have global customers leads to the identification of the global customer pressure. Determining the presence of local, regional, or global purchasing leads to the identification of possible global purchasing pressure. Understanding the nature of the information acquisition process, whether local, national, regional, or global, provides answers regarding the presence of a significant global logic.

As described in Chapter 5, the flip side of this analysis is the determination of any global logic pressure by analyzing the industry and competitive environment. Four global logic dimensions were introduced in the chapter. Global competitive logic depends on the existence of one, a few, or many competitive theaters. The global industry logic is driven by the difference or global similarity of key industry success factors that have to be met to compete in that industry, country by country. The presence of some form of critical mass is an indicator of global size pressure. And finally, the similar regulatory environment can be an indicator of global size pressure.

The seven global logic sets are combined, as detailed in Chapter 6, into an overall impression of the global logic faced by the business. The graphic of choice for this analysis is the spiderweb. However, we should not be satisfied with a simple global logic chart. Rather, we need to assess the present set of pressures and query the future pressures by understanding where pressure grows, how fast, and to what extent. This then leads to three different views: the global logic as present in a company's business today; the future global logic pressure; and the perception of the companies actions today. The last set would indicate the company's behavior, or its perception of the global logic. A gap can exist between the company's perception, the present situation, and the future or expected global logic pressure.

If a company were faced by several different businesses or segments, or multiple chessboards as determined in the earlier part of our analysis, this exercise would need to end in a multiple set of global logic spiderweb patterns.

Customer logic

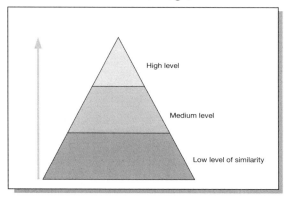

Global information logic

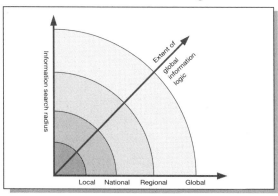

Global purchasing logic

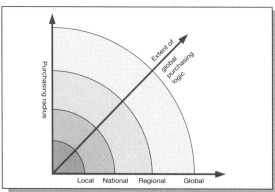

Fig 16.4   Customer-based global logic patterns

Competition

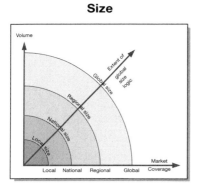

Industry

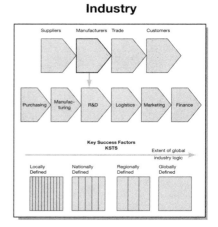

Size

Regulatory

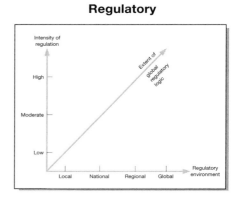

Fig 16.5 Industry-based global logics

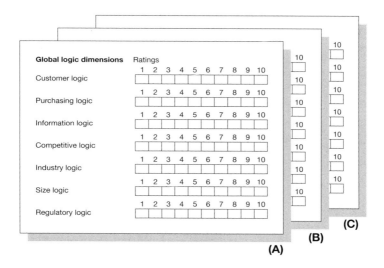

Fig 16.6   Global logics patterns

Step three: global generic strategies

As we have outlined in Chapters 9–12, the choice of any particular generic global strategy would be driven largely by the particular pattern of global logic, and the extent of the overall global pressure that created a global imperative. Consequently, Step Three follows the global logic analysis.

Possibly the most logical place to start would be to overlay the global logic pattern on a selection of the many different generic global strategies (see chapter 11). This fit would indicate which global strategies would be most suitable given the previously determined global logic pressure. It is important to recognize that the selection of a generic global strategy is made difficult due to the fact that we have been able to identify several different generic global strategies that might accommodate each of the global logic pressures. In some instances, where companies face multiple pressures from different dimensions, a firm will most likely be faced with a multitude of global generic strategies. This process of selection cannot follow strict linear analytic forms. Rather, the fitting process needs to take into account different sets of circumstances and be of a more comprehensive, holistic nature. Judgment enters the process and reasonable people may differ on their conclusions given the same set of circumstances.

A second issue centers around the extent of integration, and full or partial globalization. Confronting managers with differences or similarities in the business structure deals with the appropriate level of globalization that best represents the reality faced.

Global integration

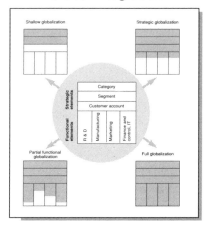

Global logic

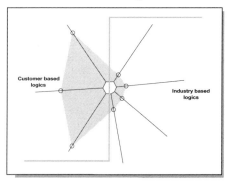

Global strategies

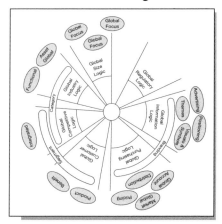

Fig 16.7 Selecting global generic strategy

Step four: selecting generic global functional strategies

Any generic global strategy has implications for functional strategies. The different levels of global integration pursued in marketing, R&D, operations/manufacturing, and finance/IT are largely driven by the desired level of globalization, and the extent to which the environment requires integration along functional lines. It thus makes sense to tackle the functional global strategies only after having assessed the overall global generic strategy as driven by the global logic faced by the firm.

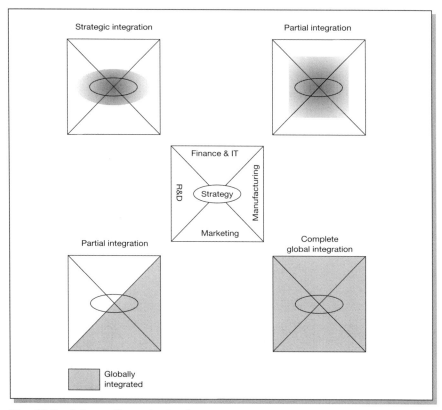

Fig 16.8   Integration strategies

⮕ Step five: making the global resource trade-off

The last step in this strategy section represents the required resource commitments needed to unfold the strategy. In Chapter 12, we have shown how a company can depict its resource commitments across different sectors, segments, value chains, and geographies. In particular, we need to understand how important it is for a company to cover the necessary geography as against emphasizing other elements in the business. The resource trade-off can be captured for the present situation as well as the future situation.

Corresponding to the resource trade off is the resource commitment of the chosen or required global strategy. This relates to the extent of required market coverage, or global reach, as against the need to commit to physical assets in many markets, and the possibility to engage in the globalization of ideas, certainly applicable if lead markets are at a distance form a firm's domestic market.

The nature of the resource constraint might force a company to make a different product/market combination selection, and to engage or disengage from multiple markets. The resulting pattern, and the desired focus, are captured in the analysis surrounding the horizontal tigers, against vertical dragons depicted in Chapter 12.

R&D

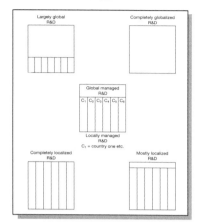

Finance

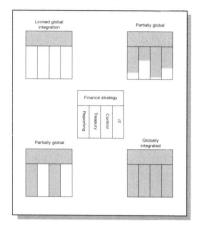

Marketing

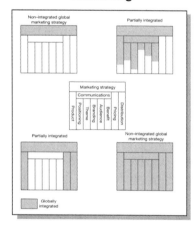

Manufacturing

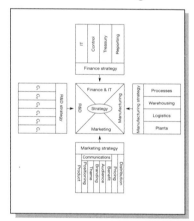

Strategy

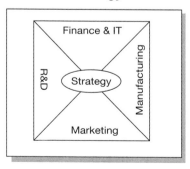

Fig 16.9   Resolute commitments

Global options

Resource trade-offs

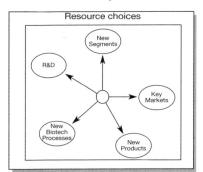 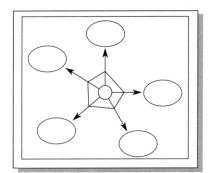

Fig 16.10   Global resource needs analysis

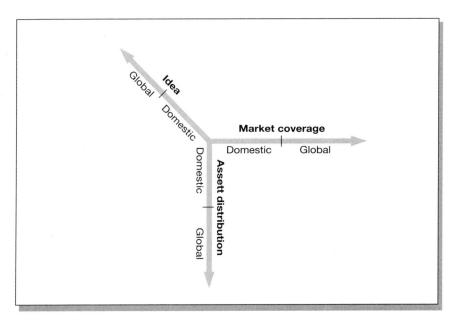

Fig 16.11   Resource commitments

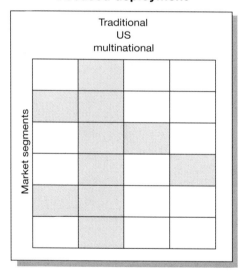

Fig 16.12   Determination of appropriate focus

> ## Step six: diagnosing global organizational requirements

With the generic global strategy adopted and the resource trade-off articulated, we can now devote our attention to the important organizational aspects. As we have described in detail in Chapters 13–15, future requirements for globalization will demand different types of organizations. In the initial assessment, we need to ascertain the organizational structure and the existing allocation of global mandates, both to individual business units, and to individual managers. The key question for managers to assess is the future allocation of global mandates at all levels to facilitate the chosen generic global strategy.

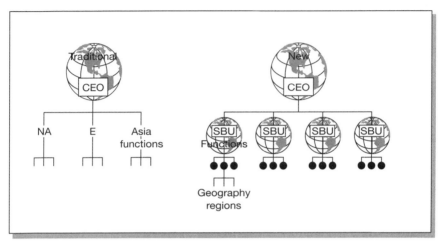

Fig 16.13 Global mandates

Multi-domestic pattern			
Responsibility / Parameter	Local	Regional	Global
New products			
Segment choice			
R&D priorities			
Product features			

Global pattern			
Responsibility / Parameter	Local	Regional	Global
New products			
Segment choice			
R&D priorities			
Product features			

Fig 16.14 Organizational charter

Aside from the organizational structure with the necessary global mandates, there will be a need to assess the appropriate organizational charter, as explained in Chapter 12.

There is also a need to assess the global mindset of the organization. In Chapter 15, we identified a number of questions, 10 in total, to assess the global mindset of an organization. These questions should be used as the background to an organizational assessment. As we identified earlier, the assessment should be done for the present situation and meet the requirements for the implementation of a firm's chosen global strategy. The comparison between the two assessments generates the gap that needs to be bridged to achieve the global objectives.

Finally, each individual manager can assess their global mindset on a personal basis. This may be done by categorizing the ability to think globally as outlined in Chapter 14. Although we have not developed a scoring mechanism for the personal global mindset, the reader can go back to Chapter 3 where we outlined the different mindsets, from domestic to global. Fundamentally, each individual manager needs to categorize their mindset personally and determine any gap that may exist between present state and requirements to carry out any assigned global mandate.

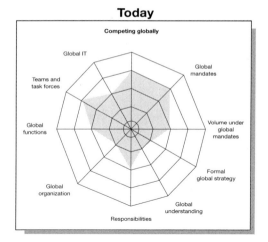

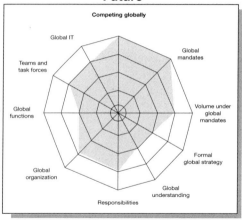

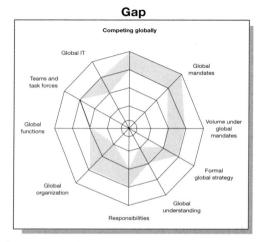

Fig 16.15 Corporate global mindset

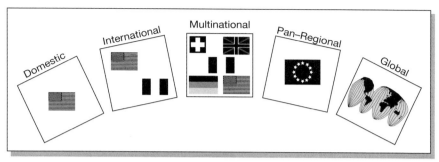

Fig 16.16   Generic mindsets

A process for engaging in global mindsets

The above analysis, described in six steps, was aimed as a guide to the practicing manager, or business teams, in assessing their own situation and determining any action to close critical gaps. We have done this by staying closely to the graphics included in our text, and suggesting a sequence that managers may follow. Our caution mentioned at the outset of this chapter needs to be repeated again. We view the description contained within this chapter as suggestive only, and would not want any manager to follow it literally. The graphics, while important, are not the only output of any global mindset analysis. The graphics remind us of steps, and they suggest a process that consists of a thorough, in-depth, searching analysis. The series of charts suggested as potential output are but stepping stones held together by an emerging, well-thought-out analysis, that captures a much richer thought process than might be suggested by this chapter.

To capture the richness of the analysis, and to engage an entire organization in the search process, companies and managerial teams alike are well advised to follow a process that allows the full engagement of all concerned. The process of global mindset should not be one restricted to a closed office. Under those circumstances, the necessary dialogue, the penetrating question and resulting answers, would never surface. Firms need to make sure that the global mindset analyses described in this book are arrived at as a genuine search where each participating individual can challenge the conventional wisdom of others. The resulting dialogue, enriched by the output and insights of many rather than the thoughts of a few, guarantees a far better result. No individual manager could possibly know all there is to question about globalizing a business. The pooling of the experience of many is superior to individual, isolated, thinking. The quality of the output is a function of the process, and needs to be considered before companies, business units, or managerial teams embark in that direction. Properly orchestrated, the process of practicing global mindsets is likely to open up new vistas for companies engaged in global competition.

Epilog

A word of caution from the author

This book was intended to challenge the minds of managers at all levels, ranging from early careers to senior management. It was based upon the author's own teaching, research, writing, and consulting experience, leveraging contacts with companies across the world. Although representing a journey over the past fifteen years, this book cannot be a finished product. Reflecting back just five years ago, it is amazing to realize how many new insights have been gained, and how many new ideas or concepts have been created. Committing it to words, publishing it in the form of a book supported by a leading publisher gives it a seeming finality not intended by the author. That leads to a word of caution to all of those who now feel emboldened enough to tackle globalization in their firms, or to contribute in more effective ways to the globalization debates raging in so many companies.

Experience with the work of other authors has taught me that some readers might be tempted to take many of our concepts literally. There are many useful charts interspersed through the text, some giving the powerful impression of details that go beyond the original intent. This book is meant as a contribution to the globalization debate, both in the managerial and academic community. Just as the ideas and concepts continue to pour out as new events occur, readers need to realize that this book was published with an artificial deadline. The conceptualization of global mindsets and global strategies will continue. New dimensions relevant to our global logics are sure to emerge. Different types of generic global strategies are likely to be identified. Tools to broaden and depict the global mindset, both individually and for companies, can be expected to emerge. In short, readers have had a glimpse of a work in progress and need to ensure they stay current, both conceptually and in terms of practice. Younger readers, with yet emerging global mandates, must realize that when they get to implement the concepts in this book, much will have changed, improved, and been rethought. A word of caution thus to all who might be tempted to take this as definitive contribution. This represents the most accurate depiction of the way I can conceptualize global business practice as of today. We cannot and should not assume that this will remain unchanged for long.

Index